'*The Pay Off* will change the way we read and think about payments. Fascinating, thrilling, intriguing and well written, with deep inside knowledge and understanding of the world of payments, Gottfried and Natasha are taking us to a future with endless possibilities, never losing sight of possible risks and wrong turns.'

Jochen Metzger, Payments Executive, Frankfurt am Main

'Whenever you buy or sell something, you use a payments system but do you ever wonder how that system works? It's like plumbing or electricity maybe, but it is actually far more complex as it is changing fast thanks to technology. You used to pay with cash, then with a click, now with a swipe or with a touch. What's next? How does all of this work? *The Pay Off* provides a wonderful deep-dive into the subject by two experts who are at the heart of the system that links all of the payments and banking world globally, namely Swift. In this book, you find so many useful insights about the past, present and future of payments that anyone who is vaguely interested in politics, economics or the world of finance should pick it up and read it. NOW!'

Chris Skinner, author, commentator and troublemaker

'Lucid and stimulating – this book sheds light on the scale (and pace) of the digital-money revolution that we are living through.'

Huw van Steenis, author of the Bank of England Future of Finance report

'An accessible, thorough primer on the money technologies that make our world go round but few really people understand.'

Lana Swartz, author of *New Money: How Payment Became Social Media*

'Payments are the most important things most people have probably never even thought about. Banks, tech companies, central banks, crypto firms and crooks all know that if you control payments, you may also control critical data and ultimately the world. *The Pay Off* cleverly dissects the workings and future of this geopolitical and technological war. A must-read for anyone in business.'

Bob Wigley, Chair UK Finance and author of *Born Digital: The Story of a Distracted Generation*

'A long overdue, highly readable and authoritative account of the uses and occasional abuses of the systems on which we all rely, and how they are still rapidly changing, that both specialists and the general reader will find informative and entertaining.'

Mark Yallop, Chair, FICC Markets Standards Board, and Former External Member, Prudential Regulatory Committee and Financial Market Infrastructure Board at the Bank of England

The
Pay Off

How Changing
the Way We Pay
Changes Everything

GOTTFRIED LEIBBRANDT
and NATASHA DE TERAN

Elliott&Thompson

First published 2021 by
Elliott and Thompson Limited
2 John Street
London WC1N 2ES
www.eandtbooks.com

ISBN: 978-1-78396-606-6

9 8 7 6 5 4 3 2 1

A catalogue record for this book is available from the British Library.

Typesetting by Marie Doherty
Printed in the UK by CPI Group (UK) Ltd, Croydon, CR0 4YY

MIX
Paper from
responsible sources
FSC
www.fsc.org
FSC® C020471

Contents

AUTHORS' NOTE

Throughout the text we have mostly used the plural 'we' to reflect the fact that writing this book has been a joint endeavour. On occasion, we have written about specific incidents and personal examples: in those instances, the text switches to the singular 'I' to indicate the difference.

Introduction

When was the last time you made a payment?

It can't have been long ago: on average people make one payment every day, though most of us make many more than that. But how often do you think about what goes into the process of paying?

Was it free to pay? Who saw you pay and how much information did they get in the process? How did the money move? When did the beneficiary actually receive it? How much did they get? How many organisations, machines or people were involved along the way? How do they link together? Who pays for them? Who controls them? And what would happen if the system stopped working?

Payments are everywhere, if you pay attention. At the cash register, to be sure, where you might use coins, a card or a phone. Online, when you take your virtual shopping cart to the virtual cash register and use your, yes, virtual card. Less noticeably you are paying when your monthly rent, mortgage payment or utility bill goes out through a standing order or direct debit. And less noticeably still, you just paid for that movie on Amazon by watching it, or that Uber ride by taking it. Be in no doubt that some of the smartest brains are working hard to make our payments easier still.

It has been argued that money is one of the three key abstractions that enable societies to function beyond the scale of prehistoric tribes (the other two being religion and writing). We all realise the importance of money, even if we aren't all equally enthusiastic about its role. But the ultimate purpose of money is of course to use it – to make payments – which is why we should all understand at least a bit about how they work.

Sexy they may not be, but payments are hugely powerful, and they matter: how we pay has a real and deep impact on our lives. Get payments right and economic activity prospers; get them wrong and economic activity can be stifled. Without payments, money doesn't work, and if it stops working, so too would (or, god forbid, will) our economies and societies. Think no food on the shelves, no petrol at the pumps, no power in the grid, and remember the words of American journalist Alfred Henry Lewis: 'There are only nine meals between mankind and anarchy.' Arguably it's less the thin blue line and more the payment system that sits between us and a total breakdown of law and order.

The richness and importance of payments make them worthy of interest at any time, but they merit particular exploration today because the 'now' in payments is far more exciting than it has ever been. Change is occurring fast – countries, indeed continents, are subverting customs almost overnight and money is pouring into the sector like never before.

Paying may be a simple, immediate act, but the payment choices we make today will have far-reaching repercussions. The way we pay is changing and the tools we use to pay with are changing too. The consequences of these changes stretch beyond our wallets; new methods of paying enable us to spend and borrow where and in ways we couldn't before. All of which is too important to ignore or leave to experts, and that's why this book seeks to explore it.

Changing how we pay brings risk as well as opportunity. Technology is transforming payments across the globe, but there is no one-size-fits-all solution, and the stakes are high.

Our societies are monetary ones; as such, they rely on everyone being able to use money. Access to payments determines whether, where and how we can participate in society. To use money, you have to be able to move money – but what if our selfish payment choices result in sections of our societies no longer being able to do so? What if the cashless choices of a digitally enfranchised metropolitan population unfairly burdened – or even excluded – those in rural communities, the poor, the elderly or the digitally disadvantaged? If some people have no way to pay or be paid, what stake will they have in society?

Then there are the questions of education and thrift. How do we teach our children about money if they can no longer touch it? How do we budget if we no longer see numbers, much less experience the pain of payment? The consequences of the unbundling and repackaging of payments are not yet well understood by those seeking to break into payments, by the incumbents being jostled in the madding crowd, or even by those who invest in and regulate payments.

How we pay determines who has access to our data, what risks we run when we are paying and how much we 'pay to pay'. This is because it's not just the methods of payment that are changing; so are the systems that support them and the owners of those systems. And alongside that, the economics of payments are changing, the politics of payments are changing and the powers behind payments are changing. Every part of how we pay is being contested by players ranging from central banks to social media giants. Each mundane payment choice we make is informing the future of payments: collectively our choices will determine which groups profit from payments and by how much; who 'owns' the power of payments, and how they might exercise it. The implications and ramifications of these changes are huge – arguably unquantifiable.

And then there is the richness of payments. Personal, painful and prosaic payments may be at the individual level, but they are also potent, political and often perverse on a collective basis. The payments universe is global, but its conventions are fiercely local. The act of paying is immediate, but the receipt of payment is often frustratingly slow; it is a bilateral operation shaped by multilateral conventions. A payment is both practice and process; it can be virtual or tangible, digital or analogue, archaic or cutting edge – and sometimes both at the same time. Cheques may be old-fashioned, but the very latest imaging technology is needed to process them.

The payments market (which arguably isn't a market at all) is both concentrated and dispersed. Payments are made to and from some 25,000 banks in over 200 countries, but almost every cross-border payment passes through one of just fifteen banks. A plethora of different technologies are deployed, but just a few underlie almost every payment. The payment network is singular and plural: like the internet it is a single system that stitches together a dizzying number of sub-systems.

Parts of this vast system are unquantifiable. There is no hard data for the most fundamental of payment types – the number and size of cash transactions. Payments can be anonymous or traceable or, in the case of cryptocurrencies, both: Bitcoin transactions are anonymous yet visible to all. The system is transparent and opaque; clean and dirty. The bad guys use it as well as the good guys.

Rich with international intrigue, geopolitics, heists and courtroom dramas, payments have it all.

There have been many audacious attempts to subvert payments for criminal gain, from the high-tech to the low-key. Remember the film *Die Hard with a Vengeance*, when the baddies try to steal the gold from the New York Fed? Two decades later North Korean hackers penetrated deep into Bangladesh's central bank network in an attempt to plunder $1 billion from its account at the Fed. Then there was the lowly assistant at Goldman Sachs who used a humble cheque book to steal millions of pounds from right under the noses of two of the bank's high-flying partners, or the diamond tycoon Nirav Modi who used an arcane payment instrument and an accommodating insider to steal $1.5 billion from India's Punjab National Bank. As the gateways to money, payments will always be targets.

Payments are important not just for what they do, but for the information they contain: payment data is highly prized by those who want to use it for financial gain, of course, but also by agencies tracking terrorists or arms dealers; international players seeking commercial or geopolitical advantage; and government agencies pursuing tax evaders – not to mention suspicious spouses spoiling for a showdown. Relatively speaking, our payment data is nowhere near as widely used as other sources of personal information, thanks in part to privacy laws, ownership constraints and the challenges in amassing and organising the material. But with profits, power and politics at stake, don't bank on it staying that way forever.

For the last few centuries, the payment and deposit functions have been as one. Banks have 'owned' payments and enjoyed the bounteous fruits of the two functions. But banks have no divine right to payments. Payments are about risk, liquidity, technology, networks and conventions. Banks are pretty good at the first two, average at the second two, and no better than anyone else at the fifth. Technology companies are, you could say, their mirror image. Best at technology and networks, they are good at building conventions, but they have no particular expertise in risk and liquidity. Nonetheless they are now stampeding into payments. With their network power and marketing nous, they are unbundling payments from deposits and transforming our payment habits in the process. The ease with which they enable us to pay is stimulating commerce. But the separation of payments from other banking services brings other consequences, as yet little considered.

It is often in the gulfs between how society *thinks* the money world works and how it *actually* does work that things tend to occur for which society ends up paying the price. Just as war is too serious a matter to be left to the generals, money and payments are too important to be left to specialists. No part of the world of money is more critical to our everyday lives than payments, and arguably no part of money is more ignored than payments. We hope to remedy that with this book, narrowing the gap between our dependency on payments and our awareness about them.

PART I

MOVING MONEY

1. What's a payment, anyway?

High in the Rhondda Cynon valley in South Wales sits the village of Penywaun, home to about 1,500 people. Located in one of the most economically deprived areas in the UK, the area's topography limits travel to two directions – up or down the valley. The village boasts a Post Office, a general store and a café, but little else in terms of commercial activity. Access to cash is critical for most residents, but the Post Office is the only source and is open only during normal business hours and until midday on Saturday. The nearest cash machine (ATM) is 1.5 miles away, a ten-minute drive or a good hour's walk there and back for someone reasonably active. With half of its households lacking access to a car and roughly one-third having some form of life-limiting illness or disability, those are certainly not options for all. There is a bus service but this brings additional costs, including for the Penywaun economy. Having travelled to access cash, where are people more likely to spend it – near the ATM that dispensed it or back home in the village that so needs it?[1]

In central London there is no such ATM shortage, but that didn't help Julian Assange back in 2010 when he gave himself up to the British police over charges he faced in Sweden. Assange was also wanted in the USA over 'Cablegate': his organisation, Wikileaks, had published several hundred thousand leaked messages between the US State Department and its embassies. It was as a result of this that PayPal, Visa, Mastercard and

---

[1]   Penywaun was the subject of a study that the University of Bristol undertook for its report 'Geographies of Access to Cash'.

others had started to refuse to process donations to Wikileaks.[2] Unable to access funds, neither the organisation nor Assange could pay their bills, not least for the servers that hosted the leaked information. Whatever you think of Assange or Wikileaks, he had at that point only been *accused* of a crime; it was unrelated to money and no judicial process had actually taken place – and yet private companies chose to rescind his access to payments. Alongside Assange and Wikileaks, the likes of InfoWars (the American far right 'news' website) and Pornhub have been subject to similar 'payment blocking'. Whatever you think of this crew, consider that such moves effectively put censorship in the hands of private enterprise.

For most of us, access to payments is unlikely to be high on the list of things we worry about – or have even thought to think about. Be honest – have you ever worried about whether you or anyone else *can* pay or *be* paid in practical terms? Contrast that with concerns about basic incomes, debt, savings, pensions and poverty, which – whether or not they affect you personally – are widespread, well understood and likely topics you hear about daily.

So, what exactly is a payment, so crucial for everyone from Welsh village dwellers to international fugitives?

Bertrand Russell famously needed the first 700 pages of his *Principia Mathematica* to define the number 'one'. Like the number one, the concept of payment seems obvious: any act in which money goes from one party to another. But there's a little more to it, of course. There will be no long, formal definitions here (although we could probably stretch them to a respectable 100 pages or so) but it's useful to look briefly at what a payment actually *is*, legally speaking.

---

[2] This was before he was holed up for seven years in the Ecuadorian Embassy in London (2012–19).

In legal shorthand, a payment is 'a way to discharge debt'. A debt could, painfully, be discharged with 'a pound of flesh'[3] or, if you're in the midst of a horticultural frenzy, tulip bulbs,[4] but for the most part debts are discharged with money. This becomes relevant when we think about the notion of cash as legal tender. It does *not* mean that merchants have to accept a $100 banknote – merchants can refuse all cash; it simply means that a $100 note is a legal way to settle a debt.

In Mark Twain's short story, *The Million Pound Bank Note*, the young Henry Adams survives for thirty days by holding (but not actually paying with) a peerless and uncashable note of that value. Few of us will accept the mere possession of money as a presumption of eventual payment, but small, simple economies could, in principle, survive without payments. Instead, they could keep track of who owes what to whom, relying on the assumption that the mutual obligations would be honoured and that – over time – they would cancel each other out.

Our favourite illustration is the story of the tourist who checks into a hotel on a small island and pays (in advance) with a $100 bill. The hotel owner uses this bill to pay off his debt with the butcher, who in turn uses it to pay off his debt with the farmer, who in turn gives it to the garage owner for having fixed his tractor, who gives it back to the hotel owner for hosting his daughter's wedding the previous month. After all this, the guest shows up at the front desk and states that he's changed his mind and decided to cancel his stay. The hotel owner gives him back the $100 and he departs. Everything is as before, except that all debts on the island have been settled.

Imagine what would happen if these debts were left open – if the butcher didn't pay the farmer, who then couldn't pay the garage owner,

---

[3] As demanded by Shylock, the moneylender, in Shakespeare's *The Merchant of Venice*.

[4] For a short period in the Dutch Golden Age, in the 1600s, a fashionable tulip bulb was worth more than ten times an average worker's annual wages.

and so on. It wouldn't be long before the entire island was in total, possibly violent, disarray.

Small or large, our economies today are plural and complex and – with the possible exception of North Korea – interlinked. Neat as it is, the island system wouldn't work for us, but payments do.

They work so well, in fact, that modern economies need payments as much as they need water, power and energy. Without smooth-functioning payments, financial markets, commerce, employment, even unemployment, would all be compromised. Look at who your country identified as key workers during the Covid-19 lockdown and you'll probably find payments staff are listed. Unless you live off-grid in splendid and completely self-sufficient isolation, you need to be able to pay and (most of us at least) need to be able to get paid.

If access to the payment system is critical for everyone, then our modern, monetary-based societies have first to ensure that they have a good system and, second, that everyone has access to it. Later in this book, we'll come to how those systems work and whether they're doing a good job.

While access to a banking system is seen as a crucial part of a country's development and necessary for lifting people out of poverty, it is not as basic a need as the ability to pay. Payments and banking don't necessarily go hand in hand, but for many people without bank accounts, cash is the only payment option. They can't easily make remote payments, are more exposed to corruption (for example, by middlemen that pay out government benefits), miss out on interest and face risks inherent in keeping cash, such as theft and inflation.

Developing economies have been able to move fast in recent years, getting more and more citizens into the financial system and out of cash-based subsistence. But their biggest advance has been in extending digital payments into the poorest and most remote rural areas.

Advanced economies have their own unbanked populations; small but persistent numbers of people who survive on cash. There is now a growing risk that these people (and potentially others, too) will be excluded from the most fundamental of financial services – the payments system.

What is ironic is that the same thing that is boosting financial inclusion in developing nations is heightening the risk of financial exclusion in advanced ones: technology and electronic payments. The same move away from cash that is helping the most vulnerable in, say, Lusaka, may be harming the most vulnerable in Louisville, Liverpool and Lyon.

Each and every payment we make informs the future of our payments, feeding into decisions about how to staff checkouts; whether to accept cheques; and if, when and where to distribute cash. If the trend away from cash continues in countries such as Britain and Sweden, then shops will stop accepting cash, ATMs will disappear and the unbanked and cash dependent will be left unable to pay or be paid.

When people have no access to payments, they will find alternatives. In extremis that may be theft, but in consensual, civil circumstances, what you pay *with*, and what you are prepared to accept in payment, is between you and your creditors and debtors. It doesn't really matter what we use to settle our mutual debts, so long as it is accepted. Banks will take your home if you fail to pay them the interest on your mortgage. In wartime, people often resort to barter. During the Nazi occupation of Holland, an entire shadow economy was effectively created to fund the Dutch resistance. The man who took on the role of treasurer to the resistance, banker Walraven (Wally) van Hall, devised two ingenious ruses to circumvent the regime.

First, he found a way to borrow money from banks and wealthy Dutch citizens. As proof of their investments – or 'in payment' for their guilders – they received worthless old stock certificates; van Hall's promise and their hope was that they could use this 'currency' to get their money back after the war. They struck a good deal. When the war was over, the Dutch government froze all bank accounts and declared banknotes null and void. Van Hall's financiers had exchanged valid banknotes that would become worthless for worthless stock certificates that would become valid.

Second, with the approval of the Dutch government-in-exile, van Hall committed the biggest banking fraud in Dutch history. With inside help at the central bank, he removed 50 million Dutch guilders (close to half a billion dollars in today's money) in promissory notes from the vault and replaced them with forgeries. He then sold the original notes for cash, which was used to fund the resistance. After the war all the loans were redeemed properly.[5]

During the Irish banking strike in 1970, the Republic's economy survived largely on the basis of uncashable cheques. For more than six months, the population effectively printed its own money. In the first half of 2020, after the Covid-19 pandemic erupted, cash ran out in parts of Papua New Guinea and residents resorted to 'tabu', strings of marine snail shells, measured in an arm's length. One-and-a-half arms will buy you a packet of rice, should you ever be caught short there. On our fictional island it's a banknote that does the rounds but it could just as well have been gold, salt, wooden sticks or even cigarettes, all of which have served as currency at some point. And herein lies the rub. As consumers, we are free to make bilateral payment choices and so too are merchants and businesses. But our choices have implications far beyond ourselves – who makes the money from payments and how, who controls payments' power, and who decides our payment futures. Our choices may also leave others unable to pay or be paid – a possibility we ignore at our peril.

To understand how to go forward, it helps to look back to how payments came about in the first place. Conventional economic theory holds that currency, the means of payment, evolved over time from the concrete to the abstract. Tribal societies simplified barter by selecting one rare and valuable commodity to trade all others against. Such commodity-based money, like seashells or gold, is nobody's debt, a feature that has special appeal to people who see debt as the root of all evil, or at least the financial kind.

The countervailing theory, espoused by anthropologists like David Graeber, argues that debt preceded money, and that from the start most

---

[5]   Sadly, van Hall did not live to see it. In early 1945, he was betrayed and executed.

money was tradable debt.[6] The economists' theory sounds plausible, but the anthropologists appear to have the facts on their side in the form of tribal societies' behaviour, past and present. Man did not live in a garden of Eden trading seashells; life was indebted, as well as nasty, brutish and short.

Our lives may be longer, but they are no less indebted. All our money now is 'debt money', representing someone else's obligation to pay. My money at, say, Citibank, is nothing more or less than Citibank's debt to me. If I pay into your HSBC account from my account at Citibank, what I've really done is transform Citibank's debt to me into HSBC's debt to you.

I could, of course, instead pay you in cash (for now), but the banknotes in my pocket are paper promises to pay by the central bank that issued them. We can quibble about what central banks would pay us if we presented them with their own banknotes, but banknotes are nothing more than liabilities on their balance sheets. Transferrable debt is what we pay with, and what we get when we are paid.

Unlike commodity money such as seashells and gold, this debt money of ours carries the inherent risk of default – but no (advanced) economy can do without it. Which is exactly why, back before he was a musical, Alexander Hamilton advocated the creation of federal debt to replace the patchwork of state IOUs that prevailed in the late eighteenth century. Seeing that the nascent US economy was being held back by a lack of currency, his intent was not so much to encourage a federal borrowing free-for-all as to create a highly liquid payment instrument to facilitate commerce.[7]

---

[6] To be fair, the theory of debt money was first formulated in the late nineteenth and early twentieth centuries by economists Henry Dunning MacLeod and Alfred Mitchell-Innes.

[7] In addition to being the subject of a Broadway musical, Alexander Hamilton was one of the USA's 'founding fathers' and the first Secretary of the US Treasury. Much of the foundations of America's financial system were laid by him.

It is perhaps ironic that to pay, i.e. to discharge our debts, we need yet more debt. When we pay our creditors, we are replacing our debt to them with money, which is just another form of debt. The point of this replacement is, of course, that our creditors would prefer their banks to owe them money (or their central banks, if we give them banknotes) rather than ourselves. The core of payments and money is therefore trust or, rather, lack of trust in each other's creditworthiness – we don't trust each other, but we *do* trust the system. Economists Nobuhiro Kiyotaki and John Moore characterised this situation in a memorable re-engineering of a biblical phrase: 'evil is the root of all money'.[8]

---

[8] The original wording in the King James Bible is: 'For the love of money is the root of all evil', 1 Timothy 6:10.

2. If money doesn't move, how does it make the world go round?

On a fateful afternoon in late 2018, *Financial Times* journalist Jemima Kelly used her iPhone to pay a £1.50 London bus fare. Fifteen minutes later, when an inspector asked her for her ticket, she found that her iPhone had run out of battery. Asked to provide proof of payment, she was eventually able to provide her bank statement, but as her bank card was not registered to Transport for London's system, it didn't prove what journey she had actually taken. A bureaucratic nightmare ensued. No matter that she'd hit the payment cap for that day anyway – she was faced with a £476 fine and a criminal conviction (later respectively refunded and quashed).[1]

This story is a good illustration of how modern payments are, above all, about information. Language can be misleading. When we talk about payments, we talk about moving money and sending money; about channels and conduits; about flows and movements; about rails and routes; about traffic, transit, travel, transfers and transmissions. All these words imply movement but, truth be told, the vast majority of payments are simply a sleight of hand: entries changed in book ledgers. And, while the technology has changed beyond all recognition, Bank of England Deputy Governor John Cunliffe was right on the mark when he described today's payments as being 'economically the equivalent of eighteenth-century bank clerks with quill pens altering their banks' ledgers to debit one account and credit another'.

---

[1]   For contactless payments, Transport for London (TfL) has a limit on how much you pay for journeys in a single day or week. Once you reach the capped amount, they won't charge you more regardless of how many journeys you make.

There's an exception to every rule and, in this case, it is of course the cash payment. If you have a bank account, your cash transaction will likely start with an ATM withdrawal and a corresponding deduction from your current account. And it will end with the merchant dropping off the physical cash at its bank, where the funds will be added to its account. Your cash payment is thus a roundabout way of moving money from your bank account to the merchant's account; the ledgers change once again. Other than cash, money doesn't really *move*; the record of its ownership is simply altered by book entry.

The same is true for gold. Gold rarely ever moves. Instead, each bar is stamped with a unique serial number. When you buy or sell gold, in most cases you are simply transferring the registration of that bar, or part of that bar, and not the metal itself. Even under the gold standard, gold largely moved by book entry only. In the early part of the last century, the bulk of the world's gold was stacked up in cages in the vaults at the Bank of England and a smaller amount at the US Federal Reserve. When foreign central banks needed to transfer gold between one another, the transfers would be recorded in the books of either the BoE or the Fed and, for the most part, the gold didn't actually move (although sometimes they would move the bullion bars from one cage to another). Two world wars and a bit of this and that, and it is the Fed that now holds most of the world's gold reserves and the BoE a much lower amount, but the same still applies.

When gold *does* actually need to be shifted, elaborate planning and expensive logistics are required. In 2019, the Polish central bank decided to repatriate the estimated £4 billion worth of gold that had been moved from Warsaw to London at the outbreak of the Second World War. The top-secret operation involved elite police forces, chartered planes, helicopters and high-tech trucks, and necessitated eight night-time flights over several months to transport 8,000 gold bars weighing 100 tonnes. A strong case for book entry if ever there was one.

Banks (still) play a crucial role in this book entry. If I have to pay you, and you and I both have an account with the same bank, it's easy; my bank simply deducts the amount from my account and adds it to yours. The 'movement' takes place on our bank's ledger. If we bank with different banks, the two banks will still add and subtract the amount to and from our respective accounts, and then, afterwards, settle the payment between themselves.

Depending on how we pay, banks (and other payment providers) conduct this settlement in a variety of ways, but they all involve changing entries in ledgers, including, ultimately, the ledgers at central banks, where commercial banks hold their own balances.

Cash aside, all payments today are therefore digital debt entries recorded in a ledger system that was invented centuries ago; an antique practice made modern by the dancing bits and bytes that animate digital ledgers lodged deep within computer systems.

Payments today are inextricably linked to money and, in turn, to banks. The money we tend to think about is the deposits we hold at banks to make our daily payments. It is these payment accounts that allow banks to create money – a skill that distinguishes them from any other business. How do they do it? To understand that, we need to take a brief historical detour.

Late medieval history and downtown Sienna are the go-to places for learning about the origins of banking, so let's imagine some medieval merchants depositing a total of 100 coins in a bank off the Piazza del Campo. The bank promises to keep the coins and make them available to the merchants whenever they want to withdraw them. The bank also promises to transfer the coins from one merchant to another on instruction by single book entry.

After a while, the bank realises that these merchants are pretty prudent types because it always has at least 90 gold coins in its vault. The bank decides it can make money by lending out some of these coins to other merchants and charging interest on the loans. So it lends out 75 of the 90 coins and charges the borrowers 5 per cent for the pleasure. While there is a theoretical risk that the depositing merchants show up simultaneously and demand their coins, the bank thinks this is highly improbable, and of course the extra interest revenue is welcome.

The merchants still own the 100 coins that they deposited. For them, this is real money that they can use whenever they need to make a payment. It is the same as having the coins in their purses, but without the bother. Meanwhile, the borrowers also have their 75 coins to spend as they need. So by taking the deposited coins and making the loan, the bank has just created 75 gold coins. Abracadabra!

Modern banks 'create' money in much the same way. Customers deposit their money at banks which in turn use much of it to make loans. The banks deposit the rest of the money at central banks to ensure there's sufficient liquidity to meet the demands of customers who want to withdraw their money. Banks can pay out the proceeds of loans in cash or deposit the proceeds in borrowers' accounts. Banks can therefore 'magically' create money out of nothing with the mere stroke of a pen – or, rather, two strokes, one on each side of the balance sheet. On the asset side they add a loan, say, $100,000 to a firm, and on the liability side they credit that firm's current or checking account with the same amount, allowing them to spend it. With those two flourishes of the pen, the banks have just created $100,000 of debt money.

Magic can also, of course, wreak havoc. Think of the Disney movie *Fantasia* in which Mickey Mouse is the sorcerer's apprentice. With his new powers, Mickey creates enchanted brooms to carry his water buckets, only to find them multiplying out of control and flooding the place. While most economists agree that modern economies couldn't function without the credit provided by money-creating banks, this practice invariably leads to booms and busts, as we experience all too often. The compromise is to permit the magic but keep it under tight control. This is why banking is heavily regulated and why central banks are so important. They are meant to be the sorcerers who prevent the apprentices (the banks) from wrecking the place.

The ability to create money has put banks at the heart of payments for the last few centuries. Increasingly, however, the way we pay is changing: new technologies are shaking things up and new competitors are vying to offer alternatives to traditional banking. Banks may need payments, but do payments really need banks?

3. Not so simple: the fundamental challenges of payment

You might well conclude at this point that all this money-creation magic is merely a smoke screen thrown up by bankers to justify their existence and rationalise their pay. After all, if payments are just changes to bits and bytes in digital ledgers, shouldn't we leave them to software engineers to handle? You're not the only one to think along those lines. Indeed, $70 billion payment start-up Stripe is based on the premise 'that payments is a problem rooted in code, not finance': it is built on just seven lines of code. As ever, the reality is a little more complicated, even for Stripe payments.

Every form of payment – including cash – has to deal with the three basic challenges inherent in any transfer of value: risk, liquidity and convention. I *won't* pay you unless I know you will deliver, I *can't* pay you unless I have the money, and I *shan't* pay you unless we have a mutually acceptable method of payment. That is where payment instruments come in: cash, cards, cheques, bank transfers and so on. Each one has to manage these three challenges. Let's take them one by one.

Risk

Payments are inherently risky. Any transaction involves the risk that someone might not get the money or the goods; perhaps because the payer does not have the funds and their cheque bounces, or because the investor has already paid for their bonds, but the seller goes bankrupt before they are transferred. This is called settlement risk.

Just like the doors are the unavoidable weak spots in the security of any building, payments are the weak spot in any storage of value. Money is easiest to steal when and where it goes in and comes out. Pirates attacked treasure ships on the high seas, highwaymen targeted travellers on the open road and pickpockets look for customers who have just taken their money out of the bank or ATM. Similarly, the private keys Bitcoin uses are most vulnerable when they are taken out of 'cold' offline storage to be used for payment.[1]

Then there is always fraud risk. Both parties to a transaction, not just the one paying, face fraud risk. The shopkeeper's customers may not be who they pretend to be and may be using stolen credit cards or forged bank-notes. Or the shopkeeper may be passing off counterfeit goods as the genuine articles to unsuspecting customers. Sometimes the two risks, settlement and fraud, combine; for instance, when the seller ships their goods but the buyer has no intention of paying, or the buyer retracts the payment after the goods have been shipped. Much to their surprise, sellers sometimes see transactions reversed and money that has been credited to their accounts is suddenly deducted from them. One popular scam deliberately exploits the fact that many banks will credit cheques to recipients' accounts before verifying whether the writers have sufficient funds. If and when they discover that the cheque writers have insufficient funds, the banks will then reverse the transactions. As this sometimes doesn't happen for several days, the victims have often already shipped the goods and end up with neither goods nor money.

Liquidity

To make a payment you need money, of the right kind and in the right place. Owning boats and castles is great, but you can't use them to pay in shops. Liquidity is key. In 1946, then Dutch finance minister, Piet Lieftinck, who had withdrawn all paper cash from circulation a year earlier in an effort to contain inflation and tax wartime profiteers, found himself in need of such

---

[1] Private keys are secret numbers that allow users to access their Bitcoins and other cryptocurrencies.

liquidity.[2] Needing to make an urgent call, he asked a passer-by for a ten-cent coin 'to call a friend' (these were the days of the public phone box). Lieftinck was understandably, if unfairly, deeply unpopular at the time and the passer-by is alleged to have replied: 'Here, have two so you can call all of them.'

You may have more friends than Lieftinck, but you still need liquidity in the form of notes and coins in your wallet – just like he did. And in the right currency because most shops won't take foreign money. To buy bonds, investors do not just need sufficient funds, they need acceptable funds in the same place that they want to buy the bonds. They may have lots of dollars in their US bank or pounds in their British one, but if the bonds are being delivered in Japan, they – or their agent – will need liquidity in the form of yen in a Japanese bank account.

Liquidity, however, has a cost. Money in a wallet or current account doesn't earn interest – and much less in Japan, where negative rates eat away at it. Banks need to keep sufficient reserves with other banks or clearing systems but it costs them; liquidity is an asset and, as with all their assets, banks need to maintain a certain amount of (costly) capital against it.

Convention

Every time we pay, we make a payment choice – an individual decision that shapes a wider system. How we pay and get paid is a function not only of how *we* want to pay or be paid but also of how those *around* us want to pay and be paid. A payments mechanism – be it bank-based, wallet-based,

---

[2] Lieftinck had withdrawn all notes from circulation, giving those who held them blocked bank credits. Banks were subsequently supplied with new banknotes, so that people could receive their wages and in the following months, de-blocking of the frozen accounts started, but a 90 per cent tax was levied on any assets accumulated between May 1940 and December 1945. This, together with further fiscal measures, helped ensure the country met American demands to qualify for aid through the Marshall Plan. After leaving office Lieftinck joined the World Bank and the International Monetary Fund.

card-based, cash-based or otherwise – is only as useful as people make it. Ultimately, it's a social construct.

Payment mechanisms also depend on unseen conventions such as shared standards, common rules and legal frameworks, and (often implicit) agreements. Some of these are technical: can my card be read by your terminal? Others are rules, such as the US and French laws that put prison terms on writing uncovered cheques (cheques for which there are insufficient funds in the account to meet them). Still others are customs; people prefer payment mechanisms that they know and feel comfortable with.

A good payment mechanism addresses all three challenges: it minimises risk and liquidity and it maximises convention in the form of acceptance and usage.

There is a trade-off between risk and liquidity even in your daily payments – how you get your groceries, whether you're an Amazon adventurer, a Netflix night-surfer and so on. By extending overdrafts, banks enable us to pay even when we have no money in our accounts, but in doing so they increase their credit risk. If the charges they raise on overdrafts are set to cover their costs (and then multiplied by several factors), the size of the overdrafts they extend us are carefully calibrated according to our ability to repay (or should be). Similarly, by accepting cheques, merchants increase their chances of selling to us, even though the money takes longer to reach them.

But it is convention that plays the biggest role in retail payments. Millions of consumers and businesses have to pay each other every day and need common systems through which to do so. Introducing new retail payment instruments is easier said than done because the conventions and tools need to be adopted by a critical mass before they can be of any real use. It's no good a shop taking payment through a new instrument if none of its customers want to use it, and it's no good consumers adopting a new instrument if no or few retailers will accept it.

Changing retail behaviour is not easy, which is why most successful payment innovations base themselves on existing conventions. Apple Pay, for example, is built around debit and credit cards. There are exceptions to this rule, but they generally start by focusing on small groups of people or businesses that pay each other regularly. PayPal, which got big by facilitating transactions on a nascent eBay, is a great example of one such innovation. Credit cards, which began by serving a small group of diners that frequented the same New York restaurants in the 1950s, are another.

These three challenges – risk, liquidity and convention – profoundly shape the entire payments' landscape and we'll come back to them repeatedly in future chapters. First let's take a closer look at the world's oldest form of payment.

PART II

HISTORY

4. The enigma of cash

Cash is simple and familiar. By far our oldest method of payment, it is unique in not depending on bits and bytes and mysterious ledgers to transfer value. It's easy, anonymous, instant and final: when somebody gives you cash, there's no risk that they don't have sufficient funds. Cash is also untraceable, you can immediately reuse the proceeds for another transaction, and its transfer is unlikely to necessitate middlemen or lawyers. Unsurprisingly, it has long been favoured by the criminal fraternity.

And not just the underworld; cash remains the world's most widely used form of payment by number of transactions. You'd think that if we know about anything, it would be cash. Think again. Much of how we use cash remains a mystery – the UK's National Audit Office found in mid-2020 that a whopping £50 billion's worth of UK notes were unaccounted for. We have no idea how many cash transactions people make, or for what value. We know (more or less) how much money people take out of ATMs and banks, but then the road stops. To continue our journey, we can only extrapolate from surveys.

Why? Because you can use the $20 bill you get from an ATM for a single payment or for twenty payments of a dollar each. The receiver(s) can return the $20 bill to the banking system or spend it, and so on. In any event, such surveys explain only part of the story because most cash in circulation doesn't actually circulate; it consists of paper money that is seldom, if ever, distributed by ATMs, such as the $100 bill or the €200 and €500 bank-notes. Not to be outdone in matters financial, the Swiss have a 1,000 franc note that is worth about $1,000. The central bank maintains the note is not used nefariously, but rather by law-abiding Swiss citizens who use it to pay their bills at the post office.

It is one of the enigmas of cash that most of it consists of such high-denomination notes, few of which are ever used or even seen by the general population. The €500 note was even known as a 'Bin Laden' because everyone knew that it existed and what it looked like, but no one knew where to find it.

The $100 note represents 80 per cent of the total $1.8 trillion worth of all US dollar notes in circulation, meaning that George Washington – whose portrait adorns the $1 bill or 'buck' – is trounced by fellow founding father Benjamin Franklin, who is pictured on the $100 bill.[1] Breaking that down by the adult population and the number and denomination of the notes that we know are in circulation, that works out to just seven notes of $10 but fifty-five $100 notes for every adult American.[2] While this distribution should make very rich pickings for thieves, it would probably jar with the experience of the average American pickpocket. We know from surveys that US consumers carry on average just $75 in their wallets. Even if we allow for cash sitting in ATMs, banks and cash tills, we can still account for only a fraction of the total amount in circulation. Which begs the question: where has all the money gone?

In the case of the US dollar, it's mostly 'on vacation'. Some 60 per cent of all dollars and 75 per cent of all $100 notes are held abroad. Successive US administrations have supported a policy of making currency available to foreign countries 'on demand', meaning they will ship physical dollar banknotes (mostly $100 bills) to these countries as people buy and withdraw dollars from local banks and exchange houses. This overseas balance has been steadily rising since the 1990s, when it stood at a mere 20 per cent of all dollar bills in circulation. It received a significant boost from the domestic currency crises in Argentina and the former Soviet bloc countries; between

---

[1]   Not just by value but also by number of notes, as there are fifty-five $100 notes for every adult American versus just fifty $1 notes.

[2]   Plus seven notes of $50, thirty-seven of $20, thirteen of $5 and fifty of $1.

1993 and 2013 the USA shipped some $20 billion per year to these countries alone. Famously, the USA also flew about $12 billion (and possibly as much as $40 billion) to Iraq in military aircraft, to pay for the reopening of government and restoring basic services. To give some idea of physical scale, $1 billion in $100 notes amounts to ten fully loaded pallets.

The euro is the other major currency with significant foreign circulation, although it's a distant number two to the dollar. Less detailed data and research is available on the euro, but the German Bundesbank, which used to distribute 70 per cent of the €500 notes produced, estimated that two-thirds of its production went abroad. A lot of those German-printed notes may have ended up in southern Europe, where the populace has more trust in euro notes carrying serial numbers starting with Germany's X symbol (than, say, in Greek-issued serial numbers starting Y). One-third of euro cash is thought to circulate outside the Eurozone, much of it in Russia and the Balkans.

Foreign usage is certainly significant but it answers only part of the question on the whereabouts of cash – and only for the US dollar and the euro. What is more, survey findings explain the whereabouts of only 5–10 per cent of most currencies in circulation. This would leave us in the dark about the rest, were it not for the fact that central banks have to check all incoming banknotes and replace those that are worn out. This process provides a valuable insight into a note's usage. The US Currency Education Program (CEP) puts the estimated lifespan of a $1 bill at just over five years, while a $100 note lasts about fifteen years. Large notes are used less frequently than small notes, but it's unlikely that they spend their entire lives in safes and under mattresses. More likely, they are circulating in the underground economy and simply frequenting the Federal Reserve less often than their lower-denomination peers.

Cash's attributes certainly make it an attractive proposition for illegal activity (Table 1). Based on the data on the amount and usage of large-denomination notes, some estimates put the size of the underground economy as high as 25 per cent of GDP, even in advanced economies like

Table 1. Attributes of different payment mechanisms from a criminal perspective.

	Anonymous?	Can be traced?	Ubiquity of acceptance	Immediacy of value transfer	Irreversible?	Constant value?	Transaction cost	Physical convenience
Bank transfer	No	Yes	Needs payer and payee to have bank accounts	Increasingly within a day	No	High	Variable	Yes
Non-bank wire transfer	No	Yes	Through agent	Increasingly real time	Sometimes	High	Variable	Yes
Bitcoin	Yes	Limited	Very limited	Instant	Yes	Extremely volatile	Variable	Yes
Gold	Yes	No	Limited	Yes	Yes	Volatile	High	Heavy and bulky
Diamonds	Yes	No	Very limited	Yes	Yes	Volatile	Very high	Very compact
Cash	Yes	No	Accepted everywhere	Yes	Yes	High	Low	Can be heavy and bulky for large values

Adapted from Peter Sands (2016). *Making it Harder for the Bad Guys: The case for eliminating high-denomination notes.* Working Paper 52, Harvard Kennedy School.

the USA. This includes tax evasion, as well as criminal activities such as drug and human trafficking. The US drugs economy is estimated to amount to $100–150 billion per year, mostly paid in cash and much of it – we have to presume – in high-denomination notes. Although interestingly, while 90 per cent of all US banknotes carry traces of cocaine, the percentage for $100 notes is significantly lower. Evidently, while the high-value notes are used to pay for drugs, an altogether different use is being found for low-value ones (see Table 1).

Economists have long pointed out the essential contradiction between governments having stringent anti-money-laundering regimes while printing large-denomination notes. Large notes are clearly convenient for those of a criminal persuasion: $1 million in single dollar bills weighs more than one tonne and has a volume of more than one cubic metre, but $1 million in $100 notes weighs about 10 kg (22 pounds) and fits neatly into a briefcase. In the even higher denomination €500 note, that same $1 million would weigh only 2 kg and fit in a small bag – or a large stomach. Indeed, an unfortunate 'euro-mule' was caught travelling to Colombia in 2004 with €200,000 in his stomach in €500 notes.

Not all criminals insist on the high-value notes, however. Two decades before our Colombian mule ingested 400 Bin Ladens, the Dutch brewing magnate Freddy Heineken was famously kidnapped. Heineken was seized with his chauffeur as he left his office to go home, just 200 metres from the Dutch central bank. The kidnappers eschewed the 1,000-guilder notes (worth more than $500) because they were worried that they would be easy to trace and difficult to exchange. Instead, they demanded that the unprecedented ransom of 35 million Dutch guilders (about $20 million) be paid in medium-denomination notes in four currencies.[3] Unfortunately this also made the ransom unwieldy: it weighed some 400 kg. Having decided in

---

[3] They asked for 50,000 each of: 100 Dutch guilder notes, $100 notes, 500 French franc notes and 100 Deutsche mark notes.

true Dutch fashion to make their getaway on bicycles, the gang had to bury the loot in woodland outside Amsterdam and had retrieved only about a quarter of the total before their stash was discovered by walkers. Although it must have been a terrifying ordeal, Heineken survived his twenty-one-day incarceration and even kept his reputation as a raconteur intact when he later described it: 'They tortured me . . . They made me drink Carlsberg!'

Former chief executive of Standard Chartered bank Peter Sands summed up the situation succinctly in *Making it Harder for the Bad Guys* when he described high-denomination notes as 'an anachronism in a modern economy': 'They play little role in the functioning of the legitimate economy, yet a crucial role in the underground economy. The irony is that they are provided to criminals by the state.' So why are some countries turning a blind eye to the use of their own high-denomination notes in tax evasion, crime, terrorism and corruption at the same time as they are inflicting ever more rigorous anti-money-laundering regulations on banks? Well, some governments *are* taking another look at high-denomination notes. But doing away with cash – or any type of payment – is easier said than done. Emotions run high, attachments are strong, habits are seemingly unbreakable – and the logistics are no walk in the park either.

Canada ceased issuing its C$1,000 note in 2000 and Singapore ended its S$10,000 note in 2014, but in the Eurozone it hasn't been quite so easy. That same year, seventeen of the nineteen central banks in the Eurozone stopped printing their infamous Bin Ladens. Germany and Austria, both cash-intensive countries, followed suit in 2019, although not without protest. At the time, Bundesbank chief Jens Weidmann remonstrated that phasing out the note would 'do little to combat crime, but damage confidence in the euro'. No longer accepted or exchangeable in any of the other Eurozone countries (or the UK), the €500 note remains legal tender in Germany and Austria, where it can still be exchanged at and recirculated by commercial banks. In theory, it will eventually be phased out as the two Germanic central banks stop issuing new ones.

This compromise may not resolve the issue at a stroke, but it does avoid a much worse outcome – undermining trust in cash. This was Weidmann's point: non-acceptance of the €500 note could make people nervous about whether similar measures might be adopted for other notes. In fear they might start refusing to use the €200 or even the €100 notes. Most importantly, this shows the importance to central banks, especially in German-speaking countries, of maintaining absolute trust in cash.

Taking more drastic action against relatively high-value notes can cause huge disruption. In 2016, India's government 'demonetised' the two largest notes in circulation – the INR 500 ($7.50) and INR 1,000 ($15) – with the aim of flushing 'grey money'[4] out into the open. At the time these two notes represented 86 per cent of the currency in circulation, although in fact the lower denominations representing the remaining 14 per cent did most of the day-to-day work.

Prime Minister Narendra Modi shocked the nation on the evening of 8 November that year by announcing on live television that the offending notes were to be banned at midnight – within just four hours. People were then given several weeks to exchange their demonetised currency for new notes at banks, but these could not be printed fast enough. The upshot was a currency crunch that left tens of millions of Indians cashless or queuing for hours each day to retrieve small sums of cash. It took weeks for things to settle down and had a significant negative impact on GDP. Meanwhile, the price of gold, India's favoured alternative to currency, rose by 20–30 per cent.[5]

The ultimate success of the operation was extremely limited. The idea behind a money purge is that only people who can justify the origin of their cash get to exchange old notes for new ones, leaving the holders of grey

---

[4] Grey money is money derived from tax evasion and or funds hidden from tax authorities.

[5] Indian households own an estimated 25,000 tonnes of gold, worth $1.5 trillion – four times the amount of domestic currency in circulation.

money with worthless banknotes. But after a painstaking two-year audit, the Reserve Bank of India reported that as much as 99.3 per cent of the junked banknotes had returned to the banking system rather than being purged. Either there was less grey money than Modi suspected or India's money-laundering schemes are more effective than its money-purging ones.

And then there is North Korea. While the hermit kingdom's government specialises in putting out positive domestic news stories, there is an offshore industry dedicated to disseminating negative ones. Both sets of stories have to be treated with some caution but, even so, the reports on the country's most recent currency revaluation put it firmly in the disastrous camp.

The current Supreme Leader's father, Kim Jong-il, ordered a sudden revaluation of the North Korean won in November 2009. The government immediately chopped two zeroes off banknotes, pulled the old notes from legal tender and limited the amount of old money that could be exchanged for new cash. Not only did that wipe out huge amounts of savings, but the old notes were pulled a week before the new ones were distributed – meaning much of the economy was shut down in the interim. Instead of reinforcing the beleaguered won, the move spurred an immediate rush to hold foreign currency as the North Koreans lost confidence in the currency provided by their government. The result was a rare domestic revolt and a dramatic collapse in the currency from 30 won to the dollar to about 8,500. By 2013, an estimated $2 billion in US dollar notes was circulating within the $21.5 billion economy – useful for Uncle Sam, not so good for the Kims.

The Indian and North Korean efforts were not so much wars on cash as attacks on certain forms of physical money. A much broader battle is underway – one that cash may not survive.

5. The war on cash

The idea of a 'war on cash' has been gaining ground over the last two decades. The fear that a powerful elite wants to take cash away and track our transactions has united libertarians, anti-poverty campaigners and conspiracy theorists in opposition. Few, though, frame their argument in such apocalyptic terms as controversial commentator Jim Rickards, who wrote in October 2019: 'Before pigs are slaughtered, they are herded into pens. Before savers are slaughtered with negative rates, they are herded into digital accounts from which there is no escape. There's no turning back at that point. The bottom line is the war on cash is real and it's not going away.'

You might be forgiven for thinking that Rickards resides in North Korea. In fact, he is based in the USA, which is also home to his arch adversary, the Better than Cash Alliance (BTCA), a coalition of private-sector companies, governments and development organisations with subtler branding and a more roseate disposition towards a world without cash.

Funded by, among others, the Bill & Melinda Gates Foundation, Citibank, Ford Foundation, Mastercard, Visa, the Omidyar Network and the US Agency for International Development (USAID), the BTCA is dedicated to promoting the transition away from cash to electronic payments. This, it claims, will reduce costs, increase transparency and accountability, diminish security risks, enhance access to financial services for the poor and drive inclusive economic growth.

If that all sounds like motherhood and apple pie, the BTCA is as breezy about the politics and practicalities of doing away with cash as Rickards is paranoid. 'Politically, the abolition of currency would run into opposition from some of the legitimately cash-dependent poor and elderly, from those for whom the anonymity of cash is desired because they are engaged in illegal activities, and from libertarians,' wrote Willem Buiter, Citibank's then chief economist. 'The first constituency can be helped, the second can be ignored and the third one should take one for the team.'

Whichever side is right (and, in truth, both have some valid points), cash is definitely in decline. It may be the world's oldest form of payment, but it is rapidly being driven to the point of extinction in many advanced economies due to habitat loss and invasive predators. So much so that some lawmakers have now declared cash to be an endangered species and passed legislation to conserve and protect it.

As ever with payments, however, big differences persist across countries and cultures. While a few countries are seeing cash usage dwindle to the extent that they are legislating to preserve it, in most countries usage is declining only slowly.

Nestled on the south-eastern edge of Europe, Albania is super-keen on cash. The World Bank estimates that businesses there receive a whopping 99.2 per cent of payments in cash and consumers make 96 per cent of their payments in cash; even the majority of pensions are paid out in cash. In total, this cash usage costs the Albanian economy 1.7 per cent of GDP. If just half of the country's cash utility-bill payments were substituted with direct debits, the World Bank estimates that Albanian consumers would save about 750 million lek (c. $6.5 million) a year, or $2.20 per Albanian per year. This amount is material in a country with a minimum monthly wage of about $190.

But back to the vanguard of increasingly cashless countries on the north-western edge of Europe. In Sweden, the Netherlands and the UK, less than half of all purchases are now made with cash and this share is declining fast. And, oddly enough, it is Sweden – the first European country to introduce banknotes – that is furthest along the road to getting rid of them.

In Sweden, cash is now used for less than 13 per cent of all purchases. Many Swedes never use cash and no longer carry it. The total currency in circulation in the country today has fallen to around 1 per cent of GDP, down from 4 per cent of GDP in 2005. The crime rate has fallen and cash is now refused everywhere, from the ubiquitous IKEA furniture stores to Stockholm's Abba museum (although the group's hit 'Money, Money, Money' is still very much on the playlist).

But then money and cash are not the same thing – and cash costs more than money. There's the printing of banknotes and minting of coins, of course, but that accounts for only some of the cost: cash also needs to be transported and distributed; ATMs need to be filled and maintained; merchants need to monitor, count and collect cash, and transport it to banks; and banks need to recount it, sort it and redistribute it. And so it goes on.

Obviously, this must all be done securely, so bank branches need special facilities and vaults, merchants need cameras and safes, and the trucks that tie everything together need to be armoured and guarded. All in all, the total cost of cash is estimated to be around 0.2–0.4 per cent of global GDP, well below the 1.7 per cent it costs in Albania, but still some 10–20 per cent of the total cost of the payment system. This amounts to around $0.40 per cash transaction, or 2.5 per cent of the value of the average $15 cash purchase.

Not only is the cost of cash substantial but much of this cost is fixed. It does not decline as cash usage declines and would disappear only if cash were abolished altogether. A good illustration is the ATM network. The cost of refilling an ATM is the same whether you are topping it up or filling it up completely. You can't close half the ATMs and expect the remaining half to still be useful – there's a certain point at which the remaining number will become as good as useless. Given that much of the cost of cash will disappear only with the last cash transaction, we shouldn't be surprised that banks and merchants in the vanguard countries are beginning to contemplate a life without cash altogether.

What would happen if this were to come to pass? Would the financial system survive? Most economists and bankers would answer broadly in the affirmative. Cash isn't a crucial function of central banking. We could continue to make deposits in dollars, euros, pounds, yen, lek and all the rest, even if their physical manifestations disappeared.

What about 'printing' money? Would central banks still be able to create money if they couldn't print it? Again, the short answer is yes. The metaphors around monetary policy are unhelpful here. Many of the headlines used to describe the Covid-19 economic aid programme involved the printing of banknotes: the Fed was 'firing up the printing press', the European Central Bank (ECB) was 'priming the money-printing gun' or, for those of a more digital bent, the 'Money Printer Go Brrr' meme. Evocative, but misleading; just as 'sending' money isn't what banks do to make payments, 'printing' isn't the way that central banks create money.

Paradoxically, printing banknotes and putting them into circulation through the banking system does *not* typically increase the money supply. Central banks create money by increasing reserves, the deposits that commercial banks hold at central banks, and reserves could exist quite happily in a world without cash.

While the private sector has ample motive to promote a move away from cash – the banks to lower their costs, the merchants to reduce commercial friction and overheads, and the card industry, wallet and e-payment providers to increase their revenue – the public sector is also keen.

More efficient, more transparent, easier for the good guys and harder for the bad guys, non-cash payments are the flavour *du jour*. Provided that the systems are robust, the electricity supply is stable and the communications networks are conversing, a world without cash would theoretically work. But those conspiring to cast off cash face significant practical hurdles and fierce opposition; and, as they have found out, our attachment to cash runs deep.

Northern Europeans are, at the risk of generalising, renowned for prizing pragmatism over sentimentalism, but even in Sweden, Britain and the Netherlands there's been some perturbation about this uber-efficient cashless future. And with good reason. Beyond its aforementioned advantages, cash has another important quality: it affords universal access to payments. You don't need to have a bank account, a card, a smartphone, a computer, internet access, 4G, a virtual wallet or even a leather one, to pay or be paid in cash. You just need to be there. Our economy depends on the payment system moving money efficiently and safely, but that's no good if it doesn't work for everyone. The system has to serve all of us, or it serves none of us.

In Sweden, the decline of cash has inspired its own protest movement. Kontantupproret (Cash Rebellion) is a network of organisations bound together by a shared interest in keeping cash alive. True to form, Kontantupproret presents the disappearance of cash as a grave threat to democracy, privacy and individual freedom.

Interestingly, the outfit is headed by former national police commissioner and president of Interpol Björn Eriksson, a man whose CV might suggest he prized legality over liberty. But as he explained to the *Guardian* in 2018: 'When you have a fully digital system you have no weapon to defend yourself if someone turns it off. If Putin invades Gotland [Sweden's largest island] it will be enough for him to turn off the payments system. No other country would even think about taking these sorts of risks, they would demand some sort of analogue system.'

Whether as a direct result of Kontantupproret's efforts or real fears about imminent invasions, legislation to preserve cash has been put in place in Sweden.[1] Rishi Sunak, UK Chancellor of the Exchequer, announced similar plans in March 2020.[2] The Swedish measures have been pushed through for two key reasons: first, to ensure that everyone, including the digitally

---

[1] In January 2020, the Obligation for Certain Credit Institutions to Provide Cash Services law came into effect in Sweden. It requires certain local credit institutions and branches of foreign credit institutions to provide cash services to consumers and firms.

[2] Delivering his first budget in March 2020, Chancellor Rishi Sunak announced that the UK government was to bring forward legislation to protect access to cash and ensure that the UK's cash infrastructure was sustainable in the long term. Budget 2020, Section 1.53.

disadvantaged, is able to pay and be paid; second, to ensure that payments can still be made if there were to be a major disruption to the system. Neither consideration is trivial.

Having reaped the benefits of a surge of economic activity away from cash, the banks, merchants and public sectors in these three countries now face a problem – *how* to cater for people who can't or won't move away from cash, and *who* should provide such services. With substantial numbers of Swedes and Britons now using only eWallets and eBanking, the bottom line has moved decisively against using cash.[3] But catering for the significant minority who are being squeezed out of payments by the demise of branch banking, the disappearance of cheques, a refusal to accept cash and the deple-tion of free ATMs (all made possible by the technological advances that benefit the majority) is proving no easy task. A 2019 study conducted by the University of Bristol, for instance, showed that in deprived neighbourhoods, where people are more likely to rely on cash, free cashpoints are rapidly dis-appearing. The contrast with more well-to-do areas with greater economic activity was stark. In one road in Clifton, a relatively affluent part of Bristol, the researchers found that 71 per cent of ATMs were bank-owned (and therefore free), while in a comparable road in the less-prosperous Easton, just 11 per cent were.

Beyond the cost of cash and the question of who has access to it, disrup-tion is another problem. When Hurricane Maria devastated Puerto Rico in 2017, cash was the only payment mechanism that still worked – but, of course, the ATMs didn't. To meet the surging demand for cash, the US Federal Reserve had to fly in dollar bills twice a day and distribute them around the island in armoured trucks. The Puerto Rican example is often

---

[3]   An eWallet is an electronic version of the physical one. It can contain your bank cards and hold cash balances. Examples are Apple Pay and PayPal, as well as Alipay and Tenpay in China.

cited as evidence in favour of cryptocurrencies,[4] but this contention conveniently overlooks the fact that cryptocurrencies rely on the very same communications networks and electricity grids as ATMs and digital payments.

Disasters come in all shapes and sizes. In February 2020, well before the US lockdown, the Federal Reserve started quarantining dollars that had been repatriated from Asia, holding them for seven to ten days before putting them back into circulation. Its counterparts in Korea and China went even further, ordering local notes from high-risk sources, such as hospitals, to be disinfected using ultraviolet light or destroyed altogether. In the throes of the Covid-19 pandemic, payment without physical exchange suddenly gained a newfound allure, as consumers and merchants avoided handling physical money following reports that it might be facilitating the spread of the virus. Digital payments surged amidst predictions that this might be a tipping point in a move towards a cashless future. It was ironic, therefore, that Wirecard, the giant digital payments provider, collapsed at exactly the time when it should have been making hay. This German firm was used by prepaid card issuers in the UK – cards that are often mooted as a 'new tech' alternative to cash and banking for the unbanked.

Mobile banking service Pockit, 'the simple, easy current account', relied heavily on Wirecard. About 500,000 UK customers used Pockit to receive their wages and benefit payments. One morning in late June 2020, they received the following notice: 'Important update: your Pockit account is temporarily inaccessible.' Millions of other prepaid card customers were also locked out of their accounts, unable to pay for anything. The reason? Auditors had revealed irregularities at Wirecard that left €1.9 billion unaccounted for on its balance sheet and Pockit's payment processor filed for insolvency. The UK's Financial Conduct Authority ordered Wirecard's UK

---

[4] Cryptocurrencies (such as Bitcoin) are 'currencies' that exist solely electronically, use secure technology and are based on a peer-to-peer or decentralised system with no central authority.

operation to halt 'all regulated activity'. Prepaid cards might have sounded like the answer to the problems of remote villages like Penywaun in Wales at one stage, but not once that €2 billion went missing.

While access to Pockit accounts was restored within a few days, the glitch highlighted the predicament faced by the unbanked. Much hope is pinned on the ability of FinTechs (start-ups that use technology to provide financial services in an innovative way; see Chapter 18) to bridge the payments divide by 'banking the unbanked' and bringing payment options to previously inaccessible places. There is some real truth in this. Technology is powering payments in Africa, India, China and beyond, bringing more people and more activity into the formal economy. Yet it comes with its own challenges, especially for those without access to smartphones or the internet. In addition, many of the providers are unregulated or lightly regulated compared with banks. Deposits with these providers aren't always covered by deposit-protection insurance, exposing customers to the risk of losing their balances if their providers get into financial trouble.

There are other concerns about the end of cash. Many of us have an emotional attachment to our currencies in physical form, and cash also plays an important educational role in our lives. Without it, money is just an abstract notion. Notes and coins allow us to touch, feel and even smell money (each to their own) and it imposes natural budgeting constraints on our spending. How do children learn about money without seeing physical currency? What will it mean for your children if their understanding of money is informed by in-app purchases, numbers on screens and one-click payments?

Reports of the death of cash may therefore be exaggerated but the 'big story' in payments is that of its steady displacement. And although that displacement may now be entirely digital, it started in decidedly analogue form at a dinner table back in the 1950s.

6. Fantastic plastic: the advent of cards

What has three types but comes in one size; measures precisely 85.60 by 53.98 millimetres (3⅜ in by 2⅛ in); has rounded corners with a radius of 2.88–3.48 millimetres (⁹⁄₈₀–¹¹⁄₈₀ in); and conforms to the ISO/IEC 7810 ID-1 standard?

The answer is undoubtably more familiar than the question. Cards are the biggest payment instrument after cash, the single most global payment instrument and a triumph of standardisation. You can't fit your American plug into an Italian socket, you can't operate French trains on Spanish rails, you can't run iOS on a Samsung phone, and you can't spend your euros on Main Street – but you can put your Brazil-issued debit or credit card into an ATM anywhere in the world.

The rise of cards has been nothing short of phenomenal. Introduced about fifty years ago, cards now account for two-thirds of all spending in stores. Some 10,000 card payments are made every second, and card usage keeps growing at more than 10 per cent every year. Unlike cash, cards are truly international.

To most of us a card is just a piece of plastic and a bill at the end of the month, but there is a lot more to the 'alchemy' of paying with plastic. This alchemy – which now extends to paying with plastic online, when no actual plastic is involved – has been conjured through trial, error, accident and an awful lot of assistance. Fraudsters have played a key role in fuelling card innovation and, capriciously, competition between card providers may have led to higher costs for merchants. The card industry has moved forwards by looking backwards and spawned sub-industries that have arguably grown as big as their parent. Its constant reinvention owes as much to the kind offices of others as to its own contrivances. But let's start from the beginning.

According to legend, the now ubiquitous credit card was, quite literally, a 'back-of-the-napkin' idea. Businessman Frank McNamara, founder of Diners Club, dreamt up the credit card over lunch in a New York restaurant while waiting for his wife to drive over with money after he'd left home without his wallet. It's a good story, but one that Diners Club's original publicist, Matty Simmons, claimed to have made up himself. In truth, he said, the concept came to McNamara one day on a commuter train to Long Island.

What's more certain is that McNamara, in the company of co-founder Ralph Schneider and Simmons, made the first credit card transaction on 9 February 1950, when he settled the bill for their lunch at Major's Cabin Grill in New York City. McNamara handed Diners Club card number 1000 to the waiter, who returned with a triplicate carbon paper sheet. When McNamara signed for lunch, the waiter pulled out sheet number three and handed it to McNamara. The top copy was to be sent to the Diners Club, and the middle copy was kept by the restaurant.

The original scheme was simple: McNamara and Schneider issued charge cards for use at New York-area restaurants. Made of cardboard, the early cards had fourteen participating restaurants listed on the back. Every month, Diners Club billed the card users for their expenditure during the previous thirty days, the restaurants received 93 per cent of the total, and Diners Club pocketed the balance. An annual fee for cardholders was introduced soon after.

Although McNamara sold out in 1952, the Diners Club card did much of the hard groundwork of signing up retailers and opening up the public's mind to cards. Within a decade, Diners Club had over a million cardholders. By that time, its most significant rival was American Express (Amex), which had entered the market with substantial financial resources. Amex's origins lay in express mail – the DHL of its time – but it had branched out into financial services in the late 1850s with money orders and, some thirty years later, hit gold when its then principal came up with the idea of the traveller's cheque. By the time it entered the card market, Amex didn't just bring money, it brought branding and a huge customer base across from its (by then well-established) traveller's cheque business.

These two, and other smaller rivals, were all 'charge' cards – like Amex still is (for the most part) today – that required users to pay off the full balance at the end of every month. They were also still made of cardboard. Amex introduced the first plastic credit card in 1959, but the real revolution started with the BankAmericard, the forerunner of Visa.

Bank of America, and a competing consortium of banks that formed what became Mastercard, laid the foundation for the phenomenal growth and success of credit cards through three key design choices. First, in the late 1950s Bank of America introduced true 'credit' cards, which allowed customers to roll their balances over to the next month instead of requiring them to pay them off in full (a topic in itself, which we'll cover in detail in Chapter 7). These cards delighted merchants because they enabled them to make additional sales to customers who wouldn't otherwise have had the funds.

Second, in the mid-1960s, Bank of America circumvented the restrictions on interstate banking that prevented it from issuing cards outside California. It did this by opening up its system and licensing BankAmericard to other banks, developing what become known as the 'four-corner model' in the process – the foundation of most modern payment systems. This made cards a whole lot more complicated to explain but was a key ingredient in their recipe for success.

The four corners refer to the four parties involved: (1) the cardholders; (2) the merchants; (3) the cardholders' banks, known as issuing banks since they issue the card; and (4) the merchants' banks, known as the 'acquiring banks' (Figure 1).

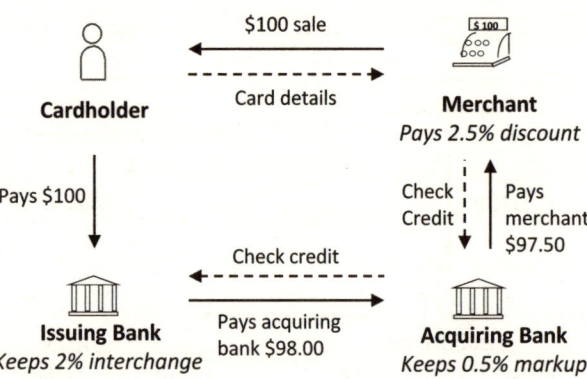

Figure 1. The four-corner model.

The model works like this: cardholders give their cards to merchants, who pass the instructions to their banks. These are the acquiring banks, which in turn pass the instructions to the issuing banks. The issuing banks then check whether the cardholders have sufficient credit/balances and, if so, debit their accounts and reimburse the acquiring banks, which, in turn, credit the merchants' accounts.

BankAmericard's third crucial innovation was the interchange fee. Invisible to the consumer, this fee keeps the whole show on the road by ensuring the basic economics of cards in the four-corner model. Without it, the issuing and acquiring banks would each make their own pricing decisions based on their processing costs. They would share the costs between cardholders and merchants, making the cards a whole lot less attractive to users.

Interchange fees are paid by the merchants' banks to the cardholders' banks, at levels set by the card networks (Visa or Mastercard). The fees vary by geography, type of card (credit or debit) and type of merchant (supermarket or hotel, for example). Typically, the fees are set at 1–3 per cent of the transaction value. They are paid by one bank to another, but nonetheless have a big impact on the cost of card transactions for both merchants and cardholders.

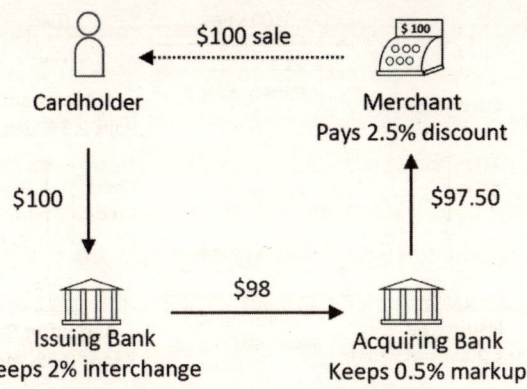

Figure 2. The merchant discount and interchange fee.

Here's how it works. Let us assume that the interchange fee is 2 per cent and the mark-up is 0.5 per cent. If a cardholder makes a $100 purchase, the issuing bank takes the 'fee' and passes on $98 to the acquiring bank. The acquiring bank will reimburse the merchant $97.50, keeping $0.50 to cover its costs. The merchant thus gets the proceeds of the sale, minus this 'merchant discount' of $2.50 (2.5 per cent of the value of the sale). See Figure 2.

So, the issuing bank gets a 2 per cent interchange fee for handling this transaction. For what exactly, you may ask? Well, the fee covers the costs involved in processing the payment but, in most cases, these are substantially lower. The margin allows the issuing bank to offer incentives to its card customers – airport lounge access, cashback on purchases, air miles and so on. There's no such thing as a free lunch, even in payments.

The net effect of the interchange fee is to make card transactions feel free, or even profitable, for cardholders, and to make the merchants bear all the explicit costs. The underlying premise is that it is the buyer, not the seller, who decides which payment instruments to use. Cardholders therefore need to be rewarded or incentivised, unlike merchants, who have little choice but to accept cards if they want to make sales. But cardholders *are* paying for cards – even when we think we aren't. Costs such as interchange and processing fees may be charged to merchants rather than cardholders, but they generally pass this cost on to their customers in the form of higher prices. Air miles, loyalty points, free insurance, cashback and other perks may make credit cards look like a great deal, but free they ain't.

What may surprise you is that these interchange and merchant discount fees differ quite significantly from outlet to outlet, reflecting not just the advantage of scale (and muscle), but also the likely risk involved. Supermarket giants pay less than corner shops; nightclubs and brothels face the highest merchant discounts of all. This doesn't reflect the prudish worldview of the card industry so much as the tendency of customers to deny such transactions the morning after. The next most expensive fees are shouldered by electronics retailers, which sell mobile phones, laptops, cameras and other easily re-sellable items. Online, just in case you were curious, it's a similar story: the porn, gambling and electronic appliance sites of the world pay much higher rates than, say, online grocers.

A senior card executive, who once had to resolve a case involving a senior oil industry figure who had gone on a spending spree, explained how it works as follows.

The oilman had used his private jet to visit brothels in four German cities, racking up the equivalent of $100,000 on his black card (a credit card with no limit). When his credit card bill arrived, he denied the transactions. The card executive was obliged to pay a call to each of the brothels, where the owners were happy to confirm the oil magnate's attendance and share the details of the services he had enjoyed. They even admitted that they might have been somewhat liberal in calculating the charges. In the end, a three-way deal was struck between the customer, the 'merchants' and the card network.

7. The mother of invention: advances in card technology

In the early 1950s, the average American consumer had less than $2,000 (in today's money) total personal debt; today, they have over $10,000 in credit card debt alone. All because Bank of America had the revolutionary idea of bringing together the revolving credit facilities provided by merchants with the charge cards (like Diners) that had to be paid off at month end.

The idea of combining convenience and lending emerged from the bank's Customer Services Research Department, run by Second World War infantry veteran Joe Williams. After his military service, Williams drove to San Francisco in search of a job. He approached A. P. Giannini, Bank of America's founder, admiring his creative and aggressive approach to banking. Giannini must have recognised a kindred spirit in Williams, as it wasn't long before Bank of America took a massive gamble on Williams' idea of launching a credit card, choosing Fresno to place its first bet. Fresno had a population of around 250,000 and 45 per cent of its households were existing bank customers. On 18 September 1958, the bank mailed out 60,000 pre-approved but unsolicited applications for its BankAmericard credit card. The fees for merchants were set at a hefty 6 per cent, but the blanket targeting of local consumers enabled the bank to swiftly sign up more than 300 Fresno merchants.

If Bank of America was circumspect in putting down this initial marker, it quickly went all-in and accelerated the roll-out. Within three months it had added Modesto and Bakersfield, while San Francisco, Sacramento and Los Angeles followed within a year. By the end of 1959 it had issued some

2 million cards across California and signed up 20,000 merchants. But problems were emerging.

Joe Williams had predicted that late payments would not exceed 4 per cent and that existing bank credit systems would hold. But he didn't set up a collectables department, and before long a staggering 22 per cent of accounts were delinquent. Police departments across the state were swamped with cases of credit card fraud, a brand-new crime, creating a tsunami of political and press trauma. In Los Angeles, prostitutes allegedly lifted cards from clients and crooks learned to spend limited amounts on each card to avoid the need for approval. Thieves stole un-embossed cards from the bank's warehouse and blackmailed the bank into buying them back by threatening to emboss the cards and run up charges.

Williams left the bank shortly after. He blamed the problems on LA bank branches, arguing that they were too lax in screening cardholders. Perhaps, but there were other problems. In one infamous example, branches were apparently asked to list customers who should never get credit cards. In a subsequent mix-up, they instead issued a card to everyone listed.

That might have been the end of it, but Bank of America persevered. It instituted a massive clean-up operation, imposing proper financial controls and issuing profuse apologies to regulators, politicians and cardholders. Against the odds, it managed to salvage the programme. Within a few years, BankAmericard turned a profit. The rest, as they say, is history.

That history is one of invention, reinvention and (when that fails) acquisition. That's not so unusual, perhaps, but there are some interesting themes within this narrative. First, how much of that history has been driven by outsiders – both fraudsters trying to subvert the system and third parties attempting to crash the party; second, how much of the success of credit cards is down to the power of the card networks; and third, how much we, the consumers, simply haven't noticed.

Right at the start, when cards were made of cardboard, all the details had to be inscribed by hand every time they were used. This was time-consuming, insecure, unreliable and vulnerable to fraud. Things moved on when Amex thought to make cards out of plastic. This advance swiftly led to manual imprinters – known colloquially as 'Zip-Zap' or 'Click-Clack' machines – that could capture the information from the embossed details on the card and transfer it onto paper slips with carbon-paper copies. Cardholders would sign the slips and keep the carbon copies (making for filthy fingers and bulging wallets), while merchants would send the originals in to their banks for processing. For large payments, merchants could telephone the issuing banks to seek authorisation – calls that took an average of five agonising minutes!

In the 1970s, the credit card industry was still struggling to develop an effective and cost-efficient way to authorise payments. Given the early unsolicited credit card mailing and the continuing problem of fraud, the need for real-time authorisation was painfully obvious. In 1973 alone, credit card losses were estimated to be almost $300 million, or 1.15 per cent of sales. It turned out the answer had already been invented.

One day in the early 1960s, Dorothea Parry had been busy with the housework when her husband Forrest, an engineer at IBM, came home to regale her with the problems he was having at work. He had been tasked with designing a machine-readable identity card for CIA officials. His plan was to attach a strip of magnetised tape to a plastic card, but glue warped the tape, making it unreadable.

The resourceful Mrs Parry suggested he use an iron to melt the strip onto the card. It worked, and the magnetised data strip, or 'magstripe', was born.

There had been no widespread agreement in the industry about the use of the magstripe on credit cards but, in 1979, then Visa CEO Dee Hock announced that all Visa cards issued after April 1980 would have to have a magstripe on the back. The Parrys' invention is now swiped through card readers more than 50 billion times a year, right across the world.

The stripe contained all the information needed to validate a payment: name of cardholder, card number, authorisation code and expiry date. It also allowed card information to be captured electronically for the first time, which led directly to the development of another game changer: the now ubiquitous point of sale (POS) payment terminal. By 1981, the credit card networks had begun to offer discounts to merchants using the newly developed automated transaction technology for all credit card purchases greater than $50. The problem was cost. The early POS terminals cost almost $1,000 – not a viable option for most merchants.

By 1982, the US-based payment technology company Verifone had figured out how to engineer and produce a terminal and get it to market for $500. Two years later, Verifone CEO Bill Melton introduced the ZON credit card authorisation system with a $125 price tag. By the time Melton retired from the firm in 1989, it had shipped the first million ZON systems. The POS terminal made it possible to conduct increasingly secure transactions, to control customers' account balances and to allow issuers to accept or refuse transactions – not least those being made by fraudsters.

The next key development in card technology was introduced by an Egyptian-born Frenchman, Roland Moreno. He was the ultimate Renaissance man – a journalist, serial entrepreneur, engineer, inventor, bon viveur, humorist, author, family man and even, for a while, broadcaster – but he is best known (at least in France) for inventing the chip that brought us the smart card.

A self-confessed 'lazy bum' and 'couch potato', Moreno claimed to have thought of the smart card concept in his sleep and apparently code-named the project 'TMR', after Woody Allen's 1969 film *Take the Money and Run*.

His original idea was to embed a 'microchip' (a miniature circuit that could store electronic data and be read and altered by a scanner) in signet rings. This was well before wearable devices were a 'thing'. He eventually switched to the more prosaic plastic card. Named *la carte à puce* (literally 'flea card' in English) after the tiny chip it contained, Moreno first demonstrated its use in electronic financial transactions in 1976 with a machine held together by Meccano. It may sound like child's play, but it was genius. This chip became the basis for 'chip and PIN' authorisation – first used in the French Carte Bleue cards, now found in debit and credit cards around the world.

The magnetic strip, electronic POS terminal and Moreno's chip were all crucial prerequisites for debit cards, which require online authorisation. With debit cards, transactions are deducted directly from the cardholders' bank accounts; they don't have to be paid off or rolled over at the end of the month. In other words, while credit cards facilitate extra spending, debit cards are for 'within budget' purchases.

From the start, debit cards were intended to replace cash, not credit cards. They offer greater convenience than cash – no more trips to the bank or wads of notes in your wallet – and better liquidity: you are debited only when you actually spend, and you don't have to 'pre-fund' purchases by taking out cash in advance. But, and it's a big but, it wasn't the credit card networks that invented them – it was the banks.

Banks started to roll out debit cards in two very different ways. First, they allowed their customers to use their ATM cards in shops. ATMs had made their appearance in 1967 and became ubiquitous in the late 1980s; banks issued their customers with ATM cards and personal identification number (PIN) codes for withdrawing cash. (Ironically, while ATMs made cash more convenient, they also paved the way for debit cards, which have done more than any other instrument to displace cash.) Second, banks gave merchants terminals that were, in effect, mini-ATMs, complete with numerical PIN-pads for customers to use. In this way, the banks slipped debit cards into their customers' wallets – the very same cards they'd already been issued with for using at ATMs.

Importantly, these PIN-debit transactions were cheap for merchants; roughly 10 cents per transaction, much less than the $1–2 they had to pay on credit card transactions. Merchants that had never accepted credit cards, such as smaller grocery shops, corner stores and independent boutiques, began accepting debit cards.

Visa and its banks did not take this incursion lying down. Instead, they introduced their own 'Signature' cards – essentially credit cards in drag or debit cards in disguise.

To the merchants, these cards looked exactly the same as credit cards and were processed in the same way; the cards carried the network's logo and customers would sign for the purchases, just as they did with their credit cards – hence the name. But for the cardholders there was a big difference. There were no monthly balances or revolving credit facilities; instead, transactions were deducted directly from customers' current accounts. The main advantage, however, was the additional reach: PIN-debit cards could be used only if a merchant had a PIN-pad terminal, but Signature cards could be used anywhere that accepted credit cards.[1]

In a way, both Signature- and PIN-debit cards were introduced by stealth, perhaps because the rationale for using either was less immediately compelling than that for credit cards. Banks had slipped PIN-debit into cardholders' wallets by adding the function to existing cards; the networks slipped Signature-debit card acceptance capabilities into merchants' credit card terminals.

So far, so clever. When the internet came along it was time for further ingenuity – in this case, a total metamorphosis. If you had a blank sheet of paper and had to invent a payment instrument for a virtual world, it's highly unlikely that you'd put a 3-inch-long plastic card smack-bang in the middle. But credit cards have made the transition to online payments so successfully that they now sit at the very epicentre of e-commerce. How did they do that?

The credit card industry picked up an early taste for remote payments. Long before the internet, Americans and Britons in particular ordered goods by phone from mail order catalogues. Then along came the home-shopping television channels such as QVC and other phone-based retailers. During lengthy advertorials, screens were emblazoned with phone numbers to ring while presenters exhorted viewers to 'call quickly while offers last'.

---

[1] From the start, Signature-debit cards could be used at all merchants that carried the Visa logo. Mastercard did the same, but with some delay, and as a result Visa remains the bigger force in debit cards.

Each performance invariably ended with the proud boast 'all major cards accepted'. Buyers just had to give their names and card numbers over the phone.

These 'card-not-present' (CNP) payments are inherently more sensitive to fraud, because there are no cards or signatures to verify; they also lead to more chargebacks because cardholders often claim they didn't receive, or didn't like, the goods ordered.[2] For this reason, CNP payments were (and still are) subject to significantly higher interchange fees, while acquiring banks also charge higher mark-ups on them. These higher margins help to absorb the associated losses and are made possible by the fact that goods sold by phone tend to have high margins to begin with.

When online shopping arrived in the 1990s, the industry's experience with phone shopping proved invaluable. Consumers were already accustomed to using their cards remotely, and the card networks were used to handling CNP purchases.

Signing up *online* merchants, however, proved altogether trickier. Merchants that sold by phone were typically large outfits, but the internet brought a multitude of smaller businesses into the equation. eBay, for example, listed all sorts of sellers, from 'mom-and-pop' e-shops selling home-made embroidery, to ordinary consumers selling everything from cars to couches.

This posed two great challenges: first, the risk that micro-vendors would keep the payments but fail to deliver the goods; and second – remember, this was pre-online banking – how to pay vendors who couldn't accept cards. At this time, merchants who accepted cards had to have contracts in place with banks. The banks were ill-equipped to serve the new breed of micro-vendor and the card networks had no way of reaching them. Enter PayPal.

---

[2] A chargeback is the reversal of a payment that is made to a cardholder when they successfully dispute a transaction – for instance in the event of the fraudulent use of their card.

PayPal solved all these problems and more. It introduced an 'escrow' account system that allowed consumers to make card payments, holding the funds until the consumers had received the goods. Using specialised algorithms and scoring systems to spot fraudulent transactions and merchants, fraud management became one of PayPal's key skills. At one point it handled more than 70 per cent of transactions on eBay, ideally positioning the company for the explosive growth in online sales that followed.

Where PayPal left off, mobile wallets like Apple Pay took over. These 'wallets' weren't meant to replace cards; instead, by storing your card data securely on your mobile phone, they abolished the need to carry your plastic with you. Just hold your phone next to the terminal and – bingo! – it's done; that coffee is yours. These eWallets have also made online purchases much easier because your card data can easily be retrieved from your mobile for purchases. Handy for indolent consumers and a cracking development for the card networks, which have effectively received a digital makeover (even if the issuers do lose some fees along the way) without having to lift a finger.

This is not to say that the card networks have been complete bystanders. They have, for instance, taken exclusivity to new heights. If you meet the requirements, you might be invited to take out a Dubai First Royale Mastercard ('the world's most exclusive card'). With a .325 carat diamond embedded into gold plate, they are limit-free, invitation only and come complete with a dedicated relationship manager. The famous Centurion American Express cards – slices of anodised titanium – come with 'concierge services' to handle special requests. Their reputation is carefully maintained through a drip of stories such as the tale of the cardholder who wanted Kevin Costner's horse from *Dances with Wolves* – the concierge tracked it down and then personally delivered it.

This 'invitation-only' approach is intended for the exclusive few. The rest of us have to make do with applying for a more 'normal' range of cards. Even so, not everyone can meet the application criteria. Life without a card isn't impossible, but it's pretty difficult. Which is why it was a gamechanger for the scale and reach of their businesses when Visa and Mastercard put their logos on pre-paid cards and started processing them using their networks.

There's nothing new or inventive about pre-paid cards: stores were handing out gift cards and vouchers way before the credit card was even conceived. And there have long been multipurpose gift cards that you buy with balances of, say, $20, €50 or £100, and give as presents, for recipients to spend at participating stores. But when Visa and Mastercard moved in on them, all of a sudden, pre-paid cards could be used at any accepting merchant, including online, as well as at ATMs. You could even have your monthly salary deposited onto your pre-paid card, a move that effectively turned it into a simple bank account – albeit one that might not always benefit from the insurance protection that bank accounts enjoy. The result was a whole new population of cardholders and an almost complete democratisation of cards.

Many people in the USA use these cards as accounts and Americans now spend over half a trillion dollars per year on such 'general purpose reloadable cards'. They have also gone global. In continental Europe, where comparatively few consumers have credit cards, pre-paid cards have taken off as travel cards, used for making hotel bookings, renting cars and funding children on a usefully limited-liability basis. The cards are also proving popular in emerging markets, where they are marketed as easy-access bank accounts. They can even be combined with other cards, such as (pre-paid) mobile telephone cards. In Nigeria, they have gone a step further: you can have your national identity card double as a pre-paid (Master)card – a 'sticky' idea, if ever there was one.

The pre-paid card's success is further testimony to the power of the card networks. Yes, they have been able and willing to innovate, to adopt and to modernise, but above all they have the scale and clout to drive mass adoption. As we've seen with Apple Pay and PayPal – and we'll see again in the FinTech frenzy – their network strength encourages outsiders to innovate through them or to build new ideas around them, which makes them even stronger. Love 'em or loathe 'em, a world without the card networks is now unthinkable.

8. Minting plastic: from credit to debit cards

In 1966, George W. Ball, a prominent US diplomat and public servant, resigned from the State Department to join the banking firm Lehman Brothers. On arrival, he was astounded by the amount of money sloshing around and was overheard asking: 'Why didn't someone tell me about banking before?'

If Ball was around today, he certainly wouldn't be working at Lehman Brothers but he probably wouldn't want to be in banking anyway; the card business is now far more lucrative.[1] Indeed, in March 2020, *The Economist* noted that, despite a precipitous fall in its share price, a humble payments processor had risen to become the world's most valuable financial services company. Visa had overtaken even the mighty JPMorgan Chase, becoming more valuable than the top ten European banks combined (though that probably says more about the profitability of European banks than it does about Visa). Mastercard, ever the Pepsi to Visa's Coke, wasn't doing too badly either; although its share of the market was only about 70 per cent of Visa's, it was still worth as much as Citibank and Bank of America put together.

The card networks – generally Visa and Mastercard in the West, Union Pay in China and JCB in Japan – connect 25,000 or so issuing and acquiring banks around the world. They are, if you like, the rails that connect the stations. They transmit information between merchants and banks and 'transfer the money' from the issuing bank to the acquiring bank – and, of course, they make a lot of money on the way.

---

[1]   Lehman Brothers collapsed in September 2008.

Visa and the other networks earn their corn primarily from the computer processing and communications work that enables us to pay by card, as well as foreign-exchange fees and annual charges levied on card issuers. Each one is small change at face value, but not when you tot it all up. Increasingly, they also offer fraud detection and other supplementary services to help feather their comfy (and coveted) nests.

The card issuers get to keep the hefty interest revenue and interchange fees (after costs). And the 'acquirers' (either banks or independent payment processors, as well as the people who make and lease the point-of-sale machinery) also take their cut from merchants – how much depends on which services the merchants use.

More valuable than banks they may now be, but originally Visa and Mastercard were privately owned by more than 20,000 banks, including JPMorgan, Citibank and Bank of America. The banks must have been kicking themselves when they saw the card networks' valuations exceed their own: how could they have let it happen?

It was like this. In 1996 a group of American retailers, led by Wal-Mart, Sears and Safeway, joined in a lawsuit brought on behalf of every retailer in the USA that accepted Visa and Mastercard credit and debit cards. Four million retailers were effectively seeking unprecedented damages ranging up to $100 billion. Collectively, Visa and Mastercard are now worth more than half a trillion US dollars, and so the potential damages involved may look cheap. But at the time their bank-owners feared they might be found liable, which doubtless played a significant part in their decision to sell the card networks off.

The retailers accused Visa and Mastercard of using duopoly power in the credit card market to take control of the debit card market. At the heart of their complaint was the so-called 'honour all cards' rule, which meant merchants had to take *all* of one network's cards if they took *any* of that network's cards. If they accepted a Visa credit card, they had to accept a Visa Signature-debit card; the same for Mastercard. Why was this so controversial?

If a customer used their Signature-debit card, the retailer had to pay the same interchange and merchant discount fees as if they'd used a credit card. The disadvantage (for the merchant) was that using a Signature-debit card didn't encourage the customer to spend more. Retailers like Wal-Mart had always accepted credit cards for big ticket and high-margin purchases – say, BBQs or semi-automatic assault rifles. But now customers were using Signature-debit cards for everyday purchases such as groceries and cleaning products, which have razor-thin margins. If they wanted to continue accepting credit cards, retailers had to accept the much more expensive Signature-debit cards. To Wal-Mart and the others, this stealth approach felt like brute force.

Visa and Mastercard settled the suit for about $3 billion in 2003 and lowered interchange fees on Signature-debit cards to about half the amount levied on credit cards. They also scrapped the 'honour all cards' rule, allowing merchants to choose which cards to accept.

It looked like total capitulation, but the card networks had in fact outflanked the retailers. Visa and Mastercard simply bought the US ATM networks that processed PIN-debit transactions, and then raised the interchange fees on these transactions to the same rate as those for Signature-debit cards, around 1 per cent of the transaction value. This effectively meant merchants had to pay the same fees on PIN-debit card payments as on Signature-debit card ones. So, while the settlement allowed merchants to accept only PIN-debit and refuse Signature-debit, the point was moot as the cards cost the same.

Having dealt themselves such a good hand, the card networks came very close to overplaying it. In 2010, US Congress took issue with the charges and passed the Durbin Amendment, which capped debit interchange fees. We say close, because the restriction wasn't all that harsh: the Durbin Amendment capped debit fees at around 0.6 per cent for the average $40 debit transaction – lower than before, but still much higher than in Europe where debit interchange fees mostly don't exist. In the few places where they do, they rise to only a third of the fees in the USA.

Less remunerative they may be, but debit cards are the truly global phenomenon. While the USA still accounts for 50 per cent of all credit card transactions, two-thirds of all debit card payments are made *outside* the USA. They continue to grow at double-digit rates: 12 per cent per year, compared to 8 per cent for credit cards.

All of which is great for Visa and Mastercard. Although they have been unable to break through Chinese bureaucracy (not for want of trying), they pretty much dominate the rest of the world. Credit card usage in continental Europe has been much more limited than in the USA, with little acceptance outside the travel and entertainment industries – but debit cards have taken up the slack, and Visa and Mastercard haven't missed a trick in getting their slice of the pie.

Europe started several years later than the USA, but the old continent rolled out ATMs in earnest during the 1980s. Because credit cards weren't widely used, Signature-debit cards were never issued in most European countries. Instead, the focus was on PIN-debit cards, which caught on with both consumers and merchants – no doubt helped by the fact that transactions were free to consumers and very cheap to merchants. While the Americans made some 240 debit transactions per person in 2019, the Dutch made over 280 and the Swedes almost 300. That Sweden has become something of a poster child for a cashless future, despite protests from some quarters, is largely due to debit cards.

When debit cards took off in Europe in the late 1990s and early 2000s, the different schemes were national. Much to the frustration of European travellers, debit cards initially couldn't be used abroad. Networks like Eufiserv (the European savings banks), Cirrus/Maestro (Mastercard) and V-pay (Visa) eventually linked these national networks, enabling customers, first, to withdraw cash at ATMs across Europe and, second, to use their cards in-store around the continent.

Visa and Mastercard steadily increased their presence in Europe. In 2016, the US-based Visa Inc. acquired Visa Europe from its European owners for a total value of €21.2 billion, while Mastercard merged with Europay in 2001 and bought the UK's Link network in 2017 for £700 million. As a result, almost all cross-border European debit card transactions and many domestic transactions run over their networks today.

There is a certain irony here: the Eurocrats had a dream of a single European payments universe, but it has effectively been realised through two US networks. The absurdity of this is not lost on the EU authorities that pushed hard for this 'Single Euro Payments Area': they never hesitate to cite the key role that Moreno's marvellous microchip played in the card business.[2]

China can lay claim to no such innovation in cards but has avoided any associated frustration. Having effectively blocked Visa and Mastercard from entering the country, China instead developed its own system, UnionPay. Launched in 2002, it is big now by any standards; there are several billion UnionPay cards in circulation, and they're accepted by millions of merchants across the world.[3] Most of UnionPay's activity is within China, but it has issued some 100 million cards outside the country that are accepted globally, albeit mostly in areas frequented by Chinese. It's not just Americans who borrow on their credit cards: Chinese credit card debt stands at $1 trillion, the same as the USA. Relative to GDP, Chinese card debt is even higher: 7.5 per cent of GDP for China versus 4.8 per cent for the USA.

Europe presumably doesn't harbour an ambition for its citizens to take on similar debt levels, but it does still want its own network. Despite

---

[2] The Single Euro Payments Area (SEPA) harmonises the way in which cashless euro payments are made across Europe. It allows European consumers, businesses and public administrations to make and receive payment transactions under the same basic conditions. A collaborative cross-industry initiative, it was pushed by the EU Commission and is supported by EU regulation (directive 2007/64/EC and regulations EU 924/2009 and 260/2012).

[3] In comparison, there are about 1.2 billion Visa cards in circulation and just short of a billion Mastercard cards, according to creditcards.com.

several failed attempts to build a European card network, the European Commission continued to call for more. Then suddenly, in mid-2020 – perhaps inspired (or incensed) by Visa's and Mastercard's valuations – a group of major European banks launched the European Payments Initiative. Aimed at creating a 'unified payment solution for consumers and merchants across Europe', the aspiration is impressive. It's an ambitious bid to overcome Europe's fragmented financial landscape. But Europeans remain stubbornly national in their payment habits, and Visa and Mastercard have long dominated the field. Changing either will not be easy.

PART III

GEOGRAPHY

9. Prisoners of geography: why our payment habits are national

If cards are so great, why do people still use other methods to pay? Why, for example, do Americans write so many cheques ('checks' in US parlance)?

One of the oldest ways of paying, cheques are perishable, cumbersome and slow – and their validity is time-limited. They have many of the disadvantages of cash, but none of its advantages in terms of immediacy, certainty, anonymity or universality. When you pay someone by cheque, they have to take it or send it to their bank, and from there it has to make its way back to your bank. Then it has to clear – and *if* the payee hasn't held on to it for too long, *if* it's in good nick, *if* the payer has addressed it correctly and *if* the funds are in their account, you will finally get paid. That's an awful lot of *ifs*.

And yet Americans still write cheques at check-out counters, where they could much more easily use cards. They still use cheques to pay invoices, even though people in pretty much every other country now use bank transfers. Some 15 billion cheques are written in the USA every year: one per week for every American! It's ironic that cheques are most popular in the country that invented cards, that spawned PayPal and Apple Pay and dreamed up Libra (now Diem), Facebook's cryptocurrency project.[1] Three-quarters of all cheques are written in the USA – no other country comes anywhere close (next in line is France, accounting for 10 per cent of all cheques written).

Economic theory holds that people choose how they want to pay based on how useful the method is to them – the benefits minus the disadvantages

---

[1] Announced by Facebook in June 2019, the Libra cryptocurrency project was renamed Diem in December 2020.

or costs. One could argue that cheques have some advantages. It takes a few days for a cheque to clear, during which time you keep the funds in your account. Furthermore, if you mail your cheques or the recipients take a while to cash them in, you enjoy an even longer hold over your money – and you can rely on the proverbial excuse for late payment: 'the cheque's in the post'. Receivers may see fewer benefits, but they can expect to get the funds, even if they take time to arrive (and even if they rely on the cheque writers having sufficient funds to ensure that the cheques don't bounce).

Another much ignored advantage is that cheques aren't prone to 'fat finger' errors, whereby the payer enters the wrong amount or the wrong currency.[2] This happens more often than you'd think – and, reassuringly, not just to us small fry. In mid-2020 Citibank mistakenly wired clients 100 times the value they were due to receive, an error of $900-odd million. The same thing happened in 2018 to an unfortunate Deutsche Bank employee who wired a $35 billion payment in error: the sum was $5 billion more than the bank's entire market value.

Equally, whereas it's hard to write the wrong name on a cheque, it's easy enough to mistake an account number in a bank transfer. This happened to US National Security Council staffer Oliver North when he was undertaking elaborate undercover deals with Ayatollah Khomenei's Iran and General Noriega's Nicaraguan rebels.[3] North was funnelling the proceeds from the

---

[2] Cheques arguably do carry the risk of 'slipping pen' errors whereby the writer enters the wrong amount; these are either rare or do not receive the same level of publicity as transfer errors.

[3] Ruhollah Musavi Khomeini, known in the Western world as Ayatollah Khomeini, was an Iranian politician, revolutionary and cleric. He was the leader of the 1979 Iranian Revolution, which led to the overthrow of the last Shah of Iran, and the founder of the Islamic Republic of Iran. Anti-Western and at odds with the USA throughout his tenure as Supreme Leader, he supported the hostage takers during the hostage crisis that led to the US sanctions that prevented North from overtly selling the arms to the country in the first place.

illegal sale of guns to the Iranian regime, via secret payments in Switzerland, to fund the rebels fighting Nicaragua's then Sandinista government.[4] During this complicated process, North mistakenly wired a $10 million 'humanitarian' donation from the Sultan of Brunei not to his own (secret) account at Credit Suisse but to that of a Swiss businessman. He had inadvertently transposed two digits in the account number. When the Iran–Contra scandal blew, North had bigger problems to deal with than the Sultan's missing millions. He was ejected from the National Security Council and moved on to become a chat-show host and, very briefly, president of the National Rifle Association.

Theoretically, a system is in place to prevent such mistakes. Bank account numbers *should* have so-called 'parity code checks' to prevent 'fat finger' errors: the value of the last digit, for example, might depend on the value and position of all previous digits. If you accidentally switch two digits the parity (check) digit won't compute, and the payment won't be executed. Either Credit Suisse's accounts didn't have such parity digits in 1986 or Oliver North made a more complex account error than a simple transposition. Given the context, it's highly probable that there's more to the story.

But parity digits aren't foolproof, as an unfortunate Englishman found to his cost in 2019 when he gave the wrong sort code to the lawyer dealing with his father's inheritance. The lawyer duly instructed the bank to send £193,000 to the account number provided, and off it went – into someone else's bank account. Quite incredibly, it transpired that Barclays had identical account numbers for two different customers, with sort codes that differed by just one digit. Sort codes don't have parity digits, which would

---

[4]   The Sandinista National Liberation Front is a socialist political party in Nicaragua that took office in 1979. Its members are called Sandinistas after Augusto César Sandino, who had led the Nicaraguan resistance against the US occupation of Nicaragua in the 1930s. During President Reagan's administration the CIA began covertly financing, arming and training rebel guerrillas who were branded 'counter-revolutionaries' by the Sandinistas, 'Contras' for short.

have prevented the mishap, so Barclays had an excuse. Even so, the bank didn't help itself by refusing to freeze and return the funds and offering just £25 to the victim in compensation.

Barclays isn't alone with these problems. When the US government's $2 trillion stimulus package came online in April 2020, the US Internal Revenue Service (IRS) was charged with paying stimulus money into recipients' accounts.[5] In many cases the cash was sent to the wrong accounts, so the IRS had to resort to mailing out cheques instead.

Oliver North's mistaken bank transfer helpfully demystifies the famous nameless, 'numbered' Swiss bank accounts of movie fame. Contrary to popular belief, these accounts are not anonymous; the banks know the names of the owners perfectly well; the 'difference' is that you can send money to Swiss accounts without mentioning (or even knowing) the name of the beneficiaries.

Despite all the publicity that these secretive Swiss accounts attract, the feature was far from unique. Until very recently, UK banks didn't check the names in transfer orders. You could literally send a payment to a friend's account, fill in 'Mickey Mouse' as the beneficiary and, provided that the account number and sort code were correct, it would arrive just fine. Incredibly, the 'Confirmation of Payee' wasn't introduced in the UK until early 2020. The UK consumers' association Which? estimated that £320 million in transfer losses (and fraud) could have been prevented if this measure had been introduced just three years earlier.

To return to the humble cheque: the principle may be the same, but cheques *have* moved with the times. In the UK, a century and a half ago you could only date and negotiate cheques within ten miles of the issuing bank. Just twenty years ago, US banks used to fly bags of paper across the country. Only after the 9/11 attacks in 2001, when all flights were grounded for a week and US cheque-processing came to a crashing halt, was there sufficient

---

[5]   The IRS is the US equivalent of Her Majesty's Revenue & Customs (HMRC).

momentum to move to image scanning. Since 2004, receiving banks in the USA have scanned cheques and transmitted the images electronically to the issuing banks. As a result, cheques have become easier to use and cheaper to process there. And yet that doesn't answer the question of why they are still *so* popular in America and nowhere else.

The reality is that our payment preferences are distinctly national. Cash usage remains high in German-speaking countries – Germany, Austria and Switzerland – even though it has been declining to much lower levels in neighbouring countries including France, the Benelux countries and Scandinavia. The Germans also love direct debits, standing instructions through which consumers authorise the likes of utilities companies and tele-com providers to take monthly invoice payments out of their bank accounts: more than two per week per German! No other country has this many – certainly not the Swiss, with less than one direct debit per month per person (so maybe it really is true that law-abiding Swiss burghers pitch up at the post office with 1,000 CHF notes to pay their bills). Only the Dutch come close, with about one and a half direct debits per person per week; perhaps because they share the German penchant for schedule and structure, albeit they don't share the same predilection for cash. Each country has its own payment mix.

The 'way we pay' has long confounded economists and researchers. They have tried to model the usage of different methods across countries using explanatory variables, such as crime rates (a low crime rate – meaning fewer thefts – might favour usage of cash) and interest rates (high interest rates might favour methods of paying that take time to clear, like cheques). But it turns out that these variables aren't great at explaining the choices we make.

Instead, researchers find that lower card usage is correlated with lower card acceptance. Of course, one wonders about cause and effect here: are cards used less in certain countries because they are accepted less, or are they accepted less because people in those places don't like to use them? The variables don't really explain the differences between countries either. If the

American preference for cheques is based on their attractiveness compared with the alternatives, then why is the cheque hardly used in other countries, where the same alternatives are available?

Part of the answer may lie in the conventions behind our payments. Every time we make a payment, we choose *how* to pay. That said, how we pay and get paid is a function not just of what *we* want but also of how those around us want to pay and be paid. A payments mechanism – be it bank-account based, wallet based, card based, cash based or otherwise – is only as useful as it is accepted. Such acceptance depends on conventions and customs, some of which are 'soft', such as cultural preferences, while others are 'hard', such as how many merchants have terminals that can read cards. Both are hard to change.

To understand why these conventions are so difficult to change, and thus explain why Americans write so many cheques, we must look at the role of two of the most significant (and fascinating) elements of payments: legacy and networks.

Almost 200 years ago, the brilliant engineer Isambard Kingdom Brunel was asked to build the Great Western Railway line from London to Bristol. He got the job eight years after the Manchester–Liverpool line had been built. Dismissing the earlier line's 1,435 mm Stephenson gauge (that's 4 feet, 8½ inches, for the metrically challenged) as too narrow, he chose a gauge of 2,134 mm (7 feet). Most railway engineers would have agreed with Brunel: the Great Western had a better gauge. Its wider adoption would have afforded the British passenger greater speed, stability and much needed capacity. By the time it was ready, however, the Stephenson gauge had already been widely accepted. Brunel eventually had to accept defeat and the Great Western line was converted. (For those interested in trains, the last broad-gauge train to Bristol was the *Flying Dutchman*, which hit the buffers for the final time on 29 May 1892; its replacement, the 11:45 from Paddington, left the following day on a standard gauge and undistinguished by any name.)

Brunel's standard fell victim to what are known as 'network effects'. This term derives from the observation that the 'value' of a network depends on the number of users. The *cost* of the first telephones and fax machines may have been high, but their *value* was limited because there was nobody to call or send faxes to. Their value increased as a growing number of people started to use telephones and fax machines. Similarly, the value of Facebook increased as more and more people adopted it. This effect is not limited to pure networks; it also applies to conventions like standards, legal systems, languages and more. The utility of each depends on how widely it is used.

In an economic sense, payment mechanisms behave like these networks: the benefit of any form of payment to each individual depends on how many other users adopt it. The value of a card depends on where you can use it. Cheques are useful (in America) because they are accepted, there are legal frameworks governing them and – just as crucially – they are part of the culture.

Network effects are everywhere in payment systems – so much so that you could write a full PhD thesis about it.[6]

The first thing to know about payment networks is that they are difficult to establish. They need a certain critical mass before they become viable – but *once* established, they have huge value. It's a 'chicken-and-egg' problem: merchants will install terminals only if their customers have cards, and customers will get cards only if they can use them at merchants. This takes us back to the way in which debit cards were introduced: PIN-debit was added to existing cards while Signature-debit cards could be used at existing merchants (see Chapter 7). Both card types broke the 'which comes first' conundrum, but in different ways.

---

[6] Which Gottfried actually did: 'Payment systems and network effects: Adoption, harmonization and succession of network technologies across countries' (The Netherlands, Maastricht University, 2004).

You may have noticed the analogy between how cards got started in the 1950s and how Facebook and PayPal took off some fifty years later. Cards developed from an agreement between a small group of diners and the restaurants in which they regularly ate in New York; Facebook started among Harvard students; and PayPal began with eBay buyers and sellers in the USA. Each then expanded by moving into similar niche communities: cards with restaurant-goers in California; Facebook with students at Stanford; and PayPal with eBay users outside the USA. They all established critical mass in small communities with similar transactional interests and then built out, focusing on particular types of activity until they reached tipping points from which they could expand laterally.

A network is a valuable thing. The Ant Group – parent company of Alipay, the world's largest and most modern payment giant – tried to buy international money transfer business MoneyGram for $1.2 billion in 2017. Why would Ant, a company that would otherwise seem perfectly positioned to wipe out traditional money transfers altogether, be willing to pay so much for this mostly analogue operation, a distant number two to Western Union? Its network – and a base of customers habituated to using it – was the real draw.

Once established, networks can become extremely powerful and difficult to dislodge. Scientific research into network effects has yielded several non-obvious and non-intuitive insights, such as the fact that the best standard doesn't always win. And, indeed, network effects make a 'winner-takes-all' situation possible: the largest network becomes inherently more attractive to almost all potential users than any other, *even* if its features are less appealing. Bear this in mind the next time you pay for something: every individual choice we make feeds into the strength of one payment network and potentially weakens another.

This same phenomenon also allows established networks to transcend major technology shifts when they occur – even if they seem to be behind the curve at the outset. Remember how Facebook deftly moved from PC to mobile rather than be displaced by smartphone-native competitors? Or, as we saw with cards, how the networks managed to pull off multiple technology migrations? However seemingly outdated an existing network may be, it's typically more practical to build on it than to start from scratch.

Our favourite example of standards transcending technology is the story of how the design of the Space Shuttle was determined by a horse's arse. The shuttle's booster rockets couldn't be bigger than the width of the railway tunnel the shuttle had to travel through on its way to the launch pad. The size of the tunnel had been determined by the width, or gauge, of the railway track.[7] When Stephenson designed the world's first railway (between Manchester and Liverpool) his track width had been fixed by the width of the track used in mines and on tramways, which – in turn – had been set by the width of the horses that drew the wagons. The wagon designers had probably used the standard width needed for chariots, which dated all the way back to the Romans. So, yes, the Romans had a hand in designing the Space Shuttle.

This is what economists call 'path dependence'. Had Brunel built his railway earlier, we might well have wider tracks; British train passengers would have more seats to sit on; and the Space Shuttle would have had bigger rocket boosters. The USA speaks English because the earliest dominant immigrants were from Britain, even though the Germans arrived later in greater numbers. Had they got there first, we might now be writing this – and you reading it – in German. The question of why Americans write cheques is thus similar to asking why the UK drives on the left, why we use(d) VHS not Betamax and why Americans (almost uniquely) measure temperature in Fahrenheit. They do – and it would be hard to change now even if they wanted to.

While path dependence sounds innocuous, the effect is often referred to as 'lock in', a term that more aptly captures the frustration of consumers

---

[7] Stephenson started with the round figure of 4'8″. The half inch was added later to give more room between the wheels and rails.

and regulators. Just as consumers can be locked into systems like Facebook or Alipay, whole countries can be locked into payment instruments, with individuals having very little choice in the matter. Consumers become prisoners of geography, their payment preferences restricted by their countries' conventions.

Frustrations aside, networks are an inexhaustibly interesting subject. They tie payment systems to the past, favouring solutions that build on what's already there. But there's a flip side to this: when there is no legacy, things can move very fast. Cast your mind back to when nascent social media landed in a large country with 300 million inhabitants, most of them equipped with PCs and internet connections, and the rapid growth of Facebook becomes easier to understand. Now imagine what could happen in another large country with a relatively underdeveloped payment system but with 1.4 billion inhabitants all equipped with smartphones . . .

10. Starting from scratch: how payments went mobile in China and Kenya

In 2019, the average person made over one hundred card payments. The resulting annual total, 500 billion card transactions, reflects the culmination of more than half a century's work of steady expansion and innovation. Impressive numbers, you might think – but think again. In the same year, some 500 billion mobile payments were registered in China alone, almost 350 per Chinese citizen. The majority of these payments were made with just two apps – Alipay and Tenpay – after roughly five years of viral adoption.

To understand just how staggering that Chinese number is, Figure 3 shows the breakdown by country of all non-cash payments made in twenty-five major countries in 2019. China accounts for 30 per cent of the population, but almost 60 per cent of all non-cash payments, some 1.2 trillion per year. The two Chinese 'super apps' account for almost a third of this, a share that's only going to grow because the apps continue to outgrow other instruments.

Alipay and Tenpay took China from a cash-based society to the world leader in terms of electronic payments in just a few years. But China wasn't the first country to witness such a phenomenal adoption of mobile payments.

In 2019, Kenya's entire population shared some 70,000 telephone lines – less than one fixed line for each 100 inhabitants. At the same time, there were almost 55 million mobile-phone subscriptions in the country – or slightly over one mobile per inhabitant. Kenya leapfrogged fixed-line telephony and moved straight to mobile phones. With a large installed base of basic mobile

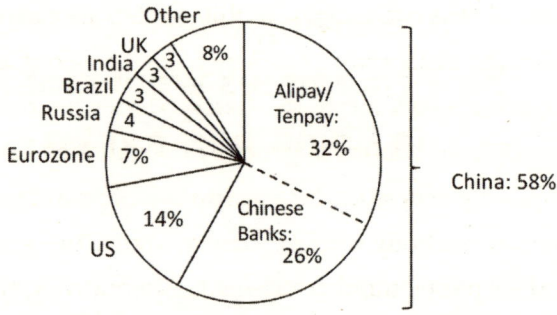

Figure 3. Share of non-cash transactions by country, 2019.

phones and no legacy payment network, Kenya used surprisingly simple technology to quickly roll out an effective payment system.

M-Pesa was established in 2007 by Vodafone's Kenyan associate, Safaricom, using simple text messages to transfer money from pre-paid balances – a currency of phone-minutes. The system worked on every phone, even simple models with no smartphone features. To allow customers to convert their phone-minutes back into cash, M-Pesa used a network of vendors who sold pre-paid phone cards. These vendors were already taking in cash from people who bought the pre-paid cards; now they were also acting as human ATMs, dispensing cash to customers while debiting their M-Pesa accounts.

The take-up of this system has been phenomenal. Ten years after its launch, practically everyone in Kenya has an account, and the system processes 50 per cent of domestic GDP in value. Compare this to Western countries, where it typically takes over twenty years for new payment technologies to achieve full adoption. Within its first decade, M-Pesa reached thirty-five transactions per inhabitant per year.

Alipay was launched three years before M-Pesa. It started as an online PC-based solution but only really took off in about 2013, thanks to almost ubiquitous smartphone ownership in a country of 1.4 billion inhabitants (compared with Kenya's 51 million).

M-Pesa and the two Chinese mobile wallets are closed systems within which users can easily transfer money to other users. Customers have to maintain account balances in the system(s) they use through being paid by other people, by transferring money in from their bank accounts or – as in Kenya – by depositing cash at appointed providers. They can then send money to anybody with an account in the same system, identifying them by their phone number or email. Alternatively, they can generate QR (quick response) codes on their smartphones, which can then be scanned by their counterparties' phones; the money is then transferred in real time.

Both Chinese super apps encourage users to keep their money inside their systems. Transactions with other users in their systems are free; if you want to send money to anyone outside them, you pay a fee of 0.1 per cent of the value transferred, with a minimum charge of 0.1 yuan (1.5 dollar cents).

The two Chinese systems are inherently peer to peer: anyone can send and receive money to or from anyone else, whether they are consumers or merchants. Similarly, anyone can act as a merchant and accept payments. Street vendors often show printed QR codes on their stalls, which buyers scan to make their payments. Apparently, even beggars now have them.

The QR code turns the traditional card model upside down. With cards, consumers are offline and just show their cards, while the merchants are online thanks to the card terminals that are connected to phonelines or the internet. With QR codes, however, consumers are online (through their phones), while merchants can be offline.

It's much easier for merchants to accept payments through Alipay and Tenpay than it is for them to take card payments. It's also much cheaper, at least for now. No wonder merchants in China have embraced the wallets at the expense of cards. The number of card-accepting merchants and card terminals in China declined by 15 per cent between 2018 and 2019, one of the very few payment statistics in China that's going down (the other is ATMs, which declined at a much slower 1 per cent).[1]

QR codes have spread throughout China. They even featured during the 2019 grand military parade marking the seventieth anniversary of the founding of the People's Republic of China. During the parade, the elite troops of the People's Liberation Army sported QR codes on their body armour, presumably for identification purposes – digital 'dog tags' – rather than to solicit donations.

Alipay and Tenpay have come to dominate retail payments in the country in record time. The average Chinese citizen makes as many payments on the two systems as the average American makes card payments.

Capable of processing over 15,000 transactions per second, the two apps aren't just great feats of engineering, they're also highly savvy marketeers. In 2009, Alibaba (the Chinese equivalent of Amazon and a close affiliate of Alipay's parent, Ant), transformed the Chinese tradition of 'Singles Day' (originally an unofficial holiday for bachelors) into a major shopping event.[2] Meanwhile, Tencent, the huge Chinese tech firm that owns Tenpay, transformed the Chinese custom of giving red envelopes filled with money at weddings, holidays and special occasions into a digital 'Red Packet' experience.

Both initiatives proved hugely successful. Singles Day has since grown into the largest shopping day in the world – great not only for Alibaba but also for Alipay, which in 2019 claimed it processed $12 billion in an hour – and $1 billion of that in the first 68 seconds.

---

[1] The number of card-accepting merchants declined from 27.3 to 23.6 million. The number of POS terminals also declined by about 3.5 million, from 34.1 to 30.8 million, indicating it was the 'single-terminal merchants' that had dropped out (data from the 2019 *Third Quarter Payments System Operations General Information Report*).

[2] Alibaba, alongside its founder, Jack Ma, is the largest shareholder in Alipay's parent company, Ant Group.

When Tencent conducted a 'soft launch' of its Red Packet during the New Year period in early 2014, the number of people using Tenpay more than tripled, from 30 million to 100 million, in a month. The following year, Tencent hit gold by teaming up with China Central Television's Spring Festival Gala – China's equivalent of the Super Bowl in terms of viewer numbers. Watched by 700 million people, that one event changed everything. Over the 2016 New Year period, Tenpay's 516 million users sent 32 billion red packets.

Almost everyone in China has an account with one or both systems, which together process a value equal to three times China's GDP every year. That's a staggering amount, especially when you compare it to the clearing houses in Western countries. These typically process eight to ten times GDP per year, but they are processing *all* invoice payments in their economies not just retail ones.

On the basis of these figures, one might fear the worst for the Chinese banks, but transactions going through the Chinese banking system have been rising quite happily (if not, perhaps, happily enough for the banks). The volume has more than doubled in the last two years, going from 150 billion in 2017 to over 320 billion in 2019 – that's 47 per cent year-on-year growth. Some of that growth is undoubtedly due to people moving their money from banks to wallets or vice versa, but it appears that the Chinese are simply making many more electronic transactions. As mobile wallet transactions are free and seamless to make, the possibilities appear endless.

Using payments as a springboard, the two Chinese mobile wallet providers have branched out to offer investment products. And they aren't doing badly there, either: on launch, Alipay's Yuebao mutual fund quickly captured $300 billion from over 325 million retail investors. For a while, the fund was the world's largest – gaining Alipay the moniker 'blood-sucking vampire' because it was swallowing up so much in savings. Both super apps also offer consumer loans, using their data on customers' payment history to assess their creditworthiness and how likely it is that they won't be willing or able to pay back the loan.

Kenya and China faced both an opportunity and a challenge: with no established systems in place they had no legacy to contend with, but neither did they have existing 'rails' on which to process payments. Instead, they both made use of near-ubiquitous mobile phone ownership – and yet the two country's systems are very different. Why? Well, partly because neither country's systems started completely from scratch: both used some form of existing base, which shaped how they then developed.

Kenya's M-Pesa was designed for basic mobile phones that could only send text messages. It also made smart use of the fact that most Kenyans had pre-paid phone accounts and capitalised on the reseller network that sold pre-paid cards. China's systems came a little later, when everybody had smart(er) phones and they were therefore able to take advantage of the functionalities these offered.

Countries never really start from zero, nor do they develop identically. Just think of English and how the British and Americans are now two nations divided by a common language. Give two countries the same technologies at the same time and the chances are that they will end up with different ways of paying that reflect their national idiosyncrasies. Path dependencies are indeed nothing if not persistent.

These path dependencies may also explain why the Chinese and Kenyan mobile wallets have not (yet) been able to repeat their success in other markets. Payments may be a scale business, but they aren't *that* scalable. M-Pesa tried and failed in India and Eastern Europe, and is struggling in South Africa; however, it appears to be doing better in the perhaps less-contested and less-developed markets of Tanzania, Mozambique and the Democratic Republic of the Congo.

Alipay and Tenpay are expanding abroad, but they are primarily doing so by signing merchants that sell to Chinese tourists. In other words, they are extending their reach but not yet their customer base. In cash-loving Germany, for example, some shops accept them (much like many shops that cater for Japanese tourists will accept JCB cards). Alipay and Tenpay are also signing up German citizens of Chinese origin, who use them to send or receive money to and from relatives in China.

Will they be able to dig deeper into the German payments market? They will have their work cut out: not only do they have to overcome the German preference for cash and predilection for privacy, but they'll also be competing with each other. And since they're closed systems, they will need to achieve critical mass before users may be convinced to stick with them. But that's the least of it – first, they would need the consent of the German and EU authorities.

Given the differences in payments (and privacy) philosophy, it does not seem likely that the EU will rush to embrace the mobile wallets offered by China's non-banks – at least on their current terms. Will Europe instead emulate the USA, where cards continue to go from strength to strength? Or will it follow India's lead in modernising payments?

11. Incredible India: the instant payment revolution

There is another nation boasting a population of more than 1 billion: India. Predictably, perhaps, India is taking an entirely different approach from China, as well as Kenya and the USA, when it comes to payments. India has several mobile wallet providers, which have enjoyed moderate success to date. But they are all now in danger of being overtaken by an initiative that speeds up account-to-account payments, makes them more accessible and easier to use – and firmly repositions banks as central players.

This is no mean feat. To understand just how remarkable India's initiative is, let's look at what happened in fast, bank-centric payments elsewhere.

Countries such as the UK have dealt with the problem of speed by introducing 'instant payment systems'. Essentially, these are turbo-charged versions of the traditional systems that banks use to settle payments between their customers – the likes of BACS in the UK, Iberpay in Spain, and so forth. While both types of system execute transfers between accounts at different banks, traditional players including BACS do this by batching thousands of payments and processing them at set times – typically once a day. In contrast, instant payment systems do this in real time, so that the money is available in seconds. Instant payment systems are available 24/7, including in the evenings, at night and at the weekend.[1]

---

[1] Such customer convenience is a source of concern for central banks though, which is why there are limits on the size of instant payments. Central banks have always used weekend closures to resolve issues with failing banks. The weekend gives banks that

First out of the gate with an instant payment system was the self-declared 'world leader in payments', the UK. Before its Faster Payments Service (FPS) launched in 2008, it took up to three days to transfer money between UK bank accounts. In spite of that, when FPS arrived on the scene take up was slow; consumers didn't seem that keen to see their money move faster. Rules were introduced requiring banks to move existing standing orders to the new platform but seven years after these came into effect, FPS was still processing only 25 per cent of the UK's transfers and direct debits.

Perhaps the new system was simply premature. Many of the instant payment services that have subsequently been introduced offer more than just real-time, 24/7 transfers. They have made it easier to pay someone else by allowing users to use 'aliases' such as email addresses or mobile phone numbers – much easier than long and unmemorable bank account details. They can be used in mobile platforms and on websites to allow customers to pay instantly.

More than fifty countries have now launched or are developing such instant payment systems. True to form, however, each country has taken its own approach, and the distinction between true instant payment systems and their 'souped-up' predecessors isn't always clear-cut.

But back to India: its solution is a domestic instant payments system combined with a superstructure that anyone is allowed to use. Customers at participating Indian banks can make instant 24/7 transfers between accounts, while this superstructure (known as the Unified Payment Interface, UPI) enables any third-party provider to initiate a real-time transfer. Firms such as Uber, Deliveroo and Google have embraced this simple way to 'inject'

---

are in trouble a respite period during which customers can't withdraw money. While people can of course still get cash from ATMs, there are limits on how much they can withdraw per day and how much the machines can actually dispense. Without limits, instant payment systems remove this 'circuit breaker' and could allow customers – corporate ones in particular – to pull massive liquidity out from a bank over the weekend, effectively accelerating its failure.

payment instructions by their Indian customers straight into the local banking system.

Technically, it's a similar set-up to the UK's FPS and Australia's so-called New Payments Platform (NPP), but India's offering has seen far faster growth and uptake.

Why? First, India's UPI allows users to pay far more easily. Instead of having to fill in account numbers and sort codes, customers can use aliases, such as mobile phone numbers. Australians can use mobile number aliases with NPP as well, but arguably the Indian system, which relies on India's ubiquitous Aadhaar national identity numbers, is better because banks already have Aadhaar numbers for all their customers, whereas users with mobile aliases have to register them first with their banks.[2]

Second, it's because UPI provides open application programming interfaces (APIs) that allow other organisations beyond the banks, such as online retailers, to initiate payments on behalf of their users. The European Commission is trying to make banks do something similar in Europe – though it has taken several years to get them to agree and the supporting regulation will take far longer to come into full effect.[3]

APIs are revolutionising financial services (as well as other industries). But what are they and how do they work?

An API is software that allows two computer applications to talk to each other. Most of us use APIs all the time without realising. For instance,

---

[2]   The Aadhaar number is a twelve-digit random number issued by the Unique Identification Authority of India (UIDAI) to residents of India who can satisfy the verification process. Any resident of India, irrespective of age and gender, can voluntarily enrol to obtain their Aadhaar number.

[3]   This is the Payment Services Directive 2 (PSD2) or EU Directive 2015/2366 that obliges banks to grant third-party service providers (that have the consent of the customer) access through APIs to initiate payments and consult account data such as balance and previous transactions.

if you choose to share on Facebook an item you like in an online store, allow an app or website to see your location or use your camera, there is an API involved.

The API description sets out how these requests – referred to as 'API calls' – need to be formatted and what information should be given in return. It can be as simple as 'ping me an account number and I will send you the current balance'. The real power of APIs is that they allow computers outside an organisation's own network to make requests. By publishing their API's specifications, organisations make it easy for outside developers to build and run such API calls.

As well as retrieving information, APIs can initiate processes, such as payments. An API call could specify the details of a transfer, including account numbers and amounts, and in return the caller would receive an acknowledgement that the payment has been executed.

Without most of us noticing, APIs have already transformed the way in which we use the internet and our mobile phones, and they are now truly revolutionising how we pay. And – sacrilege, we know, for true believers – they can achieve many of the benefits promised by the much touted blockchain technology that underpins cryptocurrencies like Bitcoin (which we'll look at in Chapter 22).

These APIs allow others – whether foreign behemoths like Amazon and Google or local Indian providers – to embed UPI within their mobile apps. The result is the 'seamless payment experience'. The apps enable buyers to pay by exchanging QR codes with merchants and merchants to present customers with electronic invoices that can be paid through UPI.

Thanks to UPI, India's instant payment system is now the world's most successful. Introduced in mid-2016, it already processes a billion transactions per month. Compare that with the UK's FPS, which, despite having launched nearly a decade earlier, processes fewer than a quarter of a billion transactions in the same timeframe. Usage of the Indian system is growing at 10 per cent per month, and more than doubling each year. This growth rate is even faster than that of Alipay and Tenpay, although admittedly UPI started later and is at a much earlier stage of adoption.

Why have countries across the world been making such huge efforts to make payments go faster? As payers, we generally don't think about how quickly someone gets their money; it's only if the person we're paying refuses to release the goods or provide the service before they receive payment that it becomes an issue. But as *payees*? Well, that's different.

Before the arrival of instant payments, when we paid by card the only thing that was certain was that the payment would be made, not how quickly that would happen. Merchants knew the money was coming, but they had to wait anything from a day to a week or more. During that time, they couldn't restock their shelves, pay their workers, reinvest the proceeds and so on. If they borrowed money to do that, it came at a cost, which in turn ate into their ability to . . . stock their shelves, pay more workers, expand their businesses. Worse, when we paid by cheque or bank transfer, receivers had neither speed *nor* certainty; until the funds cleared their accounts, they – quite literally – couldn't bank on them.

It's also a big issue for the financial sector. The longer it takes for money to get from one business or bank to another, the more credit risk that builds up in the system. That's both dangerous and economically undesirable. You want dollars to go to work, and to go to work fast.

So, the speed at which money moves really matters, and countries are jostling for pole position when it comes to instant payments – but is it a race? Payment habits are stubbornly national, so you could argue that it makes no difference if your neighbouring country goes further and faster than your own. You *could* argue that, but the efficient movement of money is crucial to every economy. You might not feel the need to keep up with any particular Joneses, but it's a mistake not to watch what they're doing, if for no other reason than to benchmark yourself against them and learn from their mistakes.

In a couple of other important ways, we should be aware that it *is* a race. There's a reason, for instance, that in mid-2020 both the European

Commission and HM Treasury started re-examining their payment strategies. A contest is clearly underway for leadership in payments – to establish standards, preserve and promote exports and influence. Less evident is the quasi-philosophical race to establish where payments should sit and who should run them; whether payments should be bank-centric or tech-centric; and whether they should be run by profit maximisers or as public utilities – or somewhere in between.

In its thinking on payments, Europe appears to be closer to India than anywhere else. The British FPS is a private-sector-funded, public-sector-driven initiative. In the euro area, a bank-owned initiative was launched in 2017, but it is complemented by the European Central Bank's own TARGET Instant Payment Settlement system, which launched just a year later.[4] The Indian initiative is similarly born of an interventionist approach and based on a private–public partnership fostered by the Indian government and the Reserve Bank of India, the country's central bank.

Although it lacks an equivalent to Aadhaar, Europe has all the other components necessary to succeed with a similar model. Not only does it have the infrastructure necessary for instant payments, it also has initiatives like the UK's Open Banking and the EU's revised Payment Services Directive (more on which in Chapter 21), both of which are helping to drive the use of APIs and easing the transfer process between accounts. Will Europe be able to combine these two elements as India has done? If it does, will it give its beleaguered banks a much needed helping hand?

---

[4] The private sector initiative is EBA Clearing's RT1. The ECB's instant payment service is TARGET Instant Payment Settlement (TIPS).

PART IV
ECONOMICS

12. Paying to pay:
the hidden costs of payments

Russia has a labour force of 72 million and an annual GDP of about $1.7 trillion US dollars. The payments industry might not touch Russia for size, but it does in financial terms. Globally, the total cost of all the payments we make amounts to somewhere between $1.5 and $2 trillion each year.

When we pay, for the most part the person we're paying gets what we send them. But the payments industry still manages to extract a healthy slice of the cake: in advanced economies, their take can amount to some $1,000 per person per year.

Savvier consumers may be surprised at this. I rarely encounter explicit payment fees, you may be thinking: I read the small print on my credit cards, and don't use them to withdraw cash; I make sure my cheques don't bounce (particularly apt for the American or French reader); when confronted by an ATM that charges for withdrawing cash, I walk around a block or two to find a free one; and – of course – whenever I want to pay someone in another country, I use Revolut or TransferWise.[1]

And yet, one way or another, we consumers *do* pay to pay. We account for a trillion dollars' worth of payment revenue, thank you very much – somewhere between 50 and 70 per cent of the total. How is it that our pockets can so easily be picked, mostly without us even noticing?

---

[1]   Revolut and TransferWise use foreign exchange rates that compare favourably to those charged by many banks and remittance operators.

The answer is complicated. Which is perhaps why neither the first generation of consumer comparison organisations (the US-based Consumer Reports, the UK's Which?, France's UFC-Que Choisir and Germany's Stiftung Warentest) nor the internet-age's MoneySupermarket.com and other price-comparison websites even *try* to offer direct comparisons of payment types and their charges.

Consumers pay in several different ways without realising it. Card fees are mostly paid by merchants, so we don't see them. But ultimately, of course, we end up paying these charges in the form of higher prices, as we saw in Chapter 6.

The second mechanism is the interest we pay on credit. Banks charge significant interest rates on credit card debt, and it can be hard to get your head around the concept of compounding – even in major advanced economies, fewer than 60 per cent of adults understand it. That's a problem. A common interest rate on card debt might be 1.9 per cent per month: that doesn't sound like much, but it works out at 25 per cent per year. At that rate, what you owe doubles in just three years and will increase by about a factor of ten in as many years.

Foreign exchange is another area where it can be difficult to calculate exactly what you're paying. Market rates vary, and by the time your statements arrive, the rates quoted will date back days or even weeks so it's hard to compare anyway. Travelex shops at airports boast 'no charges or commissions' but their rates for buying and selling are so wide apart that you could practically park your proverbial aeroplane inside them. To give a recent example, a quote of 1.40/1.12 to buy/sell dollars for euros means you will get 100 euros for $140. If you then change your mind and sell those 100 euros, you will only get $112 back. The 'round-trip' transaction will cost you $28, or 20 per cent of the initial value.

Never accept offers to be charged in your own currency at foreign ATMs or card terminals in shops. It may seem convenient, but you'll be given a foreign exchange rate that is 3–5 per cent worse than the market rate, compared with only 0.3–0.4 per cent for Visa and Mastercard. The same is true online; Amazon, for example, will use a rate that is around 2–4 per cent worse than the market.

If you struggle to understand payment charges, you're not the only one. In 2002 Mastercard acquired Europay, which held the European licence for Mastercard, along with its Maestro brand and network. Maestro was a pan-European debit network that connected ATMs and, increasingly, merchants, to facilitate cross-border transactions. Mastercard had therefore not only purchased a large credit and charge card business (which it knew well, since the business operated under its own brand), but also a debit card operation.

Shortly after the merger, a group of seasoned Mastercard executives arrived at Europay's headquarters in Waterloo in Belgium, just a stone's throw from the famous battlefield. They were horrified to discover that, in most European countries, debit cards were free for consumers and almost free for merchants: 'That's stupid – it makes no sense at all,' they are reported to have exclaimed.

But whether it makes sense or not depends on your viewpoint – and where you come from. It's not just that payment habits differ from country to country or region to region: the economics of payments, and our expectations about those economics, differ as well.

Provided we don't go into overdraft, most of us don't expect to be paying to pay through our current accounts – but don't be fooled. Banks do charge for payments, albeit mostly indirectly. Your bank offers you a package consisting of a current or checking account, plus the ability to make and receive payments.[2] This model generates almost three-quarters of the global $1.5–2 trillion payment revenue mentioned earlier (the other quarter comes from stand-alone products, mostly credit cards, which we will come to shortly). With these accounts, you generally get cheques, automated

---

[2] The USA has checking accounts; the rest of the world has current accounts. They refer to the same thing.

transfers and debit cards. You may already be charged annual fees for some services or incur regular charges on certain transactions, such as withdrawing money from ATMs owned by other banks, but because the deposit side of the balance sheet is generating less revenue in the current low-interest-rate environment, you can expect banks to soon be introducing or raising service and transaction fees.

Then there are the overdrafts themselves. Depending on where we live, banks charge us for going overdrawn in several ways; charging in advance for using overdrafts, for going into unarranged overdrafts and, of course, by raising interest on any overdrawn balances. Depending on your bank and the arrangements you chose, you can pay for the luxury of going into overdraft *ex ante* – buying the facility upfront for a monthly fee and paying an agreed rate of interest on the balance. Or you might slip into overdraft inadvertently, in which case you may face a charge that some banks even raise daily, as well as high(er) overdraft fees. What's more, for as long as you remain overdrawn, any failed direct debits, standing orders and bounced cheques might entail further charges.

Surprising as it may seem, the main source of income banks have generally relied on to cover the costs of our everyday payments is not these fees, but the interest margin on account balances. This interest margin is the difference between the interest you receive on the money in your current account (generally 0 per cent) and the interest that your money generates for the bank. As interest rates across much of the developed world are currently low, even negative, bank fees are becoming more important. For now at least, the UK is an exception because many consumer accounts have neither account nor transaction fees; this is partly made possible because UK customers, unlike those on the Continent, are avid credit card users, which is good for banks. (Whether that's good for Britain and its consumers is another matter. We'll come to that later.)

With this 'account plus payments' model, it's easy to see why you can't compare like for like. Take two people with free current accounts into which their $3,000 monthly salary is paid. Person A immediately directs $1,500 straight out again to her pension and mortgage accounts, using the balance for household spending. Person B already has a plump pension pot and no mortgage, so he leaves his salary sitting in his account. She loses virtually nothing in interest, while he, depending on where rates are, might be missing out on quite a bit. He is also paying away the opportunity cost of investing his cash.

Similarly, if two people both pay $200 a year in account maintenance fees and use their debit cards twice a day every day, they both pay just 0.27 cents per transaction. At least that would be true if they both maintain the same low balance in their current accounts. If one of them keeps most of their money in the current account to fund this spending, they are effectively 'paying' more than twice as much as the other as a result of lost interest.

Have you seen those special offers on new accounts that banks advertise with high interest rates if you pay in a minimum amount per month? They are telltale signs that banks really want your current account business. They want it because it makes money.

There are many more obvious, visible ways in which we pay to pay – making cross-border payments or ATM withdrawals and exchanging foreign currencies, for instance. What we each spend through these services can differ widely, and as we tend to face charges intermittently rather than constantly, it's easy to forget about them. But we are paying a huge amount for them – enough to support standalone businesses, many of which are doing very nicely out of the situation.

Generally, wherever you live in the world you don't pay to use your own bank's ATMs, but withdrawal fees *are* charged by the growing ranks of non-bank ATM operators. You will usually see a message along these lines: 'The owner of this ATM will charge you $2.50 for this transaction.' On top of these fees, they also charge your bank for hosting your transaction – so this first notice is sometimes accompanied by the rider: 'These fees are in addition to any fees your own institution charges. Do you want to proceed with the transaction?'

You encounter this situation a lot in the USA, where over half of ATMs are run by non-bank independent operators. The biggest one, Cardtronics, has 100,000 ATMs – more than a fifth of the US market. Even in the UK, where (visibly) paying to pay is less prevalent, Cardtronics accounts for 18,000 out of 70,000 ATMs, or a quarter of the total. A European travelling to the USA and withdrawing cash on a credit card from an ATM can get quite a shock when they return home and tot up all the charges. In a worst-case scenario they might pay for: the ATM operator's fee; their card issuer's charges for using the ATM; a fee for withdrawing cash on the card (which can rise to as much as 3 per cent of the amount withdrawn); interest on the cash withdrawn (which is raised from the point of withdrawal); a fee for a foreign currency transaction; and, oh yes, the foreign exchange rate, which may differ from the market rate by a few percentage points.[3] And, of course, if our generous traveller fails to pay off their balance at the end of the month, they will pay even more. No wonder the cards are doing so well.

Credit cards can drill deep holes in our pockets. Many of the reward cards come with annual charges; the ATM fees are, as described, pretty seismic; and the interest payable on both cash withdrawals and rolling balances is really something to avoid. That said, if you do your homework and use credit cards wisely, you can end up paying nothing at all. The perversity is that, as so often, those who can least afford it are probably paying the most.

Beyond the explicit charges for using plastic, hidden costs also exist. Visit a market or get in a cab pretty much anywhere and the seller or driver will probably now take your plastic, but they may well tell you that if you pay in cash it will be 2, 3 or 4 per cent cheaper. Restaurants, department stores, e-tailers and the rest don't (typically) do this, but you can bet your bottom dollar that they are pricing in those hefty merchant discounts.

---

[3] Look closely at your credit card small print and you will likely see that if you withdraw cash on your credit card you will be charged interest on the amount withdrawn from the point you take it out (rather than from month end).

It's not just consumers who pay to pay: businesses also pay for payments – primarily through their current accounts, although there are nuances. As well as monthly or annual current account fees, business users often face charges for all sorts of transactions, like clearing cheques and banking cash. Unlike consumer banking, credit cards don't play a major role in commercial banking, unless of course we're talking about merchants, who as we saw in Chapter 6 pay quite a bit to take cards. Instead, businesses pay (additional) fees for services such as cash management, foreign exchange and cross-border payments.

These services are often referred to as 'Corporate or Global Transaction Banking' and they represent a significant business for the large clearing banks. While businesses pay fees for all these services, they also pay indirectly by keeping significant balances in their current accounts. Liquidity requires management, so banks can then offer additional products, such as loans or overdrafts, cash pooling, netting services and more.[4]

To come back to that whopping $1.5–2 trillion annual bill: presumably businesses are footing the bulk of it? The simple answer is, no. Across the world, payment revenues are pretty much evenly split between consumer and commercial/business banking.[5] Worse, businesses have to build in their costs to the prices of the products and services that *we* consumers buy from them. In other words, we are often paying to pay in two ways.

---

[4]   This allows multinationals to combine balances from their various subsidiaries in a single balance for each currency, thus offsetting negative balances at one subsidiary with positive balances at others.

[5]   Keep in mind, though, that both McKinsey and BCG allocate the merchant discount to consumer revenue.

13. Making money by moving money: who profits from payments?

Whenever someone pays, someone else receives. The money we pay to pay is no exception, and the receivers are mostly banks. They take in most of the $1.5–2 trillion that we spend on payments every year. That amount is growing at a steady rate of 6 per cent year on year, accounting for around 30–40 per cent of overall bank revenues. But the money is not evenly spread geographically; banks in some regions rake in far more from payments than banks in others.

While all banks rely on the same economic model that we have just explored, there are huge regional differences in how much money they can make with it. These variations reflect how payment choices differ across regions, as well as the different interest rate environments – both of which are changeable. But the variations also reflect something more permanent: different countries' attitudes to paying for payments.

In the USA, the term pay-to-play describes everything from the practice of giving gifts to political figures in the hope of receiving support or investment in return to making campaign contributions in exchange for comfortable ambassadorial postings or favourable legislation. You can even 'pay-to-pray' in America. It's therefore not surprising that overt pay-to-pay charges are the norm. You might even pay for the cheques you need to make payments – while most US bank accounts provide free cheque books, they can charge $5–10 or 1–2 per cent of the amount for cashing a cheque. American regulators, politicians and the general public have historically been comfortable with that; payments are treated as a business opportunity like any other, and priced accordingly.

Europe, by contrast, tends to consider payments a utility function that should be available at low or no cost. EU regulators have stepped in repeatedly to encourage competition and lower prices and continue to do so. The result is that European card interchange fees are much lower than those in the USA, and in several cases they have been eliminated altogether. The EU has also mandated equal pricing for payments made in euros, effectively meaning that euro cross-border payments cost the same as domestic euro payments. (This Single Euro Payments Regulation was, as the name suggests, a euro regulation, which has resulted in some oddities: British banks, for instance, charge their account holders for sending or receiving *pounds* to or from other countries in the EU, but nothing to send or receive *euros*.)

Direct price regulation has been applied in the USA as well but is of an altogether less stringent nature. The Durbin Amendment to regulate interchange fees was attached to the comprehensive Dodd–Frank legislation that followed the 2008 financial crisis. The US financial industry, which you would be excused for thinking would have been keeping its head down at that particular point in history, vehemently opposed the amendment all the way to the Supreme Court. In the event, Durbin capped the interchange on debit cards at a much higher rate than had been originally proposed. The US limit stands at around 0.6 per cent – that's triple the maximum European rate on debit cards (which are, in any event, free for the most part).[1] In short, beware American payment providers bearing gifts if you are a European used to 'free' payments. They may have to put up with the European fee restrictions but, like Mastercard, they will expect to make their cut somehow.

There are also geographical differences when it comes to overdrafts. These are big business for banks everywhere, but especially so in the USA. Indeed, one US bank CEO famously named his yacht *Overdraft*, presumably to remind himself of what kept his bank afloat. While he got a bad rap

---

[1]   This is the effective cap for the average $40 debit card purchase. The actual cap is 21 cents plus 0.05 per cent.

for that, US banks on the whole still do nicely out of overdrafts, raking in a tidy $11 billion in overdraft fees during 2019 alone.

Banks receive very bad press in relation to overdrafts, much of it well deserved. In the USA, for instance, banks have been found guilty in recent years of encouraging customers to sign up for overdraft options they don't need. They have also been found guilty of prioritising outgoing payments to ensure that the biggest payments go through first, thereby pocketing fees on the subsequent ones.

All this said, most banks do at least try to make the overdraft experience uncomfortable. They make customers jump through hoops to arrange overdraft facilities. Should you go into the red without them, they bombard you with letters and reminders about the dangers of an unarranged overdraft and threats of defaulting your account. Contrast that with the frictionless way in which you can borrow through cards and other point-of-sale credit instruments, and how these actually *encourage* customers to (over)spend – or how payday loan merchants target vulnerable borrowers and charge them outrageously high rates. Perhaps (with the exception of the aforementioned misdeeds) overdrafts are as much a missed opportunity for banks as they are an income stream.

Increasingly this is the way banks see it – at least in Europe where they are faced with regulatory strictures on the one hand and competition from technology companies on the other (see Chapters 18 and 21). In the Netherlands overdrafts are capped at 15 per cent, while in the UK regulators tried to address the cost-complexity issue of overdrafts in early 2020 by prohibiting banks from charging anything other than a simple annual interest rate, without any additional fees or charges. The result? By mid-2020, when the rates at which central banks lent to banks were close to zero, European banks were charging interest on overdrafts at 15 per cent, US banks at around 20 per cent – and UK banks at a whopping 40 per cent. An example, if nothing else, of unintended consequences.

Just as attitudes to pricing differ across regions, so too do preferences for how to pay. American and Canadian consumers are heavy users of credit cards, which generate interchange fees and interest income on credit card debt. As a result, cards generate close to half of payment revenue in these two countries, whereas the interest margin on current (checking) accounts represents only a fifth.

Asian banks receive almost half of global payment revenue, but, unlike in the USA and Canada, credit cards account for just under 20 per cent of that – a huge 55 per cent comes from the margin on current accounts. This is almost the reverse of the situation in the USA, where cards account for almost half of all revenues and the interest margin for only 20 per cent. Several large Asian economies still enjoy positive interest rates and therefore solid revenues on current accounts. In China – which alone accounts for almost one-third of global payment revenues, according to McKinsey – banks earn most from the interest margin on corporate accounts. This anomaly is down to the fact that China's central bank capped the interest rates paid to bank account holders while keeping the interest rates charged on loans high in a bid to prevent the economy overheating. And, in spite of new players such as Alipay and Tenpay, Chinese customers, especially businesses, still keep ample funds in their current accounts.[2]

And then there's Europe. Where payment revenues total 2 per cent of GDP in the USA and even 3 per cent in Asia, they are a paltry 1 per cent in Europe. Few payments in Europe have explicit fees – banks rely instead on account servicing fees and interest margins, the latter making them vulnerable to low interest rate environments. With negative interest rates for the euro, Swiss franc and Danish and Swedish krone, the interest margin on current accounts is very low or even negative in Europe.

---

[2] Chinese authorities require Alipay and Tenpay to keep customer funds in custodial accounts at the Chinese central bank. Customer balances at the two wallets stand at a relatively modest $200 billion, compared with the $7 trillion that customers maintain with Chinese banks.

As we've seen, credit cards aren't widely used in continental Europe so the banks don't earn much there, and regulations limit what they can earn from interchange fees. Since payments make up some 40 per cent of all financial service revenues (the other 60 per cent comprises revenues from savings, lending, investments and insurance), the landscape goes a good way to explaining the low profitability of (continental) European banks. Britain, as ever, is an exception: with an average credit card debt of some £2,500 per household and slightly positive interest rates, UK payment revenues are closer to the global average of 2 per cent of GDP.

A similar geographic picture emerges for growth rates. For the past decade, bank payment revenues have been growing at 6 per cent per annum, well ahead of other financial services, which have seen growth rates closer to 3 per cent. Revenue growth is propelled by the ongoing move from cash to electronic payment and the phenomenal growth of online commerce, in which (electronic) payment is a key component.

Unsurprisingly, revenue growth has been fastest in the developing world, with double digits in Latin America and close to 10 per cent in Asia. North America has seen annual revenue growth of 5 per cent, well ahead of GDP, driven by rising transaction numbers as well as by mounting credit card debt. Only in Europe has the revenue growth of payments been below GDP, at just 2 per cent per year. European banks' business models are partly to blame: if they can't earn from fees, then it makes no difference if transactions increase in volume.

Now we've talked largely about banks, for which payments form an important business; with their healthy margins, they're attractive compared with other financial services. But, of course, it's not just the banking sector making a profit. Although they get most of the money that comes in from our payments, banks also face significant costs in providing payment services. A big part of this cost goes to suppliers, which, collectively, form a vast sub-industry. Go to any payments trade show (such things do exist) and you'll find scores of them: technology providers that sell or lease the software and hardware that banks use to process payments; companies that fill and manu-facture ATMs; businesses that maintain in-store payment terminals. There will be firms offering cheque processing, credit scores for card applicants, screening for compliance with anti-money-laundering regulations, and more.

Then there are the payment infrastructures such as Visa, Mastercard, the clearing houses, and Swift, the international transfer giant (though it is still bank-owned). Banks also increasingly outsource their payment services to third-party providers; most have already hived off their card acquiring and processing activities, and many are now doing the same for issuing cards. It's the same story for customer service, including call centres. The banks have to pay for all this and invest in their own IT and in shared infrastructures, reducing the amount they actually pocket from payments.

Sluggish growth and low interest rates do not generally make for happy banks. Combine that with the aforementioned fees and investments, heavy regulation, excess capacity, unionised workforces and tough employment laws, and a bank can find itself in a bind. Eurozone banks, which suffer all such tribulations, have average cost-to-income ratios of 66 per cent, com-pared with 55–57 per cent at Nordic and US banks. This ratio measures the total cost of running a bank as a percentage of its total revenue; the high ratios of Eurozone banks reflect their relatively low revenues as much as their high costs. Improving on either score is a challenge.

Cost-cutting and improving efficiency may be desirable but such man-oeuvres tend to cost money (which takes time to recoup) and are often complicated by domestic politics. Worse, it typically costs Eurozone banks more to borrow than their foreign competitors. And their ability to digitise or move their services online depends, among other things, on the overall levels of digitisation in their home countries – levels that are notably lower in a good chunk of the Eurozone than they are, say, in the USA and Northern Europe.

Let's say the European banks manage to overcome these challenges. They then need to increase their size to profit from the scale economies they can make with digitisation. Here, they face a different set of problems. They could look to merge with or acquire other banks in their home countries, but such consolidation is frowned on by competition authorities (which fear local market dominance) and governments (which fear massive layoffs as merging banks close overlapping branches). They could diversify and consolidate across borders, but then they face the challenge of bringing different markets – each with its own regulatory and legal infrastructure, insolvency laws and judicial system, not to mention payment instruments and habits – onto a single IT platform. Little wonder that European bank executives were described as being 'depressed, despondent and concerned' in the *Financial Times* in late 2019. It's hard to imagine that much has cheered their spirits since then.

All of which is to say that the European banks are in something of a predicament. Well, so what? Actually, we should all be worried, especially within the Eurozone. Unprofitable banks may well choose to consolidate or retrench (leaving us with less choice and less competition), to pile on risk or to underinvest (leaving customers, taxpayers and savers vulnerable). You might not want your bank making a mint, but you don't want to put its back to the wall either – at least not for as long as you depend on it. And depend on banks, we do.

Beyond Europe, banks are doing a bit better, but there's no room for complacency. Yes, banks make billions in revenue from payments, but they also fund much of the infrastructure that makes it possible for us to pay, and they provide the liquidity that lubricates the payment system. As banks face performance pressure, they may scale back these investments or stop certain payment services altogether. So far there is no evidence to suggest that newcomers to the payment field would be willing to pick up the slack and invest in the essential plumbing behind the scenes. Nor is it clear what could provide liquidity if the banks don't. We'll come back to this later, but now let's take a closer look at some of the other challenges facing banks.

First up, a concern that is older than the banks themselves: theft.

PART V

BIG MONEY

14. How to steal a billion: fraud and theft

In the Netflix hit series *Money Heist*, a gang of multi-disciplinary thieves, coordinated remotely by a criminal mastermind known as the 'Professor', breaks into the Spanish Royal Mint – colloquially known as the Casa de Papel ('House of Paper', the series title in its original Spanish). Rather than simply grabbing the loot and running, as the police expect, they barricade themselves in along with their hostages and keep the presses (and the series) running. The aim is to stay in situ for eleven days, printing €2.4 billion in untraceable notes.

Inventive and dramatically fertile the plotline may be, but, despite the cleverness, this is an analogue heist at heart; it wouldn't be the modus operandi of anyone as ingenious as the Professor in today's digital world. This isn't just an idle thought. In the realm of payments, combating cybercrime has been a major challenge for some time.

Money Heist first aired in 2017, more than a year after cyber thieves very nearly pulled off a virtual transcontinental theft of $1 billion from a central bank and three years after the Carbanak hacking group had compromised the systems of one hundred banks in forty countries, stealing up to $1 billion in the process.[1] Why bother with guns, hostages and getaway headaches

---

[1]   The Carbanak gang derives its name from the banking malware used in countless high-value cyberattacks. The gang is perhaps best known for hacking directly into bank networks using compromised Microsoft Office files, and using that access to force bank ATMs into dispensing cash. Russian security firm Kaspersky Lab estimates that the Carbanak gang has probably stolen upwards of $1 billion.

when you could steal as much or more from the comfort (and safety) of your sofa? A mint may be the ultimate cash machine, but it is not the mother lode. And the way to hit the mother lode is digital.

Whether onscreen or in real life, both analogue and digital payments carry the risk of theft or fraud because they are the gateways to money. A payment is like the drawbridge of a castle; when down, the whole edifice, however impregnable, is vulnerable to attack. And like a drawbridge, part of the role of each payment method is to manage the risk of attack. Thieves and fraudsters are an inventive and resourceful lot, however, and they know that there is advantage to be gained through technological leadership.

Even the straightforward 'smash and grab' has been updated for the modern day and gone at least 'semi-tech'. Perhaps it's all down to the decline of branch banking, but cash-loving criminals now tend to head for the ATMs rather than holding up counters with guns. The smashing part generally involves ripping the ATM out of the wall using high-powered stolen vehicles, but this technique is not universal. In 2019, ABN AMRO had to shut down half of its ATMs because criminals had found a way to insert explosives and blow them open rather than up.

Then, we have counterfeiting. The 'evil twin' is almost as old as cash itself and remains a highly popular and profitable pursuit. When the UK issued a new £1 coin in 2017, it did so primarily to combat the counterfeiters: an estimated 3 per cent of the old coins were imposters. In 2013, the USA replaced all of its C-notes (slang for $100 bills) with a new design, partly to defeat a wave of fake 'nearly perfect' ones – named 'supernotes' – that were allegedly being produced in North Korea. Counterfeiting today is quite a feat, given the extensive security measures used in modern banknotes: holograms, microprinting, metal threads, raised letters and colour-shifting ink.

The card fraud industry is every bit as vibrant and dynamic as the card sector itself – and has also been updated for the digital age. The early cardboard cards were simple to replicate and forging the cardholder's signature never posed much of a hurdle. When embossed plastic cards arrived, criminals retrieved old paper carbon slips from rubbish bins and used the data to punch fake cards. And when magnetic strips were added to credit cards, they quickly figured out that the information the strips contained was the same as the embossed letters on the cards. They therefore continued to fish old carbon slips from bins and simply programmed the data onto the magnetic strips of their fake cards.

As a countermeasure, the card companies added a three-digit CVV (Card Verification Value) code to the magnetic strip – but not to the card itself. This worked in shops, but not over the phone: users could give their numbers and expiry dates but didn't know their CVV codes. So, the card networks then had to add a second three-digit code, the CVV2, which is printed on the back of the card. This meant CVV2 cardholders could provide their codes to merchants but, because they weren't embossed, they didn't show up on the carbon copies.

Game over? Not a bit of it. The fraudsters swiftly moved from reading paper slips to 'skimming' magnetic strips (including the CVV codes) by, for example, mounting little readers in merchant terminals and in ATMs. The industry responded by adding Moreno's chips, which are harder to copy than magnetic strips, to cards. It also introduced PIN codes to replace signatures, which had always been vulnerable to fraud.

As the card industry threw up defences, the fraudsters went wholesale, hacking merchants' computer systems in search of customer card details stored to facilitate repeat online purchases. When giant US retailer Target (not, with hindsight, a great choice of name) was hacked in 2013, criminals bagged the details of 40 million credit and debit cards, as well as the records of a further 70 million customers. The card industry countered with tokenisation, whereby sensitive account details are replaced by a unique and temporary digital identifier – or 'token' – to be used online, in-store and in-app. Payments can be processed without exposing actual account details.

In addition to these 'hardware' measures, banks and card networks use pattern detection to help identify fraudulent transactions, where algorithms play an increasingly important role. The end result is that the card industry has managed to keep fraud at around 0.1–0.2 per cent of the total card spend. That's an amount easily absorbed by an industry that enjoys profit margins way in excess of these losses, but it's always going to be playing catch-up.

Meanwhile, there's email and social media fraud to contend with. The advent of email afforded fraudsters greater reach than ever before; in contacting thousands of potential targets, they will inevitably trick a number into providing sensitive information such as usernames, passwords and credit card details, a practice known as 'phishing'. The arrival of social media allowed them to take this to the next level. With 'spear-phishing', fraudsters could target their victims more precisely, sending customised messages to specific individuals or organisations, either to steal data for malicious purposes or to install malware on users' computers.

Particularly lucrative is the practice of 'executive whaling' or 'CEO-fraud', whereby criminals send fraudulent communications that appear to have come from senior staff within the receiver's organisation to trick employees into making large payments, disclosing sensitive information or granting access to computer systems. Social media offers scope for precision, for example by checking on Facebook or LinkedIn when the CEO will be on a long flight, when senior executives are all attending conferences or when newly arrived employees, who are less likely to query instructions, can be targeted.

This happened to Ubiquity Networks, a Silicon Valley start-up, in 2015. The Chief Accounting Officer, who had been in the job for only a month, received emails purporting to come from the founder and CEO, as well as from a lawyer at a London law firm. The emails explained that Ubiquity was conducting a confidential acquisition and instructed the CAO to send wire transfers to accounts at banks abroad. Over a period of seventeen days he made fourteen transfers to accounts in Russia, China, Hungary and Poland for a total of $46.7 million, most of which was never recovered. The company became aware of the fraud only when it was alerted by the FBI, which had been watching the account in Hong Kong where some of the transactions were sent.

Ubiquity is certainly not the only one. Other victims include US payment transfer company Xoom (lost $30.8 million in 2015), FACC AG in Austria (lost €50 million in 2016), Crelan bank in Belgium (lost €70 million in 2016), Leoni AG in Germany (lost €40 million in 2016), Facebook (lost $100 million in 2017) and Google (lost $23 million in 2017), to mention just a few.

While I was CEO of Swift, the company's finance staff received a fraudulent email purporting to come from me. Swift's then francophone CFO identified the scam mail, alerting me to it with the damning aside: 'Gottfried, while I know you speak French, there's no way this comes from you. It's in perfect French – even the accents are correct.'

Or there is dating-app fraud which brings a fresh frisson to the online dating scene. Thieves take advantage of people's vulnerabilities as they look for potential matches online, and then lure them into sophisticated fraud schemes. According to Interpol, which issued a warning on dating app fraud in early 2021, this part of the cybercrime industry has thrived on the back of Covid-19 lockdown loneliness.

The way it works is like this: first the criminals establish artificial romances with their targets through dating apps. Once communication is regular and trust is established, the criminals start sharing financial tips with their victims and encouraging them to join an investment scheme with pyramidic levels of status, dependent on the amount they invest.

Those that fall victim to this then download a trading app and open an account, into which they start paying, all under the watchful eye of their new 'friends'. Everything is made to look legitimate: screenshots are provided, domain names are designed to be eerily similar to real websites and customer service agents pretend to help victims choose the right products.

Until, that is, the day that all contact stops, victims are locked out of their accounts and left confused, hurt and – presumably – much the worse off.

Counterfeiting, phishing, whaling, credit card, dating-app and crypto fraud – all have their downsides for the criminal would-be billionaire, however. They may be relatively low tech or require physical presence; depend on malicious insiders or social engineering; or be limited in scale, risky at the exit points or easily detectable. In other words, they'll only take you so far. So, what do you do if you really want to steal a billion? Head for the real payment gateways: the banks and the systems they use to make the big payments.

Only a few actors are capable of mounting such an assault because certain preconditions must be met. As with any crime, it is essential that you face no risk of being caught or no penalty if you *are* caught; that you have an enormous cyber armoury at your disposal; and that you have nothing to lose – including your own financial system. One contender springs to mind: North Korea.

The Lazarus Group, North Korea's state-sponsored hacking outfit, had already gained notoriety in 2014 with its hack of nuclear power plants in South Korea and its subsequent attack on Sony Pictures. In apparent retaliation for Sony's release of the film *The Interview*,[2] the group released confidential emails, pre-release movies and copies of scripts. Although alarming and embarrassing for South Korea and Sony, respectively, neither episode was particularly lucrative for Lazarus or North Korea. But taking these notable scalps gave it confidence and it wasn't long before it went for the money shot.

Improbable a target as it might seem, these 'armed robbers of the internet' (as the *LA Times* dubbed Lazarus), decided to go after Bangladesh. Why? Most likely a combination of different factors: a diplomatic grudge between the two countries; poor security; weak local governance; hefty overseas balances; and the compelling addition of a Sunday-to-Thursday working week.

---

[2] Seth Rogen's comedy about a plot to assassinate North Korea's dictator, Kim Jong-un.

The heist began at some point in early 2015, when Lazarus broke into the internal network of the Bangladeshi central bank. It sent job enquiry emails, attached to which were CVs containing malware.[3] This gave it a foothold in the bank's systems from which to have a good dig around.

Over the following months the group explored the central bank's internal workings, eventually finding its way to the bank's payment gateway for its international transfers.[4] Using tailored malware, the group penetrated the payment gateway and eventually overrode the bank's required credentials. One February morning Lazarus sent thirty-five fraudulent payment instructions over the Swift network, requesting the transfer of $951 million from Bangladesh Bank's account at the Federal Reserve Bank of New York, where (like many other central banks) it maintained an ample balance of dollar reserves.

The Fed received the instructions and executed five transfers of $20 million each, before blocking the rest. One of the five executed transactions was to a bank in Sri Lanka, which spotted the fraud and blocked the receiving account before the money could be taken out. The other transfers went to four hitherto unused individual accounts at a bank in the Philippines. From there, the money was quickly withdrawn and channelled through local casinos. Only about $15 million was ever recovered.[5]

The timing was impeccable. The fraudsters had carefully scheduled their attack to occur on a Thursday evening after Bangladesh Bank staff had gone home for the weekend (which in Bangladesh, as in many Muslim countries,

---

[3]   According to the FBI, the fraudsters had started their reconnaissance of banks in Bangladesh in October 2014, well over a year before the heist. See www.justice.gov/opa/press-release/file/1092091/download.

[4]   This gateway is used to send and receive international payment instructions over the Swift network and forms part of the bank's local payment infrastructure.

[5]   Some $15 million is believed to have been recovered from the casino owner, who apparently was kind enough to return his commission for laundering the money.

is Friday and Saturday), and ahead of a Filipino holiday on the Monday. To buy further time, the malware erased their tracks by turning off a function that printed out all the bank's transfer instructions immediately after they were sent. The malware even went so far as to alter the confirmation statements that the Fed sent back to Bangladesh Bank, removing the fraudulent transactions and replenishing the account balance.

Ironically, the program the group used might have been too sophisticated for its own good: it caused the bank's system to crash and alerted a Bangladesh Bank employee who had come in on the Friday to check things over. The employee couldn't restart the terminal but decided to leave it for the next day. When he and his colleagues managed to reboot the system, they discovered that something was seriously wrong: files were missing or had been altered. Furthermore, there were enquiries from the Fed about suspicious transactions. By that time, however, the USA was closed for the weekend.

When news of what had happened eventually emerged, it sent shockwaves through the global payments community. Not only had the fraudsters pulled off a theft from a central bank and abused the trusted international payments network, they had also used sophisticated malware typically used only by nation states. Worse still, they clearly had access to correspondent banking expertise – people who knew how to format Swift instructions, and how to route them through intermediary banks.

With the world's media and forensic investigators focused on the case, it soon became clear that the problem was far bigger than Bangladesh. It wasn't long before new cases emerged elsewhere. As the deputy director of America's National Security Agency was later to put it, all the indications were that 'a nation state is robbing banks'. To date, only one member of the Lazarus Group has been identified; an arrest or a trial seems unlikely.

Following the Bangladesh Bank fraud, Swift and its banks launched a comprehensive program to secure the banks' payment gateways and prevent such frauds. Although attempts likely still continue, so far this seems to have been effective as no Bangladesh-type frauds have been reported in recent years.

Advanced technology isn't the only game in town, however: it's possible to extract large sums through low-tech fraud if you focus on other payment 'gateways'. What you need is a good deal of patience, a tame insider and a bank with weak controls. Nowhere does this seem to be better illustrated than in the case of the Indian diamond tycoon, Nirav Modi, and Punjab National Bank (PNB).

The Wharton-educated and Hollywood-loving jeweller-to-the-stars was a denizen of the Forbes Indian billionaire list and the owner of a New York store opened by none other than Donald Trump. But Modi's passion for publicity backfired badly in 2018, when an explosive story gained him more brand recognition than his promotional budget could ever have achieved.

It began with the revelation that PNB, India's second-largest state lender, had uncovered a $1.8 billion fraud. PNB issued a criminal complaint, subsequently published by India's Central Bureau of Investigation, stating that the main beneficiaries of the alleged fraud were the jet-setting jeweller and his uncle, diamond trader Mehul Choksi, as well as their respective companies.

Modi had allegedly financed his meteoric expansion using an arcane trade-finance instrument specific to India: a letter of undertaking. This is issued by a bank acting on behalf of an importing client and is sent to the bank acting for the exporter, typically in another country. The letter effectively tells the exporter's bank: 'You can lend the money to the exporter; I know the importer and guarantee that they will pay your exporter in six months.'

It seems Modi had a helpful insider at PNB who, over the course of seven years, issued over 200 of these letters to foreign subsidiaries of other Indian banks. Those banks then advanced the sums to firms that, in turn, shipped diamonds to Modi. Modi is alleged to have used the proceeds of each new letter to pay off previous ones, steadily increasing the amounts each time. His apparent accomplice inside the bank had access to PNB's payments gateway and sent the letters using Swift messages. Because PNB had no additional controls, such as cross-checking messages, the bank remained blissfully unaware of the guarantees it was doling out. By the time it discovered the fraud, PNB had effectively guaranteed close to $2 billion to other banks.

Unlike the Lazarus Group, Modi currently resides in a cell in Wandsworth prison, south London, pending a request for extradition by the Indian government. If extradited and found guilty, Modi faces a life sentence in one of the world's most unpleasant prison systems.

Modi's incarceration aside, these incidents neatly demonstrate the clear appeal of cross-border digital payments fraud. Targets can be anywhere in the world and proceeds can be routed to countries with lax money-laundering controls. The cases also helpfully illustrate how payment gateways are to money what drawbridges are to castles. Security around payment gateways is vital – and sometimes the lack of it can be alarming. As soon as organisations plug holes, criminals will simply look for new ones, exploiting any advance in technology every bit as fast as the industry. So long as we continue to pay each other, the payment pipes will be the targets.

15. Invisible plumbing: the mechanics behind payments

Across the world, huge volumes of payments flow every day – moving vast amounts of value around. All this happens through a tangled network of networks. We talk about the 'payment system', but really that covers both a system of systems and the many systems that make it up. Truth is, the infrastructure behind our payments is vast, multi-faceted and complex. There are the retail behemoths like Visa and Mastercard but also systems you may never have heard of, such as the Bank of England's Clearing House Automated Payment System (mercifully shortened to CHAPS) and hundreds of others the world over: some big, some small; some single purpose, some multi-purpose. Much of this complexity is due to history, as banks in different countries or regions built local infrastructures over time that were later cobbled together into one system.

We saw in Chapter 9 how payments are fiercely national, and they are, but not that long ago they were regional; about 150 years ago, moving funds within countries was little easier than moving funds abroad. In the UK, cheques were accepted nationally only in 1853 – until then you could write them only within a ten-mile radius of the issuing bank. In the USA, it was not until the dawn of the twentieth century that cheques were widely accepted across state lines.

At the turn of the eighteenth century not only were there no direct debits or credit cards, but you could clear bills (the precursors to cheques) only at the issuing bank – or at a bank located nearby and willing to clear its bills and assume its risk. Needless to say, this limited the possibilities of payments, making them time-consuming to process, expensive and slow to use.

As the eighteenth century progressed, banks began working in geographic clusters; in major cities they banded together to clear the bills en masse, thereby allowing money held by a customer at one bank to be used to pay a customer at another bank. This clearing took place in 'cycles' at agreed times and at agreed venues – in London, during the unlikely, but doubtless enjoyable, lunchtime slot at the Five Bells tavern.

Despite its improbable location, the London Clearing House and others like it quickly became the workhorses of domestic interbank payments. In the early days, clearing cycles ran weekly, before moving to daily cycles in busier cities. With the emergence of cheques in the mid-eighteenth century, banks in smaller cities began holding so-called 'correspondent accounts' with banks in larger cities. These intra-regional account networks enabled money to flow across regional, city and state lines. Payments were slower than they would be *within* a given state or region, but money could still move.

In some countries, this tradition of in-person clearing lives on – today, in at least one developing market, cheque clearing is still executed in a park under the shade of a large tree. Representatives of the banks arrive on scooters carrying bags filled with cheques deposited by their customers; they sort the cheques into neat piles according to issuing bank; then each scoots off again with the cheques issued by its own bank.

Most clearing systems today, however, are quietly buzzing away processing cheques, credit transfers, standing orders and direct debits on an entirely automated basis throughout countries and currency zones. Each bank in any given country could, of course, in theory still deal directly with every other bank. But given that there can be anything between a few hundred and several thousand banks in any particular country, this approach would quickly become time-consuming, messy and expensive. Instead, the clearing houses receive instructions from all banks in their country, process them collectively on a regular basis, send the sorted cheques and instructions back out to their banks, and then calculate which banks owe which banks and how much. Each participant bank is sent a single set of debit and credit instructions, showing which customer accounts to debit and credit, as well as a single set of net balances showing each bank what it owes to or is owed from other banks.

With this each bank knows how much it can expect to be paid in and from which banks, and how much it needs to pay out to other banks. It can then debit and credit the individual customer accounts accordingly.

Today these infrastructures are fully automated and are known – rather unimaginatively – as automated clearing houses (ACHs).[1] It used to take a full working day for an ACH to clear payments, but many have got faster and now process multiple cycles or batches each day. If you've ever been told 'you should get your money in the next batch', this is what's meant.

In the case of direct debits, which are initiated by the payee's bank, the payer's bank may find there are insufficient funds in the payer's account. In such cases, and again depending on where you live, it may charge the payer an eye-watering penalty and send the transaction back to the ACH, which will reverse it in its next batch. Of course, the availability of funds may be simply a question of timing, as was neatly illustrated in early 2019 when a processing error by UK mobile phone provider Three Mobile led to direct debit payments being taken four weeks early from 550,000 customers' bank accounts. Some were left with empty accounts while others reported facing fees for going into their overdrafts and/or cheques bouncing, as well as charges for late payment fees from other service providers. The result was uproar on social media channels, profuse apologies from Three Mobile and castigation by *The Sun* newspaper under the headline 'Mobile Moan'. 'Say Watt' was the *Sun*'s headline when energy company E.On made the same

---

[1]   These ACHs have equally unmemorable names such as BACS (Bankers' Automated Clearing System) in the UK, STET (Systèmes Technologiques d'Échange et de Traitement) in France and NACHA (National Automated Clearing House Association) in the USA. The Eurozone is considered domestic in this context, and indeed has several ACHs that operate across borders but within the single currency.

mistake in December 2020, charging 1.5 million customers two weeks early (and apparently ruining Christmas for more than a few of them).

The systems that today support all this payment activity overlap and connect in a web of seemingly unfathomable interdependent complexity that no one with a clean slate and a right mind would set out – or perhaps even be able – to design. Huge numbers of payments flow through a labyrinthine network of networks. Every day the entire system shifts trillions around, backwards and forwards: from you to me and him to her; from company to company; bank to bank; and country to country.

History aside, a certain amount of complexity is unavoidable because small payments and large payments require different 'pipes'. Payments come in many different shapes and sizes, from 50 cents to $5 billion. Whether it's my phone bill or your lunch, corporate payrolls or drug deals, dividend payments or divorce settlements, each payment has to be accommodated. We like our payment choices: you might choose to pay your tax bill by cheque, but you probably prefer to receive your salary by automated bank transfer; you perhaps like the certainty of paying for utilities by direct debit, the security of making larger purchases by credit card and the ease of making smaller ones by debit card; and you probably pay for the odd incidental in cash. Horses for courses.

Table 2 shows how we can divide payments into three broad transaction types. The top row represents what we buy in shops, markets and online. These alone represent almost 2 trillion payments per year, more than one per day for each person on the planet.[2] Most are small – an average size of around $20 – but in total value they represent $40 trillion per year, or roughly half of global GDP.

The second row shows the invoices we pay to, and the money we get from, businesses and governments – rent, utility bills and taxes, as well as our

---

[2]   All figures presented in the table are for the 25 CPMI (Committee on Payments and Market Infrastructures, part of the Bank for International Settlements (BIS)) countries.

Table 2. Overview of major payment flows.

Payment flow	Transactions (billion/year)	Total value ($ trillion/year)	Average value ($/transaction)
Purchases	1,800	37	20
Invoices	300	900	3,000
Financial	2	5,000	2,500,000

Figures for 25 BIS/CPMI countries, 2019.
Source: BIS, author analysis.

wages, salaries and social benefits. This row includes the business-to-business payments that underpin supply chains and the general commerce that is the engine of any (post-)industrial society. These transactions are less frequent than our daily purchases, around one per week per person globally, but they are much bigger, averaging around $3,000. In total value, they represent well over ten times global GDP.

Last, but certainly not least, in the bottom row you see the financial flows between banks and other financial players, such as pension and hedge funds, as well as the large borrowers – companies and governments. These wholesale payments are much lower in number, not even one per year per person, but they are hefty in size: averaging over $2.5 million each. In total value, they represent some $5,000 trillion every year – seventy times global GDP.

These three categories are necessarily broad and contain lots of different payment flows, each with particular characteristics and needs. But the systems that support the different payment flows are all mutually dependent – small money can't move without the big money, nor big money without the small money. Behind the things that we can see – the point of sale terminals, ATMs and so on – lies the really important infrastructure: the payment *systems* that perform the alchemy that enables money to 'travel' from A to B. Most of this plumbing is invisible and, while in any given country or currency zone it constitutes a single connected 'system', it is made up of individual components that can vary significantly. The systems all have to address the three key challenges we encountered in Chapter 3: they have to minimise risk, minimise liquidity and maximise convention (meaning they must be widely accepted by merchants and widely used by customers).

The role of convention is most significant in retail payments, in which solutions need to be easy for consumers and network effects favour systems that connect many counterparties – the more the merrier. As we saw in Chapter 3, this explains why retail systems tend to be highly local and have a tendency to remain that way. Meanwhile, settlement risk and liquidity are most relevant in the bottom row. Why? Because trillions in value move daily through these systems. Wholesale payment systems *have* to be built around a conscious trade-off between liquidity and risk, as we will explore in Chapter 16.

You can see this trade-off in action by looking at how clearing houses operate. One of the key features of clearing houses is that they 'net' the payments. This doesn't mean that they deduct tax or national insurance from the payments (God forbid!); rather, it means the banks can offset their positive balances (what they are owed *by* others) against their negative balances (what they owe *to* others). At the end of each netting cycle, banks simply settle the net values between them.

This arrangement doesn't just reduce the overall processing costs for banks, it also saves them valuable liquidity because they require only sufficient funds to settle the net amounts.

There are, however, two big disadvantages to netting systems. First, they are relatively slow. Traditionally, netting is done at the end of the day, or even overnight, meaning payments can take at least a day to reach the other bank – sometimes even longer.

Second, netting systems are risky. Should a bank collapse during such a cycle, all of its payments up to that point have to be rolled back. Even if a receiving bank had already paid out the money to its customers, it would not receive the underlying funds from the now failed sending bank. In practice, this means that banks credit their customers only at the end of the netting cycle, when all net amounts have been properly transferred between banks. This may not seem ideal for customers, but it makes things a whole lot more efficient and affordable for banks.

For our standard daily payments, netting risk is manageable. It's only when we hit the really big numbers in the bottom row of the table that netting doesn't work so well. If these high-value payments take a day or more to become final, the banks involved face significant exposure if anything goes wrong. Should a bank fail in the interim, it could go down owing its counterparties several times their capital, making them fail as well. One failure could lead to systemic collapse. In June 1974 Germany's small and little-known Herstatt Bank demonstrated this in glorious Technicolor, giving the world a compelling reason to find a better way of dealing with high-value payments.

When regulators discovered that Herstatt had lost more than ten times its capital after a series of disastrous bets on the dollar, they suspended its licence. A bank needs only to lose its capital to fall into bankruptcy, so this was big. Even so, Herstatt was the thirty-fifth-largest bank in Germany – its failure should have been a purely domestic matter, were it not for the fact that Herstatt was involved in significant US dollar–Deutsche Mark trades with other German banks. These banks had already sent their Deutsche Marks to Herstatt in Frankfurt and were waiting to receive their dollars in New York, which was several hours behind. The dollars never arrived because Herstatt declared itself bankrupt before the New York markets opened for the day.

Herstatt's New York bank, Chase Manhattan, froze Herstatt's accounts and stopped paying out dollars on its behalf. The impact on the entire New York financial system was immediate and explosive. Liquidity – the funds banks hold to help process payments – dried up as trust between banks evaporated. The volume of payments between US banks fell by 60 per cent and interbank interest rates rose significantly, which naturally trickled down to customers. The consequences weren't limited to the USA either; the fall-out sailed right back across the Atlantic to Europe. And all because a small German bank had failed.

16. How to move a trillion (or why we need central banks)

In the 1997 movie *Men in Black*, a secret government agency polices alien refugees on earth while keeping extra-terrestrial activity a secret from the general population. It's unlikely that many central bankers model themselves on the men in question, but you can think about the role they play in the global financial system in much the same way. Central bankers are all too aware of the dangers within the financial system – that it can blow up or melt down with devastating consequences – and they do their utmost to prevent existential perils. We, meanwhile, largely remain blissfully unaware. Well, that's the theory. When things go wrong, as they did so spectacularly with Herstatt Bank, their job is first to deal with the immediate crisis, and then to stop it happening again.

The lesson learnt from Herstatt was that large debts between banks should not be left open; they should be settled through payment as soon as possible. This required a new piece of financial plumbing in the form of big pipes between banks and central banks. Really big pipes – pipes that move billions in the blink of an eye and trillions before lunch.

It can be difficult to visualise the volumes handled by these systems. When billions and trillions started to feature regularly in daily news bulletins during the 2008 financial crisis, there was much confusion over the numbers. At least some of this was down to the fact that in English-speaking countries, a trillion is a million million (with 12 zeros), whereas in many non-English-speaking countries it is a million times larger (with 18 zeros). Helpfully, the need to explain just how much money underlies these large numbers fired up a cottage industry of bloggers. One solution they offered was to visualise the numbers in physical money. A million dollars' worth of

$100 bills (they say) fills a briefcase. For a billion dollars (1,000 million) you apparently need ten fully stacked pallets of $100 bills. For a trillion dollars you would need a full-size international football (soccer) pitch – and you'd have to stack your pallets three-high.

Netting, as we saw in the previous chapter, is most definitely not the answer to the problem of moving such large amounts. What you really need if you want to move a trillion is a system that settles large-value payments between banks one-by-one and in real time; and one in which these payments are 'final' and cannot be rolled back. The solution the central banks reached was the real-time gross settlement (RTGS) system. You can think about RTGSs as playing the same role as the $100 bill passed round the small island in the story in Chapter 1 – albeit on a significantly larger scale. They allow all mutual debts between banks (in a country or currency) to be settled immediately instead of accumulating like dry tinder waiting for a spark.

When CHAPS, the UK's RTGS, came online in 1996, the then Bank of England governor, Edward George, described the system as 'Nirvana'. Perhaps you have to be a central banker to find Nirvana in an RTGS, but if you *were* a central banker you'd be a cautious type of person and you'd want to know that the vast exposures that build up among banks are settled between tea trolley rounds and before you pop out to deliver a speech.

While processing each payment gross and in real time eliminates credit risk (and helps central bank governors sleep at night), it is an expensive business. Not because of the cost of building and installing the systems (after all, these are run by central banks), or the man or machine power needed to run and maintain them, but because of what actually fuels these systems – money itself. Just as the island needed its $100 bill to fuel activity, RTGSs need liquidity and they need it in spades.

To put the numbers in context, consider this. CHAPS processes roughly £365 billion a day.[1] That may look like a huge IOU, but the sums are dwarfed

---

[1]   In the first six months of 2020, the average daily value was £365 billion.

by the two largest high-value payment systems – Fedwire for the US dollar and TARGET2 for the euro. Each of these behemoths processes $3 trillion per day. The total risk-bearing capital of all the banks in the world is close to $6 trillion. This means that the combined daily volume processed by just the US dollar and euro RTGSs is equal to the total capital base of the entire global banking system. To put it another way, if these payments were to collapse or be revoked ex post, the entire banking system could be, er, broke.

While gross settlement reduces risk, it requires much more liquidity from banks than the net-settlement equivalent. Banks need to pre-fund the RTGSs with a lot more than a $100 bill to make these large payments. Since liquidity on this scale is expensive for banks to maintain, the RTGSs are designed to minimise the amounts needed. They do this by allowing participants to run negative balances secured against collateral (that is, overdrafts secured against government bonds), and by running algorithms that execute payments in an optimal order. The bigger, most advanced RTGSs allow participating banks to limit the funds they must post to as little as 1 per cent of the daily cleared value.

According to Diana Layfield, an executive on Google's payments team, the greatest accolade a payment system can aspire to is to be forgotten about. By that definition, RTGSs score very highly; most of us don't even know they exist. And why would we – these systems seem to be billions of dollars and millions of miles away from most of our everyday payments. But that doesn't mean we aren't dependent on them: a painful lesson we learn only when they *stop* working.

Thankfully major problems are rare, but when they do occur, their impact is immediate, as unlucky British homebuyers discovered to their cost in October 2014. 'I rang my solicitor this morning and he said that they hadn't received any funds and that nothing had come through from my mortgage provider,' Colchester resident Joe Friedlein told reporters, before tweeting: 'This has to be top of my "what I don't want to happen on the day that we are moving house" list.'

Friedlein's experience was no exception: several hundred UK house sale payments failed to go through that day because of an outage on CHAPS. The CHAPS service had added one new bank to the system over the weekend and removed another; when it was restarted at 6 a.m. that Monday morning, the system had crashed.

'My 10-year-old can transfer money on a smartphone but the Bank of England system crashes when they carry out an update!' bemoaned another affected house buyer, interviewed by the BBC. The UK's National Association of Estate Agents warned of the 'cascading' effect of the delay on payments scheduled for later in the week, and a *Financial Times* headline screamed, 'BoE payments failure delays thousands of house purchase deals'.

News of the outage dominated the UK media that day and, predictably, nearly all coverage focused on the impact on house sales, quietly sidestepping the 70 per cent that did go through and ignoring the fact that property sales account for just 0.1 per cent of the total value transferred through CHAPS.

The media's decision to focus on the housing market was probably a reflection of the British obsession with property. But it also masked a failure of imagination as to what a more prolonged outage might mean. Alan Greenspan, who served as chair of the US Federal Reserve from 1987 until 2006, suffered no such illusions. Freed from the constraints of office, he wrote in 2007: 'We had always thought that if you wanted to cripple the US economy, you would take out the payment system. Banks would be forced to fall back on inefficient physical transfer of money. Businesses would resort to barter and IOUs; the level of economic activity across the country would drop like a rock.'[2]

---

[2] Within a year of Greenspan's warning, the US economy had of course dropped like a rock, but it had nothing to do with the payment systems. He had accurately portrayed what would happen if payments were taken out; he just hadn't considered what else might trigger the same outcome.

Indeed, as the *Financial Times* put it when it revisited the CHAPS episode a few years later on its *Alphaville* blog: 'A long-standing . . . collapse would have constituted nothing less than a systemic collapse of the sterling monetary market with potentially catastrophic consequences for the UK economy. Think human sacrifice, dogs and cats living together, mass hysteria.'

Could the failure of these high-value payment systems really herald such an apocalyptic scenario? To answer that, it helps to visualise the payments machinery by analogy with the rail system (no disrespect to our long-running plumbing metaphor). The rolling stock is the money, the stations are the payments gateways (Visa's card readers and the ATMs) and the branch lines are the retail rails that funnel the money to them. To connect and power all this requires some heavy-duty trunk lines and some major junctions; these are your RTGSs.

Payments coming through these trunk lines include urgent and high-value payments for businesses and occasional big-ticket items like house purchases for consumers. The RTGSs also process the settlement payments of other domestic systems, such as the interbank netting systems we encountered earlier.

These trunk lines and major junctions must have sufficient capacity to carry thousands of passengers (retail payments in our analogy), but they also need to be strong enough to support the huge freight trains carrying thousands of tonnes of iron ore and steel (the high-value and wholesale payments between banks). This part of the infrastructure absolutely *has* to work or the whole network will fail.

So, to return to cohabiting cats and dogs, how *would* we fare if the RTGSs were to go down for more than a day? You might think that since we survived just fine without them less than forty years ago, we would still get by today. Not so fast. We also survived without the internet, mobile phones and personal computers. Imagine a world without these things today. Of course, there would be workarounds to fall back on – landline phones, postal services, bricks-and-mortar shops and banks – but those systems don't work for the capacity we now need. There would be plenty of things we *couldn't* do and many other things that we *wouldn't* do; commercial activity would plummet and the cost of doing business would increase exponentially.

A modern economy without the RTGS would be an altogether more severe trial than the inconvenience of life without Google, Facebook and email. You might think we could at least keep calm and carry on with our daily shopping because these small retail payments would continue to flow through the card networks and interbank systems; however, that ignores both the mounting exposure between banks and how the groceries get to the shops or the petrol to the pumps. Payments made *by* supermarkets and oil companies fall into the high-value bucket, while their imports depend on cross-border and foreign-exchange settlements. While firms would probably let their customers' debts accumulate for a few days – much like the islanders in the first chapter of this book – at some point they would stop. No more goods in supermarkets, no more oil at the pump, no more salary payments and so on.

Keeping these big-value systems working is clearly important for the smooth running of society. But they also play a major role when disaster strikes. In the wake of a crisis, central bankers need to act as financial firefighters, dousing the flames of financial disruption and potential panic with massive liquidity. They rely on pipes like the RTGS systems to carry this liquidity to wherever the fire is.

There is no better illustration of this than the 9/11 attacks on Lower Manhattan, which hit the nerve centre of the global financial system. The thirty-two-storey building adjacent to the World Trade Center was a critical hub for telecoms conglomerate Verizon, containing what was arguably the densest knot of cables and switches anywhere in the world. It housed more than 4 million data circuits, ten cellular towers, 300,000 dial-tone lines, the New York Stock Exchange's communications and the city's main emergency switch. When the towers collapsed, steel beams pierced the front of the Verizon building, copper wires and optical fibres were wrenched from their sockets and water flooded the lower floors. All power was lost.

While the devastating consequences of 9/11 were far wider, the attack on this part of the payments nerve centre required action. The Federal Reserve stepped in quickly. It bought $30 billion worth of government securities, effectively making the cash available in loans by adding it to banks' reserve accounts so that they could make their payments. The Fed lent another $45 billion directly to banks, providing yet more liquidity to make payments. Because dollar borrowing was becoming increasingly expensive abroad, the Fed also made dollars available to foreign banks through swap lines with other central banks around the world. In total, the Fed 'injected' some $100 billion in liquidity in the days after the attacks and so helped prevent the collapse of the global financial system.

After September 11, a lot of work went into improving the banking sector's physical redundancy and resilience; regulators told banks to build back-up sites in remote locations, set up dual communication systems and more. But then the next crisis came along and, of course, it was entirely different.

The 2008 crisis didn't involve power and telecoms outages, floods or travel disruptions, so few if any of the measures put in place helped. When the investment bank Lehman Brothers failed during the weekend of 13–14 September 2008, it made Herstatt's failure look like a kids' game and put international financial relations to the test like never before. This time it wasn't just the Fed – central banks around the world found themselves having to bring in the heavy lifting equipment. In fact, they threw everything they had at it, including government-led programmes to buy bad assets from banks.

Lehman Brothers wasn't a big shot in the payments business; in fact, it wasn't even in the business at all. But it *was* involved in a dizzying network of transactions, many of which involved long-term and complex derivatives, securities and foreign exchange trades. And it was trading with a range of counterparties all around the world. Hence it was that the unfortunate KfW wired its side of a €426 million payment swap to Lehman after the US bank had already declared bankruptcy (earning itself the moniker of Germany's 'dumbest bank' in the process). The French bank BNP Paribas was exposed to the tune of €400 million, and the erstwhile Royal Bank of Scotland a further £1 billion. In total, Lehman's UK entity alone went down owing a total of £36 billion in liabilities.

Where Herstatt's failure revealed the fault lines in the foreign exchange market and 9/11 exposed the fissures in the securities market, Lehman's failure laid bare the world of derivatives. In particular, it shone a light into the murky world of 'credit default swaps', which are instruments devised to enable investors to insure against the risk of companies defaulting on their debt. These derivatives had morphed from quite sensible risk-management tools into what Warren Buffett dubbed 'financial weapons of mass destruction' within a very short period.[3] The market had exploded in size from less than $1 trillion in 2001 to $60 trillion in 2008 and had become far more complex. Most of these credit default swaps weren't being used for corporate debt; rather, they were being used to insure against defaults on sub-prime mortgages, and many were also part of complex financial transactions involving European and Asian banks.

Fortunately, the pipes held throughout this financial crisis. Payments flowed smoothly once the world's central bankers had injected funds to replace the now dried-up liquidity between banks. Without the big money RTGS systems, it could have been much worse. Unlike Voltaire's summary of the Holy Roman Empire ('neither holy, nor Roman, nor an empire'), the global financial system is very well described. And the crisis only served to demonstrate, just in case we hadn't spotted it earlier, just how enormous and interconnected it has become.

While credit derivatives lived down to Buffett's description during the financial crisis, they have, together with their more mundane cousins,

---

[3] Warren Buffett, also known as the 'Sage of Omaha', is an American investor and the chairman and CEO of US investment firm, Berkshire Hathaway. He first made the comment in his annual letter to Berkshire shareholders in 2003.

interest rates and foreign exchange derivatives, once again become indispens-able tools for the financial industry. Like the markets for securities (stocks and bonds) and foreign exchange, they are a central component of the global large-value transfer system.

The world's largest banks play a crucial role in this system. They domin-ate the securities, derivatives and foreign exchange markets. They provide the liquidity for payments and settlements and they are also the major partici-pants in the supporting infrastructures.[4] JPMorgan alone moves $6 trillion in wholesale payments each day.

While the individual league tables differ, the top players feature on every ranking: JPMorgan, Citibank, Deutsche Bank, HSBC and Bank of New York, to name a few. The skew to the West in this list is down to history, geography and (most of all) the dollar. Buyers and sellers need deep, liquid markets, which gives these large players an advantage.

What should we make of these complex, little-understood financial markets? Are the big players simply pumping ever larger amounts of risk around in a high-stakes game of pass the parcel, putting us all in danger? It may look like that from some angles, but the global large-value transfer system is an integral part of the engine that enables us to pay and borrow and that oils the wheels of commerce and trade. No one has yet found a better way to do that. Without foreign exchange markets, there would be fewer, slower and more expensive cross-border payments and therefore less trade. Without interest rate swaps there would be no defined-benefit pensions, no mortgages or loans – or at least far fewer – because the banks and other providers would be able to offer them only when they found investors ready to take the opposing risk. And without banks and capital markets for stocks and bonds, businesses would have much less access to funding.

We can debate whether banks behave well or badly; whether they pay their senior staff too much and their depositors too little; whether they lend

---

4   Such as central counterparties and central securities depositories.

as much as they should to whom they should; and so on. But, on balance, we need them. And the bigger they get, the more we need them – as we learned to our cost with Lehman Brothers.

Central banks haven't sat idle since Lehman failed; in fact, they went into overdrive. They wanted to do away with banks being 'too big to fail', while also making banks stronger. To achieve this, they required banks to hold more capital, to report regularly on their activities and to pool their risk in central infrastructures to improve transparency and help neutralise the effects of any individual bank defaulting. These infrastructures are set up to withstand collapse, not least through the stringent access requirements they impose on participants. But regardless (or because) of these impositions, the fact remains that most of these banks are still too big to fail, as are the central infrastructures they rely on. Policymakers seem to have taken up Andrew Carnegie's advice: 'Put all your eggs in one basket and then watch that basket.'[5]

We have seen systems like Visa or CHAPS go down temporarily but, so far, not for more than one day. This is just as well: a system outage for, say, a week could severely disrupt the global economy and potentially undermine entire societies.

The 2020 Covid-19 pandemic served up a massive economic shock and curtailed a great many personal and commercial freedoms in a way that would previously have been unthinkable to generations accustomed to living in peaceful, democratic societies. But we could still pay and be paid, and we could still go out to buy food and fuel. Now imagine the pre-Covid scenario in which we still have personal and commercial freedoms – but our payments stop working. Even if we found ways to buy groceries, the supermarkets wouldn't be able to re-stock their shelves; we wouldn't be able to pay for fuel or transport; and providers wouldn't be able to pay their staff

---

[5] Andrew Carnegie (1835–1919) was a Scottish-American industrialist and philanthropist. Having led the expansion of the American steel industry in the late nineteenth century, he became one of the richest Americans in history.

or suppliers. Would we see a return to rationing, black markets, even martial law? How long before economies and societies broke down completely?

Fortunately, there are some institutions focused on this very problem. The Financial Stability Board (FSB) is an international body that monitors the global financial system: its mission is to promote international financial stability and it has had its eye on payments for a while now. The central banks also have payments firmly in their sights, not least through their work at the Basel-based Bank for International Settlements (BIS).

No examination of our global payments system (nor any self-respecting conspiracy theory) would be complete without the BIS. But what does it actually do? Founded in the 1930s to facilitate the post-First World War reparations that Germany had to pay under the terms of the Treaty of Versailles, its original members were the central banks of the European countries involved in those reparations. Established as a bank with its own balance sheet, the BIS will sometimes intervene on behalf of a central bank to shield its identity and prevent speculators from taking advantage of sensitive information. Over time, the BIS has also evolved into something resembling an association of the world's central banks. It sets standards for banks, helping them to operate across borders, as part of its mission to promote global financial stability through international cooperation.

Is that enough? Only time will tell. The ongoing revolution in payments poses enormous challenges to regulators. The FSB, central banks and the BIS are engaged in a constant game of review and catch-up, augmenting their rules and expanding their remits. They face persistent opposition from lobbyists and special interest groups, whose remit is to dilute legislation and regulation. The banking and tech sectors, with their substantial tax revenues and large employment figures, have significant political clout and the resources to employ armies of highly paid lobbyists – often former regulators and public sector officials – to work their interests and slow-walk regulation. And all the while, the rapid pace of change persists, meaning that any advance can quickly be overtaken by events.

17. If money never moves, how do you send it abroad?

Cross-border payments are the payments that *everyone* loves to hate. They are routinely described as expensive, slow and opaque. And as anybody who has tried to send a couple of hundred dollars halfway across the world can confirm, this reputation is not undeserved.

Cross-border payments can involve obscure bank codes, unrecognisable account formats and requests for details that appear completely irrelevant to the task at hand. If you've ever sent one you might recall needing to indicate who bears the charges, which can be substantial. If you stipulated that you, the sender, would pay them all, you may have found that the recipient's bank still deducted an additional fee. You may not have discovered this until a week after you submitted the payment and likely you had to rely on the recipient advising you that they had received the money – and how much – because chances are that your own bank didn't know.

In the last few decades, the demand for cross-border payments has exploded, especially at the low end. Increasingly, we now buy online, often from digital shops halfway across the world. Each year, 200 million international migrant workers send an estimated $600 billion to their home countries. Add to this over 5 million international students paying for tuition and living expenses. And while Covid-19 has clearly put the brakes on international travel, business travellers and tourists also need cross-border payments for hotels, taxis, shopping and so on.

The geography of economic activity has changed beyond recognition, but payments have not kept up. This is all the more surprising given the available technology: we can email, chat and videocall with anyone anywhere in the world, in real time and often for little or no cost. We can use our debit cards to withdraw local currencies from ATMs all over the world; and we can hand over our credit cards in virtually any shop, anywhere, and pay instantly for goods and services. Why can't the same banks that perform cross-border card transactions so seamlessly do the same for cross-border transfers?

The problem lies with borders, currencies and – to a lesser extent – scale. Banks and currencies (with the exception of the euro, of course) operate within borders and most payments are made within, not *across*, them. Despite widespread talk of 'sending money abroad', no 'money' is actually 'sent'. What use would it be, after all, if pounds were sent to Frankfurt or euros to London? When you stop to consider it, it's obvious that money doesn't 'move abroad'. The vast majority of foreign payments were – and are – handled through a system called correspondent banking. The system was designed precisely to avoid the need to ship gold and other coinage around.

How does correspondent banking work? The principle is much the same as when my brother in the Netherlands says to me: 'You still have a US bank account, right? If you pay this US invoice on my behalf, I'll reimburse you in euros in your Dutch account.' Imagine that on an industrial scale. Unlike me, of course, the banks don't do it for free; to service the cross-border needs of their customers, large banks will maintain hundreds or even thousands of accounts with other banks around the world – all of which need funding.

Let's take the example of a US firm that needs to pay a supplier in China (putting trade wars and tariffs to one side). It's a big US firm and it banks with a large US bank. Being big, this bank will already be doing business in China and will therefore have an account at a bank there. It will send this bank an instruction to pay the Chinese supplier out of this account. The Chinese bank will check the US bank's account and, providing there are sufficient funds, will process the payment. In doing this, the Chinese bank is acting as a 'correspondent bank' for the US bank.

Sometimes it takes multiple 'hops' to get a payment to the final destination. If the US bank was a small community bank, it would probably not have a correspondent bank in China. In that case, it will use a larger US bank to act as intermediary, asking it to send the payment through to its Chinese correspondent. If the Chinese supplier also banks with a small bank, then the Chinese correspondent will have to process the payment through the domestic payment system. You can begin to see why these things take time and cost money . . .

In a way, correspondent banking resembles airline connections. You *can* get from any airport in the world to any other, but not necessarily directly – the journey may involve several different legs. Which brings scale into the equation. The reason that you can't fly from any airport to any airport is because there isn't sufficient traffic to sustain the flights. Just like the airline system, correspondent banking has its major global cross-border payment hubs, the equivalent of well-connected airports like Heathrow, O'Hare and Changi. These are the dozen or so global transaction banks, each of which has correspondent banking relationships with thousands of other banks. At the next level down are mid-size banks that serve as 'regional hubs', processing payments for other banks in the area and passing them on to one of the global banks. The remaining banks are smaller and mainly process payments for their own customers, relying on the services of other banks for sending the transactions abroad.

Like air travel, payment journeys can be long, but most involve only one or two 'legs'. Seventy per cent of cross-border payments involve only the sender's bank and recipient's bank or one additional intermediary, often one of the big hubs. Only a very small number of payments require longer 'chains' of banks.

The correspondent banking system enables a huge amount of value to move around the world: close to a trillion dollars per day in total, comprised of some 2 million individual payments with an average value of nearly half a million dollars.[1] These movements include commercial payments for shipment of goods and other business-to-business invoices, as well as financial flows, such as cross-border securities and derivatives-related payments.

You might wonder how banks keep their correspondent banking accounts funded. After all, it's not just individual consumers who can't move money across borders – neither can banks. To explain how this works, let's go back to the example of our Chinese and US banks and their customers.

If the US bank keeps paying invoices in China for its US customers, it will have a nice accumulation of dollars in the USA but its account with the Chinese bank will run dry. To rebalance that account, it uses the foreign exchange market. Our US bank in need of yuan will look for a counter-party, say, a Chinese bank, that needs dollars and is willing to sell yuan. This Chinese bank will then transfer the yuan to the US bank's account in China, while the US bank will transfer dollars to the Chinese bank's account at a US correspondent. In other words, the two banks turn two cross-border transactions into two domestic ones.

Although the correspondent banking system has moved with the times, much of its terminology reflects its fourteenth-century Venetian roots. For instance, in our example, the US bank will refer to its account at its Chinese correspondent as its 'Nostro' account, *nostro* being the Italian for 'ours', while, confusingly, the Chinese bank will refer to the same account as being its 'Vostro' account – *vostro* being Italian for 'yours'.

The term 'correspondent banking' also dates from when banks used to send their instructions in letters that were carried on ships. Similarly, while the term 'wire transfer' comes from the time of the telegraph, it too

---

[1]   This includes domestic correspondent banking, which makes up a third of the total. It covers the domestic legs of international transactions, as well as pure domestic correspondent banking, whereby banks in the same countries use the Swift system to settle through accounts they maintain with each other.

continues to be used today, not only for cross-border transfers but also for long-distance domestic payments in the USA. This is because US banks used to be licensed only at state level and had to rely on domestic correspondents to execute their inter-state payments. The telegraph was gradually replaced by the teleprinter, better known as the telex, which was in turn replaced by Swift, the global electronic cross-border network.[2]

The Society for Worldwide Interbank Financial Telecommunication, to give it its full title, started with an idea that could have germinated only in the late 1960s or early 1970s. The vision was certainly of its time: a single shared system could be created to interlink banks the world over, overcoming problems of cost, security, timing, trust, language and technology.

Swift, though, was no pipe dream. It went live in 1977 with 239 banks in fifteen countries. Every participating bank got a 'Swift terminal' through which it could enter instructions, send them to its correspondents and retrieve the instructions sent back *to* it *by* its correspondents. Swift now connects more than 10,000 banks in every country except North Korea, which send some 30 million messages per day over the network. About half of these relate to payments, but the Swift network is also used for communications related to securities and foreign exchange settlement, as well as trade finance and letters of credit (which we'll discover later in this chapter).

The correspondent banking system is all-encompassing, allowing payments to reach any bank anywhere in the world, no matter what language it uses and domestic conventions it follows. To enable this, the payment instructions are necessarily quite complex; they need to accommodate a wide variety of banking practices, addressing systems, currency conversions, charges, remittance information, data protection and financial crime

---

[2]   The term teletype is helpfully descriptive: a telex is like a typewriter operated remotely over a telegraph line. On the sending side of the telegraph wire, a typist entered characters on a keyboard; on the receiving side, a machine printed the characters on a paper ribbon that could be read by (some) humans.

regulations, and more. Swift standardises the format of these instructions as envisaged by the 1970s visionaries; it also assigns each bank an eight-character address, known as the Swift or BIC code.[3]

Since the instructions sent over Swift move trillions between accounts right across the world, the network is highly secure and provides the tools for banks to authenticate the instructions.

If you still don't like the sound of correspondent banking and you aren't moving big money, there are other ways to 'send money abroad'. The oldest is Hawala, an informal payment system still used throughout the Muslim world. Originating in the eighth century, it predates correspondent banking, although the underlying mechanics are similar. Like correspondent banking, it relies on intermediaries maintaining accounts with each other. But Hawala intermediaries are dealers, often merchants (not banks); the accounts are informal; and it relies on an honour system for enforcement.

With Hawala, money is sent through 'hawaladars', as Hawala dealers are called, who keep informal journals of all their transactions. A customer in, say, Dubai will give 500 dirham to a local hawaladar to send to Pakistan. This hawaladar will contact a colleague in Pakistan and ask them to pay out the money in rupees, minus a commission, to the receiver. Both hawaladars will then update their records to reflect the transaction. They can just record that the sending hawaladar now owes the receiving hawaladar 500 dirham or the equivalent in rupees. Or the two hawaladars may have other business dealings with each other and offset the transaction against those. Alternatively, they could aggregate several transactions and send the balance through another channel, such as other hawaladars, the banking system or the remittance operators.

The system is built entirely on trust. There are no formal contracts between hawaladars or recourse to courts if they fail to maintain their

---

[3]   BIC used to stand for Bank Identifier Code. Since non-banks can now also join the network, the name has changed to Business Identifier Code. Just to confuse things, the BIC may sometimes also be referred to as the 'telex code'.

commitments. Instead, they lose their honour and status as a hawaladar. Volume data is hard to come by, but by many estimates the Hawala system processes billions each year. US officials estimate that some $5–7 billion flows into Pakistan alone each year through Hawala. The lack of formal channels or record-keeping has attracted the criticism that the system frustrates efforts to trace illicit money, thereby potentially facilitating money laundering and terrorist financing.

Both correspondent banking and Hawala date from a time when cross-border payments mainly served international trade. But the world has moved on. Over the last couple of centuries the drive to create national payment systems has been facilitated by technology, fuelled by regulation and, most of all, driven by need. Today, technology affords us a similar ability to innovate in international payments, and need we have aplenty.

So, the race is on to disrupt international payments. There are roughly three types of contender. First, the card networks. To their credit, they have done a good job of providing convenient, real-time payments for ATMs, shops, hotels and restaurants, and of course e-commerce. They are not free, though, and come with explicit fees as well as implicit costs through foreign exchange rates that differ from the market rate. Traditionally, they have not been convenient for person-to-person payments, but the card industry is working hard to change that. PayPal is a good example, allowing a cardholder in the USA to use their card to make a payment to a person in India, for example.

Second, the money remitters, of which Western Union is traditionally the biggest; it processes some 250 million cross-border remittances per year, with an average value of $300. By maintaining accounts in all countries it serves, it can transfer money in a matter of minutes. It will simply pay out to the receiver as soon as it has received the money from the sender, and then wait for the settlement to find its way through the traditional banking system. These traditional remitters increasingly face competition from a new breed of online money transfer services (which we'll look at shortly).

Third up are those who aim to make use of the domestic instant payment systems that are emerging everywhere (see Chapter 11). Interlinking these would allow consumers (and their banks) to use them for cross-border payments. The instructions would hop from the system in country A to the instant payment system in country B, where customers would receive funds much as they do domestic transfers. This process is not actually as easy as it sounds: there are some hurdles to be crossed, such as currency conversion (and sometimes currency controls) and screening for compliance with sanctions or anti-money-laundering regulations, from which domestic payments are often exempt.

One could argue that retail players such as the Hawala network and the newer contenders mentioned above perform the same function as correspondent banks: they take in money in one country and pay it out in another, converting currencies in the process. But they do it for much smaller payments and, because they *are* smaller amounts, they can then bundle (or 'net') them into a few large transfers through the correspondent banking system.

Your traditional correspondent banker may smile at these contenders, pointing out that they do not work for the larger payments that grease the wheels of international trade and finance. Where the average payment is some $500, the average payment that goes through correspondent banking is closer to $500,000. The total value transferred through correspondent banking is more than 500 times the value transferred by cards, far too much to pass through a single bank.

Large payments require significant liquidity from banks. I can easily accommodate my brother's $100 payment, but if he were to ask me to pay $100,000 on his behalf, I'd tell him to take a hike; I wouldn't have nearly enough liquidity in my US account and, dear to me as he is, I am not going to store funds of that amount on the off-chance that he might want to use them. Similarly, the interbank settlement exposure from all these payments would be unacceptably high – so high that not even the largest bank could provide the required liquidity to act as a single settlement bank.

What's more there are rules to worry about. Cross-border payments are screened to check that they are not breaking sanctions or anti-money-laundering regulations (which we will dive into in more detail in Chapter 29). While these regulations apply in principle to all payments, including smaller and domestic ones, attention is generally focused on the larger cross-border flows that can attract the headline-grabbing fines. This compliance requires sophisticated systems as well as a great deal of human input, and the large clearing banks will typically have several thousand people working on the problem.

So, there *are* good reasons for banks to keep using the correspondent system, even if it is centuries old. No alternative can provide the liquidity that's needed to clear the $1.5 trillion that it moves every day, at least not at an acceptable risk level. Even so, one might still legitimately ask why banks have been taking days to move transactions from one country to another, or why they have been unable to trace such payments en route.

Corporate customers might point out that the slow pace at which money moves across borders is lucrative for banks: were interest rates at 3 per cent, keeping a $1 million payment for a day would yield a bank $100. Keeping the entire daily flow of $1.5 trillion for a day yields the banking system $150 million, or close to $40 billion per year. Like the proverbial turkeys that wouldn't vote for Christmas, banks may well have an interest in keeping the system slow and the whereabouts of payments vague.

Until, that is, they suspect that someone else might be about to sit down and eat their lunch. Enter Taavet Hinrikus and Kristo Käärmann.

Taavet and Kristo, two enterprising Estonians, were living in London in the late 2000s. Taavet worked for Skype and got paid in euros but needed pounds for his day-to-day living costs. Kristo earned in pounds but needed euros to pay his mortgage in Estonia. They both became frustrated with the high fees charged by their banks for transferring money back and forth between Estonia and the UK. And (just like my brother with me) they soon realised that they could avoid the banks by pooling their needs and wants with friends and family.

They started doing just that. Taavet transferred his euros from Skype to pay Kristo's mortgage and Kristo sent his pounds to Taavet to pay his London bills. Two opposing cross-border transactions were thus turned into two local transactions.

This basic idea became the foundation of TransferWise, a successful start-up in cross-border payments that processed some 40 million transactions in 2019, with an average value of $3,000. Like Western Union and other remittance operators, TransferWise maintains bank accounts in several countries and turns cross-border transactions into local transactions. But while the remittance operators typically serve one-way corridors (the USA to Mexico, Spain to the Philippines, Dubai to India), TransferWise focuses on country corridors with flows going in both directions – Germany to the UK or Sweden to the USA. It also caps transaction sizes.[4] These two limitations ensure that TransferWise needs to send only small net amounts through correspondent banking to balance its accounts – a neat feat that allows it to charge comparatively low fees of around 0.6 per cent, including foreign exchange fees.

TransferWise (like many of its FinTech peers in cross-border transfers) isn't doing anything magical; however, from a standing start in 2011 it reached unicorn status in 2016 and is now widely heralded as one of the UK's greatest FinTechs.[5] It is currently valued at several billion dollars.

Facing increased pressure from non-bank competitors like TransferWise, banks finally took action to speed up cross-border payments and increase transparency. In 2017, the global payments innovation (gpi) was born,

---

[4]   The maximum amount of money TransferWise allows you to send depends on the currency: $1 million for US dollars, $1.2 million for euros but only $10,000 for Indian rupees.

[5]   A unicorn is a term that denotes a privately held start-up valued at over $1 billion. The term was apparently coined in 2013 by venture capitalist Aileen Lee, who chose the mythical animal to represent the statistical rarity of such successful ventures.

marking the most significant advance in cross-border payments since the founding of Swift almost fifty years earlier.

Part convention, part technology, gpi was the brainchild of the global transaction banks and Swift. It solved a major underlying problem with correspondent banking: there was no way of treating a payment – say, from you to me – as a single transaction because every message (or leg) in a payment's journey was disconnected from the others. In practice, this meant no clarity on which stage a payment was at or whether it was moving slowly or swiftly; nor was there visibility on costs and charges. It also meant that if, like the hapless Bangladesh Bank, you realised you were the victim of a fraud, you couldn't stop the payment because you had no way of knowing where it was in the chain.

With gpi, the payment route is now visible end to end and the banks involved have to commit to sending the money on as soon as they receive it, which greatly speeds things up. Because payments are trackable, gpi allows the sender and receiver to know where the money is and whether it has arrived. And while banks now have to be even quicker off the mark in spotting frauds, they can at least stop the payout immediately.

Perhaps thanks only to the threat of disruption, thousands of correspondent banks are now embracing gpi. Not all, but most correspondent banking payments are now trackable, and all should be processed end to end within twenty-four hours, half of them within thirty minutes. If your bank doesn't do this with your payments, ask it why.

Is that as good as it's going to get, you might ask? No. Like everything else with payments, we can expect that cross-border payments will be subject to further change. Banks are keen to hold on to this business, while both FinTech and BigTech[6] are keen to win it. The regulators and legislators, meanwhile, are hot on the heels of them all.

---

[6] The dominant companies in the US information technology industries: Amazon, Apple, Google, Facebook and Microsoft.

In fact, the cross-border payments 'problem' is one of the few issues that all governments seem keen to tackle – and just as well. Looking back at the three things that precipitated the growth of national payment systems in the last few centuries, we clearly have both the technology and the need – but not yet the accompanying regulatory environment. But there *are* signs of progress. Every year the heads of state of the nineteen countries with the largest- and fastest-growing economies, plus the European Union – the so-called G20 – gather to discuss the most important financial and economic issues of the day. Agreeing an agenda for the 2020 summit was never going to be easy, but one thing all participants agreed on was the need to improve cross-border payments. According to the G20: 'Faster, cheaper, more transparent and more inclusive cross-border payment services, including remittances, would have widespread benefits for citizens and economies worldwide, supporting economic growth, international trade, global development and financial inclusion.'

In such a fractured geopolitical landscape and testing economic environment, it remains to be seen how quickly both governments and the private sector will act on their commitment to the cause. But the trajectory is undoubtedly towards making cross-border payments cheaper, faster and more transparent for everyone, especially the smaller users. One day, it may be possible to send a payment, like an email or chat message, anywhere, anytime, at the speed of light and for next to nothing.

Until we get there, however, we must to keep working with what we have. Take for instance a fourteenth-century invention, the Letter of Credit, through which $2.8 trillion is funnelled. More than 10 per cent of all cross-border trade relies on this arcane payment instrument, but it's a complicated beast; few payment experts even understand it. So let's go with the short-form explanation.

Imagine you are a Venetian merchant about to bring in a shipment of silk from China. You have a potential buyer in Flanders but you do not know or trust him, and you have to ship the goods before he will pay – in fact he may not be able to pay until he has turned the silk into garments and sold them. How do you ensure that you get paid?

The Letter of Credit solves this by involving two banks: your bank and the buyer's bank. The Letter is a guarantee by the buyer's bank in Flanders that effectively says: 'If you show me proof that you shipped the silk, I will pay your bank; I will then recover the money from the buyer, but I may give them a few months' credit so they can process the silk and sell the clothes.' If the merchant is unable (or unwilling) to pay, his bank will still have to pay your Venetian bank, as long as you have provided the documents with proof of shipment.

The Letter of Credit played an unexpectedly important role in the aftermath of the 1961 Bay of Pigs fiasco when the failed invasion of Cuba led to more than a thousand CIA-financed anti-Castro commandos being taken prisoner there. Fidel Castro finally agreed to release them in exchange for $53 million worth of food and medicine, but insisted on a guarantee that the ransom would arrive before releasing the prisoners.

Henry Harfield, a great US authority on the instruments, was enlisted to find a solution and resorted to an elaborate and cunning adaptation of the Letter. The Banco Nacional de Cuba would get access to $53 million credit from a bank to purchase the supplies once Cuba had 'shipped' the prisoners. No US banks could extend this credit because of a US embargo on the country, so the Royal Bank of Canada (RBC) was cajoled into fronting the credit. The Red Cross would act as the 'buyer': each time it shipped supplies, the line of credit from RBC would be reduced by the value of the supplies shipped by the Red Cross.

If the Red Cross failed to ship (i.e. failed to pay for the prisoners), Cuba could draw on its credit and RBC would be able to recover its money from the Red Cross. RBC didn't, of course, wish to get into a situation in which it would have to foreclose on the Red Cross, so a behind-the-scenes backstop was guaranteed by JPMorgan and Bank of America, for $26.5 million each. Harfield's scheme worked. The prisoners were released, no US cash touched Cuba, the supplies were received by Castro, and Harfield received a signed letter of thanks from the White House – presumably from President Kennedy.

Esteemed authorities such as Her Majesty's Revenue & Customs and the World Bank caution against using Letters of Credit on the basis that they are confusing and restrictive and entail 'expensive delays, bureaucracy and unexpected costs', but banks continue to process some 15,000 of them per day, with an average value of $670,000 each.[7]

Harfield, a lawyer as well as a banker, profited from the complexity and bureaucracy of Letters of Credit and would no doubt be well pleased at their survival. But even he sounded a note of caution in later life when he observed that related litigation occurs in spurts, 'generally following periods of adverse or unusual business conditions'. His observation was prescient. Only a few months into the Covid-19 pandemic, the first signs of Letter of Credit litigation were already emerging. The April 2020 collapse of Hin Leong, one of Asia's largest oil traders, was precipitated when banks refused to give it any more Letters. The firm went down owing $3 billion to more than twenty banks.

Whatever losses Hin Leong's banks ultimately have to write off, a healthy chunk will likely relate to the Letters they had previously extended to it. Fortunately for those banks, the instruments are supported by solid conventions: they are embedded in most national legal systems and they are governed by rules set out by the International Chamber of Commerce (ICC). And, of course, there's an army of lawyers ready to advise on them.

---

[7] 'Although letters of credit can be useful, it's often best to avoid using one for a transaction. They can sometimes result in expensive delays, bureaucracy and unexpected costs. As a general rule you should probably only consider opening a letter of credit as an importer if your supplier insists on it or if national exchange controls require it.' (HM Revenue & Customs, August 2012).

But – and there always is a 'but' – the naysayers have a point: Letters of Credit involve a tremendous amount of cumbersome, *real* paperwork: the original documents have to be signed, safeguarded and presented for payment. Unlike money, the Letters actually *have* to move, although that may change – indeed, further proof that there's life in Letters of Credit yet can be deduced from the dozens of FinTechs frantically trying to gain fame (and fortune) by dragging them into the digital age.

PART VI

THE TECH REVOLUTION

18. Crashing the party: challenging the role of banks

Jack Dorsey effectively revolutionised the world with the 140-character news story. The CEO and co-founder of Twitter, Jack frequently finds himself in the news for blocking tweets and suspending accounts. Less famously, he is playing an equally revolutionary role in the payment industry as co-founder and CEO of a company called Square.

Together with Square co-founder Jim McKelvey, Dorsey came up with the square 'dongle': a small (and, of course, square) piece of hardware that turns any mobile device into a credit card terminal. What's particularly ingenious about Square is that it did this by re-imagining the 3.5-millimetre headset socket, at that time the only standardised way of feeding data into and out of mobile devices. The square dongle reads the data from the magnetic stripe on cards and transmits it to an app on the mobile device through its audio socket. Square effectively transformed a lowly and largely ignored hole in our phones into a multi-billion-dollar prospect, bringing smaller merchants like market traders and taxi drivers into the e-payment age. Square is currently valued at close to $100 billion.

Square is a prime example of a FinTech. While the application of technology to finance can be dated back as far as finance itself, the term 'FinTech' dates only to around 2008. We can debate cause and effect, but excitement about the convergence of technology and finance coincided with the explosion in public fury about the financial sector. Born at the apex of the financial crisis, the term really hit the public consciousness in around 2013 when investors started piling into the sector thick and fast. It's no coincidence that 2013 was also the year Bitcoin (of which more later) arguably went mainstream, with its price rising from $10 in January to $1,000 by year-end.

Beyond the helpful political tailwinds and huge hype that accompanied the emergence of FinTech, there are real underlying reasons why these companies hold such promise.

For one, FinTechs are unencumbered by legacy infrastructures. As a result, they can offer innovative, transparent and inexpensive financial services that banks have (or had) failed to offer to their customers. Unfettered by anything as mundane or expensive as local branches or overseas networks, their digital platforms are instead able to accommodate different languages and diverse local requirements, enabling them to scale up quickly.

Another important reason is regulation. Banks may have only themselves to blame for much of the existing legislation, but regardless they are tied up in it. Banking is heavily regulated, checked by rules that address three distinct and sometimes contradictory issues: customer protection, making sure banks don't fail and tackling financial crime. Throw in rules on competition and then multiply by the number of jurisdictions in which a bank operates. Then contrast that with FinTechs, which are able to unbundle parts of banking and enter into some (but not necessarily all) of its businesses – offering payments, say, without deposit-taking. All of which allows them to operate with far less regulatory encumbrance.

FinTechs are also able to attract talent: newsworthy and nimble, they are unfettered by the red tape and bureaucracy of banks. Where their staff are painted as hungry young sneaker-wearing digital-natives, bankers are depicted as comfortably girthed middle-aged bureaucrats with at least one foot in the past – and both in brogues. Ever keen on a tax-take and a photo op, political leaders are anxious to see the next PayPal built in their backyard. They have bent over backwards to attract FinTech business and are quite happy for their regulators to hold FinTechs to lower standards.[1] The

---

[1] Such as letting them use a regulatory sandbox – a framework that allows FinTech start-ups and other innovators to conduct live experiments in a controlled environment under a regulator's supervision.

regulators have meanwhile been keen to encourage competition, hoping that new providers will challenge banks on price and service and reach under-served markets, such as the unbanked.

The FinTech revolution has largely lived up to its billing thus far, unleashing a wave of innovation in financial services and repairing some of its prevailing shortfalls. These innovations offer consumers more choice, better-targeted services and keener pricing. Small businesses are able to get access to new forms of credit. Banks are becoming more productive, with lower trans-action costs, and the financial system itself is becoming more resilient, with greater diversity, redundancy and depth. Fundamentally, financial services are becoming more inclusive; people are better connected, more informed and increasingly empowered.

Needless to say, venture capital money has pooled behind FinTech, much of which is backed by the belief that banking in general and payments in particular must be ripe for disruption. Similar to what has been happening in music, retailing, travel and cars, these investor-cheerleaders believe banks are 'facing a Kodak moment' – for those of us who remember Kodak, that does not mean a photo opportunity for senior management.[2] Over the past few years, investors have sunk some \$30–40 billion per year into FinTech.

Few, if any, parts of the financial sector have been spared FinTech's atten-tions, but perhaps none have received quite so much attention as payments. Globally, payment revenues have grown at 6 per cent per year over the past ten years, a pace that is expected to continue for at least the next five years; what's more, it's double the growth rate of other financial services. It's also an increasingly technology-intensive area in which scale economies can

---

[2] Kodak was the dominant producer of photographic film in the days before digital cameras. The company's ubiquity was such that its 'Kodak moment' tagline entered the common lexicon to describe events that demanded to be recorded for posterity. Kodak began to struggle financially in the late 1990s as a result of the decline in sales of photographic film and its slowness in transitioning to digital photography.

deliver huge rewards. Most banks are ill-equipped to adapt to this; technology is not their forte, and all but a few banks are relatively small, operating within a fragmented industry. Globally, even the largest banks have market shares in the lower single digits, while many technology players dominate their sector: think Oracle in databases; Amazon in cloud computing; and Apple, Samsung or Huawei in mobile phones.

That might sound surprising given how we tend to think about the big banks, but the numbers bear it out. Citibank and JPMorgan are arguably the largest banks by most metrics, but JPMorgan's market share of US retail and commercial banking is around 5 per cent, while Citibank's is even lower. These two behemoths have (just) 300 million customers between them. Compare that with, say, Google's 40 per cent and Facebook's 20 per cent share of the US online advertising market, and several billion users around the globe.

Given the relative disadvantages of the incumbent banks, you might wonder why the FinTechs have not yet put them out of business. The night is still young, of course, but those FinTechs that have tried directly competing with banks – the so-called 'challenger' or 'neo-banks' – might well find it closing in quite soon.

For the most part, this type of FinTech offers full payment accounts based on cards. Their offering sounds very similar to pre-paid cards (see Chapter 7), but they typically target existing bank (or bankable) customers, offering cooler and cheaper alternatives to bricks-and-mortar banks. With no branches or paper, they are all about mobiles, cards and apps; their services include spending overviews, currency switching at competitive exchange rates, and investment and lending products. You may have already come across Monzo, Starling and Revolut in the UK or N26 in Germany.

The neo-banks distinguished themselves by offering very low rates and transaction fees – so much so that Monzo's yearly revenue per customer is around $7 while Revolut's is $10. Even if their costs are extremely low, that's wafer thin. Within months of the onset of the Covid-19 pandemic, they were all feeling the pinch. Monzo was forced to raise between £70 and 80 million in May 2020 to help it through the pandemic and, in so doing, faced a drop of almost 40 per cent in its valuation. And while Revolut and N26 started the pandemic cash-rich, plummeting transaction volumes meant they were soon cutting staff salaries to weather the storm.

There are others, including Moven, Saxo and bunq (yes, the Dutch did pick that name for a bank), none of which has made headlines with significant valuations. The UK's MetroBank is valued at just £240 million at the time of writing. Simple, a full online bank, was acquired by Spanish bank BBVA (Banco Bilbao Vizcaya Argentaria to give it its full name, which is anything but simple) for a nifty $117 million in 2014, but since then BBVA has had to write off nearly all of it.

The bricks-and-mortar banks may seem staid by comparison to the young pretenders, but they still have the best customer base – older customers who tend to save more and are less likely to switch providers. In contrast, most mobile customers tend to be price-sensitive and younger – rarely the most profitable clientele for banks. Overall, although mobility is increasing, there is still some truth in the saying that 'people change their spouse more often than their bank'.

While these neo-banks have perhaps not been the success that their investors hoped, they have benefited consumers. They may not have the same heady valuations as the FinTech firms that serve, rather than challenge, banks, but they have done everyone a great service by shaking the banks up. If your bank now offers you a well-functioning mobile app, more detail on your spending, cards that support touchless and/or mobile payments, or the option to use most products and services remotely, then you have this crowd to thank for it.

19. Cashing in on cards: the rise of the acquirers

The neo-banks may not be keeping banks up at night, but there are other stars in the FinTech firmament whose investors have been handsomely rewarded with astonishing valuations. We already saw in Chapter 8 how Visa is now worth more than any bank, but if it's a bit last century to qualify as FinTech proper, consider PayPal. Now valued at close to $275 billion, its price has risen more than fivefold since being spun off by eBay in 2015.

It may have struck you that PayPal, Visa and Mastercard are all in the business of card payments. This is not coincidental. As we'll see, with the exception of the mighty Chinese duo, Alipay and Tenpay, most payment FinTech giants are in the card business.

Table 3 shows 2020's most valuable payment companies. None of them are challenger banks, all of them service existing banks and most of them specialise in facilitating card payments to merchants. Each one is worth more

Table 3. Largest payment companies, by market value.

Payments company	Market value ($ billion)	Payments company	Market value ($ billion)
Visa (US)	511	FIS (US)	88
Mastercard (US)	356	FiServ (US)	76
PayPal (US)	274	Global Payments (US)	64
Square (US)	98	Adyen (NL)	58
Amex (US)	97		

Market values on 1 January 2021. Table includes only listed companies.

than $50 billion – more than the value of almost any European bank. These companies' profits are driven by merchants' willingness to pay for the ability to accept card payments.

Several of these firms are active in merchant acquiring – the same acquirers that we met in Chapter 8, but now with a twist. The acquirers then were banks – partly for simplicity's sake, partly because that's how it used to be. Since then, digitisation has brought new ways of selling, and a new breed of dedicated non-bank acquirers, as well as an entirely new species of payment 'facilitators' or 'aggregators', has emerged – between them propelling cards deep into the digital future.[1]

When acquirers process payments for merchants they receive a percentage of the merchants' take, the 'merchant discount', which is typically in the order of 1–3 per cent. This includes the interchange fee, which is passed on to the cardholder's bank, as well as fees for the card companies. They ultimately pocket between 0.25–1.5 per cent.

In return, acquirers provide two key services for the merchants: first, they enable merchants to take multiple payment instruments (cards of various types and brands, mobile wallets, transfers – the more the better for the merchant); second, they help to detect and prevent, or at least reduce, fraud and chargebacks. This service includes detecting transactions made with stolen cards, but also identifying cases in which customers falsely deny having made purchases or claim to have cancelled subscriptions, received damaged goods, and so on. Acquirers build risk management into their systems, running sophisticated algorithms to spot suspicious transactions in real time and minimise losses.

Companies in this business include those you may never have heard of – the aforementioned Square, Stripe (which we encountered in Chapter 3),

---

[1] Some facilitators and aggregators are acquirers in their own right; others rely on official acquirers to connect them to the Visa and Mastercard networks. In practice, they all sign up merchants and process their payments minus the merchant discount.

Adyen and Paytm (all four of which are worth over $10 billion each) as well as more familiar names like Klarna and PayPal.

Acquiring is patently a good business to be in. The business model is clear: the acquirers take their cut from the merchants who use their services, the cut ranging from 0.2 per cent of a transaction for a high-volume online acquirer to 1.5 per cent for a player that focuses on smaller merchants, such as taxi drivers.[2]

While it's true that this new breed of acquirer has built its business off the back of the card networks' legacy infrastructures and the card issuers' customer bases, their ingenious tweaks have truly revolutionised the way that we pay and can be paid. The business hasn't just been good for *them* – it has enabled a huge range of merchants to 'set up shop' with hitherto unthinkable ease. Sometimes the best ideas really are the simplest.

We already saw in Chapter 7 how PayPal stepped into the credit card cycle in a way that no one had before, providing a nascent eBay community of small merchants with a convenient way to get paid. PayPal did this by effectively taking on the role of merchant. Working with a traditional acquirer, PayPal would accept the buyer's card. Once the goods had been received by the buyer it would pay the funds into the eBay seller's PayPal account before ultimately receiving the money from the actual acquirer.

Or how about Stripe, a company that is to the online shopping world what Jack Dorsey's Square is to the physical one. Stripe is the brainchild of brothers Patrick and John Collison, who hail from a village in Tipperary 'with nothing but mooing cows'. These are no ordinary siblings: before they could legally drink in Ireland, they had won the country's Young Scientist of the Year award and gained access to MIT and Harvard. And before either had turned twenty-one, they had sold their first start-up for $5 million, making them both millionaire undergraduates.

---

[2]   Adyen's revenue divided by its processed volume. These fees come on top of the interchange fee, so the merchant discount will be significantly higher.

Founded in 2010, Stripe was built on the premise 'that payments is a problem rooted in code, not finance'. The foundation of Stripe was thus not a piece of hardware but a simple API call (see Chapter 11) – just seven lines of code that any developer can drop into their own code. This API call asks for an amount, a currency, a method of payment (with details such as name, card number, expiry date and so on), and an email address to which to send the receipt. The call will then reply to say whether the payment has been approved and set the processing and payment in motion. It's an all-in payment solution for e-tailers, combining the payment gateway with payment processing, making it a convenient way (if not necessarily the cheapest option) to handle e-commerce. Like Square, Stripe has expanded into other services, such as financing and payroll processing for smaller businesses.

There's a small but important nuance in what platforms like PayPal, Square and Stripe do, which is to front the transactions, acting as 'master merchants'. This makes it easy for new merchants to sign up, allowing the platforms to reach parts of the economy that cards had never before touched. It's also obviously good business; however, acting as 'master merchants' means the platforms typically work with traditional acquirers that handle chargebacks and the other housework that goes on behind the scenes. To cover their own costs, traditional acquirers will give these master merchants a choice: either exclude customers who generate high chargebacks or face higher processing fees. Players like Stripe and Square chose the former: as a result, they have to tread a careful line in terms of the types of business they accept. Stripe, for example, refuses businesses that are illegal (drugs, marijuana, pirated music), and also those that are: regulated (alcohol, online pharmacies), 'shady' (multi-level marketing) or financially risky (concert pre-sales and airline tickets). It also won't take on products that might be associated with money-laundering and fraud or that might damage its brand (such as porn or sex toys). Square seems to be okay with alcohol and the sex industry, but not pornography. It too prohibits anything illegal but also has an outright ban on the sale of ammunition or weapons.

This selectivity – especially when combined with market power – raises some interesting questions about financial inclusion, censorship, civil liberties and more, but it doesn't seem to be harming the companies themselves. Square went public in 2015 for $3 billion and is currently worth around $100 billion. Stripe remains privately held, but an April 2020 financing round valued the company at $36 billion and by November of that year the company was seeking financing at a $70–100 billion valuation – more than ten times the value of Ireland's biggest banking group – and a figure that makes John and Patrick the youngest self-made (paper) billionaires to date.[3]

There's also a new breed of acquirers who do what traditional acquirers used to do – but better. FinTech supremos Pieter van der Does and Arnout Schuijff are a case in point. Their latest vehicle is Adyen, Surinamese creole for 'again'. Adyen's story began in 2004 when the Dutch duo sold their first start-up, Bibit (meaning 'sapling' in Javanese), to WorldPay, the Royal Bank of Scotland's former merchant acquiring business.[4]

Bibit had specialised in acquiring online merchants and it was this expertise that WorldPay wished to add to its portfolio. The expertise, however, departed WorldPay soon after the acquisition and by 2006 had started Adyen. Pieter and Arnout wanted to do Bibit 'again', using the benefit of hindsight to get the tech right from the start. It worked like a charm. High-profile online merchants such as Facebook, Uber, eBay and Netflix signed up in short order, attracted by the global platform's proposition of unified commerce across different countries and through different channels. In 2018, Adyen went public with a valuation of $8 billion; on the first day of trading it soared to $15 billion – more than the whole of WorldPay, which had been sold for $10 billion just a year earlier. At the time of writing, it's nudging $60 billion.

---

[3] At the time of writing, Ireland's largest banking group, Allied Irish Banks, was valued at $5.5 billion.

[4] There is a pattern here, as Indonesia and Surinam are both former Dutch colonies.

Beware of assuming that acquiring always leads to FinTech gold, however. The infamous Wirecard was also in the acquiring business. Billing itself as 'beyond payments', Wirecard is a remarkable example of how FinTech euphoria camouflaged gross financial misconduct. When we started writing this book, Wirecard was also worth more than $10 billion; however, that was back when it was still Germany's FinTech posterchild rather than a national embarrassment.

The company was founded in 1999, during the so-called dot-com boom, and went public in 2004. In 2015 it began a meteoric rise, becoming Germany's great technology hope and its stellar stock-market performer. Wirecard's remarkable growth saw it expand beyond Germany into Europe, the USA, the Middle East and Asia. By 2018 it was one of the thirty most valuable German companies listed on the Frankfurt Stock Exchange and had overtaken Deutsche Bank, Germany's largest bank.

In its own words, Wirecard was 'the global innovation leader for digital financial technology'. It worked with household names such as Qatar Airways, KLM and Transport for London, handling debit and credit card payments. Less celebrated in its official literature (although highly visible on its customers' own sites), however, was the company's penchant for processing payments for porn and gambling websites, clients typically avoided by most FinTech acquirers.

If this didn't set alarm bells ringing, they should have sounded loudly when allegations began to emerge about the veracity of Wirecard's financial reporting and the real size and shape of its business. *Financial Times* journalist, Dan McCrum, had been scrutinising the company since 2014, after receiving a tip-off about its accounts, and the scope of his investigation only expanded as he and his colleagues discovered more about the company's numbers and business practices.

Wirecard responded by issuing vehement denials and rebuttals and by launching legal actions against its naysayers, not least the *Financial Times*.

Extraordinarily, Wirecard managed to keep the German regulators onside until the very last minute. BaFin, the German financial regulator, even banned investors from betting against Wirecard shares for two months and brought a criminal complaint against the journalists who had reported the allegations.

Undeterred, the *Financial Times* doggedly continued to investigate Wirecard through 2019 and into 2020, while the company accused the newspaper of reporting on fake information and attempting to manipulate the market by discrediting the company. But by June 2020, amid lurid reports of London-based short sellers being harassed, a former Libyan intelligence chief masterminding surveillance operations against critical investors, and the firm's chief operating officer fleeing to Manila, things went south. Wirecard's audit firm, EY, finally admitted it could not confirm the existence of €1.9 billion supposedly held in trust at two Asian banks – a quarter of the company's balance sheet. The document certifying the existence of these accounts turned out to be a forgery.

Germany's answer to Silicon Valley saw its stock market value collapse. Marcus Braun, Wirecard's long-time CEO, resigned and days later was arrested on suspicion of false accounting and market manipulation. Jim Freis, a former director of the US Department of the Treasury's Financial Crimes Enforcement Network (FinCEN), was hurriedly bumped up from chief compliance officer designate to interim CEO, and within a week the company had filed for insolvency. Leaving behind many unanswered questions about how criminal activity could have reached such scale unnoticed by regulators or investors, Germany's FinTech posterchild had become Europe's Enron.

20. Live now, pay later: the allure of invisibility

'Alas! how deeply painful is all payment,' laments the narrator in Lord Byron's *Don Juan*. The act of making a payment may have got a whole lot easier since Byron's day, but no one has been able to make it ultimately less painful. That's not to say that the payments industry doesn't dedicate a whole lot of time and effort to making the *act* of paying less painful. It does, and with good reason: we like ease and merchants like sales. The easier it is for us to spend, the better it is for their businesses.

We haven't so far looked at the psychology behind payments, but it's an area that many people focus very closely on. Companies that provide – or hope to provide – payment services want to make their products more successful. Academics want to understand the socio-economic effects of our changing payment habits.

As a payments specialist at Google, Diana Layfield is part of the former group. Her observation that 'people don't want to make payments, they want to do what a payment facilitates' offers a clear signal into what Google and others are trying to do with their payment products: make them less painful.

The ultimate example is Uber, the taxi app, which makes the act of payment completely invisible: you just step out of the taxi and you've paid. This is made possible because Uber stores customers' billing and payment information. As we write, there are efforts underway to apply this to many other sectors, such as bars and restaurants: no more need to catch the waiter's attention, wait for – or even look at – the bill before handing over a card. As with the new Amazon Go shops, the mere act of walking (or crawling) out of an establishment will trigger the payment. As we move to the internet of things, we should expect more innovation around this 'embedding' of payments.

All of which sounds great. As we saw with PayPal, Stripe and Square, making payments easier for individuals creates business opportunities and drives commerce, the engine of our societies. But is the art of making payments smooth, effortless, frictionless, however you want to label it, *only* a force for good?

The reviews from the academic side – behavioural economists, psychologists and anthropologists – are mixed, despite a good number of them being in the employ of the providers. Overspending and fraud are two of their biggest concerns. While temporarily taking away the pain from payments helps fuel modern economies, there is indeed a dark side. In the movie *The Joneses*, marketeers pose as a suburban family with a goal of enticing their neighbours to consume to the hilt. Frighteningly it works a treat.

Whenever we pay, unless we are paying into our own savings accounts or our pension pots, perhaps it's helpful to feel that little bit poorer for the experience. It is certainly the case when we pay with hard cash. Cash makes the impact of spending immediate and visceral. Non-cash payments, by contrast, soften the blow. That is why people trapped in debt are often advised to switch to cash. Indeed, there is ample evidence that people spend more when they use payment instruments other than cash. This effect is felt even if that other instrument happens to be physical, like scrip money.[1] ClubMed used to offer its guests the option to use beads on strings as a portable alternative currency. While wearing beads is clearly more practical than carrying cash onto beaches and into swimming pools, guests also spent those beads more freely than the cash they used to buy them.

---

[1] 'Scrip' refers to any type of substitutional currency that replaces legal tender. Scrip has also been widely used in localised commerce when traditional or legal currency is unavailable or in short supply.

The debate over whether modern methods of paying make it too easy to spend has been fuelled, of course, by the huge growth in 'frictionless payments' – payments that we don't even experience and that take us further away from the physical act of paying and the realisation that we are spending.

In 1999 Amazon patented 1-click shopping, a concept that was made possible by keeping its customers' payment, billing and shipping information on file. While the idea may seem obvious with hindsight, the patent was strong enough to force US bookseller Barnes & Noble to settle a lawsuit brought by Amazon in 2002. Apple took a more cautious approach and purchased a licence for its iTunes store in 2000, long before Barnes had settled. Perhaps fortunately for mobile commerce in general, Amazon's patent expired in 2017.

The model is certainly a marvel of consumer friendliness, especially compared to shopping in physical stores. No need to go to a shop, and no need to get out your wallet. Just a quick search and a few clicks stand between the impulse to buy and completing the purchase. It's particularly convenient for shopping on mobile screens, which are less suited to re-entering detailed information at checkout. It does, however, lend itself to overspend (a problem Amazon hasn't yet got a solution for and, given the incentives not to, perhaps never will).

Amazon was not the first to file credit card data to facilitate repeat sales. Magazines, for example, had been doing it for years as a way to renew subscriptions 'invisibly' – you could call them 0-click renewals. But Amazon did blaze new trails when it started offering its platform, with the stored customer information, to other retailers. Both Amazon and its partners found that 1-click shopping reduced the risk of shopping carts being abandoned and increased conversion rates.

On the negative side, 1-click shopping is vulnerable to fraud because customers are not asked for any additional information, such as card CVV codes at the point of payment. However, by using algorithms Amazon has become pretty good at spotting criminality. Its fraud capabilities have allowed the e-giant to take it one step further and offer payment-as-a-service through what is now called Amazon Pay, used by e-stores ranging from Dyson to Liberty London.

It's not just Amazon and Uber that make payments (too) easy. Have you noticed how pretty much all e-commerce sites now remember anything you abandon in your basket, and how they offer to store your card details, making it so much easier to pay next time? Games offer an even more seamless experience with 'in-app' purchases. UK father Doug Crossan was 'horrified' when he discovered that his thirteen-year-old son Cameron had run up £3,700 on his credit card. The card was linked to an iTunes account on the iPad that his son used to play games. Cameron racked up more than 300 'in-app' purchases on games such as *Plants vs Zombies*, *Hungry Shark*, *Gun Builder* and *N.O.V.A.* The games were free to download and use, and Cameron claimed to have assumed that his purchases were free as well. Five-year-old Danny Kitchen meanwhile spent £1,700 buying virtual weapons and ammunition in iPad game *Zombies vs Ninjas*.

Cameron and Danny were young and it's easy to see them as vulnerable; however, adults who aren't particularly financially literate can be just as vulnerable. Combine the ease with which we can now spend with low levels of financial literacy, and you can see a problem looming. According to Standard & Poor's global financial literacy survey, just 33 per cent of adults worldwide are classified as financially literate. On average, Europe scores more highly at 52 per cent, but huge variations exist. While countries such as Denmark, Sweden and the Netherlands sit at the top of (some of) the global league tables, Portugal and Romania are near the bottom. In the UK (which sits plumb in the middle of the European rankings), the Money Advice Service estimates that nearly 50 per cent of working-age adults have a numerical ability equivalent to that of an eleven year old.

There is plenty of research indicating that different representations of money can affect consumer behaviour. Unsurprisingly, the spending patterns of many have changed significantly with the arrival of new technology;

far from checking receipts line by line, millions now wave cards at tills for contactless payments without even checking the amounts they are being charged, much less verifying the maths behind them. This has implications for fraud, of course, but also for consumers' ability to monitor expenses or to stay within budgets.

According to MIT professor Drazen Prelec, who studies the psychology of money, instruments that introduce a temporal delay, disconnecting the pleasure of buying from the pain of paying, are particularly insidious when it comes to overspending. Prelec conducted an experiment to test his thesis. His research team organised a silent auction for tickets to sold-out Boston Celtics basketball games. Half the bidders were told they could pay only with cash and the other half were told they could pay only with credit cards. On average, the credit card buyers bid more than twice as much as the cash buyers, suggesting that the psychological cost of spending a dollar on a credit card is only 50 cents.

If you have ever wondered why it's still common to see signs on shop doors and at cash desks bearing the logos of the card networks or the different ways you can pay, well, now you know. It's not just about branding or customer information. Ample research has shown that the mere presence of a credit card logo is sufficient to prime consumers to think about a product's benefits and so to be more inclined to pay, whereas cash is more likely to make you think about the cost. Next time you're in a car showroom and the salesperson asks whether you want to pay by card, you'll know that it's not a stupid question, it's a primer to make you purchase.

Our willingness to spend more with cards helps to explain why merchants are prepared to pay the fees that accompany them. The problem is that this also makes it easier to run up credit card debt, which is expensive for cardholders. The interest gets added to the balance, leading to a vicious cycle that can trap people in debt. There's a whole body of research into the risks of credit card spending and borrowing and a good deal of regulation in place now to deal with it. But while governments and regulators have taken action to protect unwitting borrowers from card issuers, card lending is now a bit last century. A whole new universe of point-of-sale lenders has emerged, taking the 'buy now pay later' model to an entirely different level.

Back in 2005 three aspiring Swedish entrepreneurs had an idea for a better online shopping payment experience. Sebastian Siemiatkowski, Niklas Adalberth and Victor Jacobsson entered their idea for the Stockholm School of Economics entrepreneurship award. They lost, but undeterred founded Klarna a year later.

Klarna's model is different from that of the credit card companies. Consumers sign up to the service and when they reach the checkout at any of Klarna's 200,000 participating merchants, they leave their email and shipping address. They then select how they want to pay from various options: these will generally include paying in four instalments spread out over two months at no interest; deferring payment for 30 days, again at no interest; or engaging in a financing plan for up to thirty-six months (for which Klarna will charge an interest rate of up to 20 per cent per year). Klarna pays the merchant directly after the purchase and takes on the risk of the customer not paying.

Arguably, Klarna does for the online world what cards like American Express do for high-street shopping. They both operate a three-corner model, through which they sign up merchants and shoppers but not banks (Klarna is now officially recognised as a bank). This is different from the four-corner model used by Mastercard and Visa, which sign up only banks, not merchants and consumers. Like Amex, Klarna makes money by charging merchants fees, although its fees are lower, at around 2 per cent, compared with 3–4 per cent for Amex.[2]

Klarna has been a staggering success from a business standpoint: today, the company is worth more than $10 billion. Its 90 million consumers are

---

[2]   While some sources put the fee at 3–6 per cent, Klarna's commission revenues are about 2 per cent of its processed volume.

only a one-click process, a speedy 'soft' credit check and a mere twenty-five seconds away from paying for their purchases on borrowed money. Consumers who sign up or download the app are told where they can spend the money they don't have, which is mostly in fast fashion and beauty stores given Klarna's millennial target market – short on cash but keen on clothes. For delinquent borrowers, there's an added bonus: those soft credit checks don't trigger official records of your borrowing.

The business model is clearly popular, despite concerns being raised about whether it encourages younger customers in particular to rack up debts they can't afford to pay off: alongside Klarna, there's now Clearpay, Laybuy and more – Amazon and PayPal have climbed on board, among others. For merchants, this is great news. They don't just get to sell to people who might otherwise not have the cash, without any risk to them; they also get additional reach on the back of their (often extensive) marketing, as well as full payment services.

The ubiquity of invisible payments may be firmly established for many of us at this point and the accessibility of point-of-sale borrowing inevitable, but these aren't the only directions in which payments are now going – they are also going social. How do you feel about the idea of publicly sharing the details of your payments?

21. The new oil?
The importance of data

Lana Swartz, an assistant professor of Media Studies at the University of Virginia, spends a lot of time thinking about money and payments. You might wonder why a media-focused academic would do that – unless, like her, you see how we pay as a form of communication. If you do, you might also believe that payments aren't just about communicating, but also about how – and where – we interact with each other.

Swartz offers Venmo by way of an example. For young Americans, Venmo is currently the payment weapon of choice, widely used to send each other small amounts of cash. The free app has grown from transferring $59 million a quarter in 2012 to about $35 billion per quarter in 2020. But it has also successfully turned money transfer into another mode of teenage interaction. Venmo users 'share' their transactions with others (with *everyone* else, by default; with friends only, for more timid sorts), allowing them to see what they've paid to whom and when.

'Venmo isn't a wallet, it's a conversation!' Swartz says. Venmo has claimed that this public sharing of private data is the magic ingredient that fuelled its growth, reminiscent of the famous tagline 'Sharing is caring' of the mega-network The Circle in the eponymous book by David Eggers (the tagline went on to state that 'privacy is theft, and secrets are lies').

To some extent this notion is going back to basics: money *is* a social construct and paying is a very social act. From its very start, money has been linked to data: 'money is memory', as Swartz would put it. The first known instances of human writing aren't literary; somewhat disappointingly, they are neither poems nor letters, but clay tables that record ownership and debt. Payments generate records almost by definition, and when they don't, we tend to run into problems. For most of us, making a payment without leaving a trace now takes some doing.

There's a paradox here. When we pay in cash, we engage in a direct, face-to-face communication, but our transactions are traceless and therefore anonymous. Conversely, when we pay electronically, we engage in remote, de-personalised communication and yet leave behind indelible records of these 'conversations'. Venmo's model re-personalises electronic payments by making payment conversations public.

While you *can* adjust your Venmo privacy settings, the company (which was acquired by PayPal in 2013) is doing very nicely from its data feeds, having captured 52 million users. But while Venmo makes data its unique selling point (USP), it doesn't actually monetise data. It makes a living the traditional way, out of the transaction fees we explored in Chapter 12, charging around 3 per cent on all card and business payments.

Quite a few others believe there is serious money to be made from payment data, touting it as the new oil. Are they right and, if so, would it be preferable to 'pay' with our privacy rather than our money?

To explore that question, we come back to the two Chinese giants, Alipay and Tenpay. In both cases, the mobile wallets are free to use within the parent companies' closed ecosystems, and customers can engage in pretty much everything under one virtual roof: paying, shopping *and* social media. Where a British or American consumer might use several different mobile apps for these activities, Chinese customers don't leave their provider's app. How do Alipay and Tenpay make these wallets pay? By using customers' payment data to offer them financial services, in particular loans and mutual funds. With that information, Alipay can assess both *when* a customer might need a loan and *whether* they are likely to pay it back. Alipay's credit business is so huge that it now issues about one-tenth of China's non-mortgage consumer loans. Research conducted by Bernstein and the *Financial Times* estimated that Alipay's parent, Ant, had disbursed a total of Rmb1.7 trillion of outstanding consumer credit loans by June 2020, more than the retail loan book of any Chinese bank.

This isn't the only way in which our payments data could potentially prove remunerative. Providers of payment services could follow the Facebook model of using our data to create targeted marketing and advertising – or selling it to third parties to enable them to do so. We might prefer to pay for our payments with data rather than money: as the saying goes, 'if it's free, you are the product'.

What Alipay and Tenpay have done is little different from the approach long used by banks, the traditional custodians of our payment records. Banks have always used our payments data to their advantage – offering us premium accounts, credit cards and saving vehicles when they've seen our income rise; mortgages and pension products when we've reached a certain age; loans and overdrafts when we're caught short. But they haven't tended to do this on such an industrial scale.

In fact, they can't, at least not in Europe. Where American regulators are somewhat laissez-faire in their approach to the tech industry's use of personal data gained through social media, their European counterparts have taken a firmer line. The European attitude to banks using financial data is even stronger. Take the example of the Dutch bank ING. In 2014 the bank announced that it would run a test to see whether it could successfully target its customers with adverts based on their payment data. A public storm ensued and both the Dutch data privacy authority and Dutch conduct authority said no, forcing the bank to abandon its plans.

Five years later the bank tried again, this time limiting itself to using customers' payment data solely to offer its own products and services; obviously, the bank planned to do this in full compliance with data privacy regulations. No matter. It was a case of déjà vu: a media storm, followed by questions in parliament and a refusal from regulators. This time, the privacy authority didn't wait for the conduct authority to come up with an opinion; it wrote to inform ING that such marketing was simply *verboten*.

Compare that with Amazon, which will use your data to give you suggestions on what to buy (if you find those of limited use, be patient – AI may improve things); allow you to borrow money at checkout; and send you reminders about products you have previously looked at. Banks have a fair point when they moan that others use our data in ways they can't. But they have a bigger problem to worry about where data is concerned: open banking.

The concept of open banking stems from a 2015 investigation by the UK Competition and Markets Authority (CMA), which found that 'information asymmetries' gave incumbent banks an unfair advantage; consumers were losing out because competitors couldn't get a look-in. In simple terms: your bank holds lots of information about you. By looking at your payments, for example, your bank might spot that you are likely to buy insurance or an investment product. Your bank is also better placed to assess how risky it is to grant you a loan. Because outside competitors can't see your incomings and outgoings, they aren't in a position to offer you the most favourable terms, so you tend to be stuck with whatever rate your bank offers you.

To loosen the banks' grip on data, the UK industry was made to move to Open Banking, so called because you can give others permission to access your bank data – literally bringing them into your payments conversation.[1] If you apply for a loan at another bank or a FinTech, for example, you can allow it to retrieve your recent payment history from your bank.

The EU passed similar legislation later the same year, but for different reasons: its PSD2[2] regulation is rumoured to result from the effective lobbying of one specific FinTech. German start-up Sofort – meaning 'right

---

[1] 'Open Banking' was mandated by the Competition and Markets Authority in the UK and is capitalised. Elsewhere however the generic global non-capitalised term 'open banking' is used. *The Pay Off* follows this (albeit confusing) convention.

[2] The revised Payment Services Directive (PSD2 – Directive (EU) 2015/2366). This regulation built on the original Payment Services Directive (PSD), which was intended to harmonise payments across the EU and increase pan-European competition.

away' – is (or was) a so-called 'screen-scraper'. Screen-scrapers are basically firms with software that can retrieve customer account data from eBanking websites using the login codes that willing customers give them. They then use the 'scrapes' to offer financial services to customers, including account aggregation (you get information on accounts at multiple banks on one screen), bill payment and bookkeeping. Best known of the screen-scrapers are the US firms Mint and Plaid.

At the time of its EU lobbying efforts, Sofort enabled its customers to make online purchases by initiating transfers from their bank accounts. Customers would hand Sofort their eBanking login credentials, and Sofort would log in to the bank websites on their behalf, initiate their payments and process the confirmations. Not long after the company had its business up and running, the banks introduced changes that made it harder for third parties to login on behalf of their customers. Sofort cried foul and accused the banks of shutting out competition.

PSD2 aimed to level the playing field for FinTechs like Sofort (which by then had been acquired by Klarna). The regulation forced EU banks to enable third-party service providers to initiate payments and read account statements on behalf of their customers. PSD2 also subjected these third-party providers to regulation. Using the occasion to introduce yet more acronyms, the directive requires PISPs (payment initiation service providers) and AISPs (account information service providers) to qualify for licences before gaining access to bank APIs.[3] Whatever you think about PSD2, the idea of regulating this so-called screen-scraping activity seems a good one, since third-party access to bank data looked set to become the Wild West.

---

[3]   An account information service provider (AISP) offers account information services as an online service to provide consolidated information on one or more payment accounts held by payment service users with one or more payment service provider(s). A payment initiation services provider, or PISP, provides online services to initiate payment orders at the request of payment service users with respect to payment accounts held at other payment service providers.

This was certainly the case in the USA, where screen-scrapers have even been known to sell customer data to hedge funds.

Whatever the origins, both UK's Open Banking and the EU's PSD2 were designed to ensure that banks would enable third-party providers to work securely, reliably and rapidly with the banks' services and data on behalf and with the consent of their customers. While PSD2 does not explicitly require banks to use APIs to meet these obligations, APIs were generally seen as the best way forward. This explains why this API access is referred to (even outside the UK) as 'open banking'.

From Korea and Singapore to Australia and Canada, open banking is now a reality throughout much of the world. In the USA, however, open banking initiatives have a lot of catching up to do. No doubt this is in part thanks to a complex regulatory regime, which gives plenty of regulatory bodies the opportunity to weigh in and be lobbied on. Nonetheless, it's happening there too. Open banking should be good for us as consumers, of course. It will enhance competition and give us access to better and cheaper services without having to switch our bank accounts – *if*, that is, we take up everything it has to offer.

If you were to conclude that everybody should be happy with PSD2 and open banking, you'd be mistaken. For starters, some FinTechs were unhappy. The EU's new model required the banks' cooperation whereas previously the scrapers didn't need any such cooperation – instead they'd relied on software. Several FinTechs had invested in that software and feared that PSD2 would do away with their advantage, allowing anybody to do the same.

The banks weren't keen, either. One of their big fears was that having to open up their payments data to third parties, while also being unable to use it themselves, could propel a tech industry takeover of their territory. They pointed to India, where UPI has enabled Google and Amazon to successfully launch wallets that allow customers to pay in stores as well as online by accessing the funds in their bank accounts using APIs. The banks feared a future in which the current bank-centric model could be inverted: payments would no longer be a service they could offer to complement their balance-sheet business. Instead, payments would form a core part of data-driven platforms, feeding the owners with the payment data gold dust we discussed earlier. In this vision, arguably their worst nightmare, banks would be relegated to playing the role of utilities, bearing the costs of maintaining the underlying infrastructure while tech players control the customer interface and exploit the information they gain.

In arguing their case, the banks are quick to point out that they are held to much stricter standards than FinTech and BigTech and they're right about that – for now, at least. If regulators have championed the appearance of FinTechs in particular and the use of technology in general, one of the trickier aspects of their work in recent years relates to how they regulate them. While banks are firmly inside the regulatory perimeter, non-bank providers of bank-like services often aren't. As the banks see it, a tricky problem for regulators could prove an existential one for themselves.

The higher standards banks are held to don't just apply to data, marketing and advertising. They also relate to consumer credit, for example, where European banks face strict standards on their lending practices, while FinTech and BigTech don't – yet.

Quite reasonably, German banks have been quick to point out that it would be cheaper for consumers to finance impulse purchases by going into the red on their current accounts, compared to using the option to repay in instalments offered by 'buy now pay later' companies such as Klarna (particularly feared by the German banks since it bought Sofort). Continental European banks' interest rates often compare favourably with Klarna's 20 per cent – especially in the Eurozone, where interest rates on overdrafts are often set at 10 per cent or lower.

Playing fields have a habit of levelling themselves out, but whether banks will fare much better when that happens is questionable. FinTechs are nimble – and in many cases have deep pockets with which to fight battles. BigTech firms enjoy both those advantages; what's more, they not only have the business models to exploit data but also the technological skills and scale to deal with thousands of banks' APIs and to develop and use algorithms and artificial intelligence to crunch through mountains of data. Frankly, banks don't.

Of course, the likes of Google and Facebook already have so much data on their users that one wonders whether payment records could actually raise the sea level of the oceans they already swim in. Perhaps, instead, the tech giants envisage owning banks as subsidiaries, insurance against possible future developments in how we pay or to make it easier to connect their own services with the financial system.

Google buying Goldman Sachs is an interesting thought but hold it for now because a couple of issues need to be addressed before data can really fuel business. First, is the question of regulation. There are already concerns about the power that, as *The Economist* put it recently, 'a handful of unelected executives' now wield over our online conversations. BigTech platforms are increasingly in the business of setting the boundaries of free speech. Before handing over our payment data, arguably we or our regulators – or both – should require reassurance in the form of some standard-setting.

Second, public trust in the large tech companies is another hurdle. A recent survey in Holland showed that just 2 per cent of consumers were happy to share their payments data with BigTech, while less than 5 per cent would trust BigTech with payment initiation services. And yet those same consumers trust their intimate information, conversations and images to Facebook, WhatsApp and Messenger, in exchange for the convenience of these services. Perhaps it's just a matter of time – or financial incentive.

While BigTech firms have the financial clout to fund more consumer services in exchange for payment data, the business models behind Apple Pay, Amazon Pay and Google Pay (revived after initial failures) don't seem to be based on data use – though that doesn't, of course, mean that they never *will* be. What the tech crew will do with our payment data when they've captured market share remains an open question. Google has made great inroads in

India with its Tez payment app (now part of Google Pay), for example, but to date has not explained how it intends to make money out of it.

BigTech firms have the capacity to develop products and build up their share of the market for a decade or so before they need to start making money from them. They may be banking on our willingness to give up our privacy but if so, their strategies presuppose our regulators allowing them to monetise our data – which isn't a given. They will also have to reckon with geopolitics, as Europe and India view American and Chinese BigTech firms with particular suspicion. But perhaps that's all immaterial because a completely different form of new technology is being used by other players keen to reshape the fundamentals of how we pay. Advocates of cryptocurrencies think they have the answers – but are they asking the right questions?

22. In code we trust: meeting the cryptocurrencies

L ate in January 2018, I was attending the World Economic Forum in Davos. Walking back to my hotel one day, I passed a gaggle of people hanging about on the pavement. Sporting beards, face and neck tattoos and partly shaven heads, they looked like clubbers on a vape break. They were standing outside a door marked 'CryptoHQ'. I was intrigued.

CryptoHQ was packed. It was dark and there was a bar and loud music. I felt hopelessly out of place, twice everyone else's age and the only person in a suit. Nonetheless, I struck up a conversation with a man who ran a company that 'did something with blockchain'. I asked him what the business model was. 'I just raised $20 million through an ICO,' he said. 'That pays for everything.'[1] No wonder he seemed to be enjoying life.

Upstairs was a better-lit room, some fifty chairs and a podium. The chairs were all occupied and a few people were wearing suit jackets. I began to feel more at home. The young man on the podium was explaining how he was going to put woven skirts made in Indonesia on the blockchain; he was looking for investors. Another man asked the room whether anyone wanted to invest and several jacketed hands immediately went up. Time for the next pitch.

I watched several pitches, each lasting about five minutes. It took me back to a scene in *The Big Short* in which an investor discovers that Florida lap dancers are doing buy-to-lets on multiple condos. The investor decides

---

[1]   An initial coin offering (ICO) is the cryptocurrency industry's equivalent to an initial public offering (IPO), enabling firms to raise funds to create new coins, apps or services.

to short subprime mortgages right then and there.[2] But while he experienced this epiphany well before the 2008 crisis, the crypto-crash was already underway when I was wandering around Davos' CryptoHQ: Bitcoin had peaked at $20,000 several weeks earlier, on 17 December 2017, and was now on its way back down to $3,000.

Bitcoin did not, however, go down to zero. Instead, it recovered somewhat and has been trading between $4,000 and $30,000[3] over the last few years – a wide range by any definition, but an especially wide one for a currency.

Bitcoin first appeared in 2009, right after the financial crisis, and was conceived as a technological utopia – an alternative to banks and money, whose failings had just become all too apparent. Bitcoin does away with the need for intermediaries like banks, and authorities such as central banks and governments. With Bitcoin, the integrity of payments – and indeed money itself – rests on trust in computer code and cryptography.

As crypto visionaries and enthusiasts see it, Bitcoin and other cryptocurrencies are superior alternatives to our current payment systems and could even replace much of our financial system. There would be no more need to put our trust in intermediaries like banks. Instead, trust is achieved by recording transactions in immutable shared ledgers that are open for all to inspect and see. That's a significant claim to make, but then cryptocurrencies have come a long way.

The mechanisms behind Bitcoin are pure genius. What's more, they actually work. I am therefore compelled to try to explain what Bitcoin is. If I leave you as (or more) confused than you were before, don't worry; you

---

[2]   Shorting is a trading technique whereby investors sell stock they don't already own, hoping to buy it later at a lower price and thus make a profit.

[3]   As this book went to press, Bitcoin had surged to well over $50,000. We have here used the $30,000 rate (the rounded rate on 1 January 2021) for converting Bitcoin to US dollars.

and I will be in good company. It's not easy to understand and it's even more complicated to explain. Few crypto enthusiasts understand it entirely.

The first thing to know is that Bitcoin relies on cryptography, computers, the internet and some people called miners – most of whom hang out in colder countries where their work costs less (much of the electricity used by data centres is used for cooling computers).

Bitcoin uses public–private key encryption. These keys come in pairs: a private and a public key. The keys are essentially long numbers – really long numbers. As the name implies, a private key is kept secret and a public key is published. If I use your public key to encrypt something, you (and only you) can use the corresponding private key to unlock it. I can also use my private key to encrypt something. You might wonder what use this is, since anyone can then use my public key to unlock it and read it. However, using my private key demonstrates that it was me (and only me) who locked it. This feature is used for signing documents: by using my private key to lock the document I show that I sent it and that it has not been modified since. I use my private key to sign transactions, thus proving that I actually own the Bitcoin I am transferring.

Bitcoin, like other cryptocurrencies, takes the form of electronic tokens that can be transferred online. If you want to pay me 0.02 Bitcoin (worth about $600), I will (happily, thank you) give you my public key. This public key serves as the 'address' to which you then send the Bitcoin. You can think of it as my account number. Since I have the corresponding private key, I can then later prove to others that I do actually own the Bitcoin you just sent me. Importantly, your transfer to me does not consist of a token for each Bitcoin or fractions thereof. It consists of one token worth the exact amount you paid me, 0.02 BTC in this case.

Now let's assume that I want to spend those Bitcoin to pay someone else BTC 0.01. I can't simply transfer the token you gave me because it is worth double what I need to pay. It's for this reason that Bitcoin transactions do not transfer existing tokens. Instead, each transaction takes one or more tokens as input and *destroys* them while simultaneously *creating* new tokens as output. So to spend part of the BTC 0.02 you sent me, I will perform a transaction that *destroys* the token you sent me while *creating* two new tokens as output, each of which has to be assigned to a public address (public key) of a payee. I will send/assign the first token to the public key/address of the person I need to pay, and the second token back to myself, as change.

Figure 4 demonstrates how this transaction would appear on the public ledger/blockchain. It shows one input, for BTC 0.02 (around $600), with its public key/address (14R534V. . .). Since this input is the token you sent me earlier, this is the address that I gave you when you paid me. Because I have the corresponding private key, I can prove that I own this input token.

```
Inputs:
14R534VhdJKtGsxprPZnC6hZPK8kuMhe1e          0.02 BTC

Outputs:
1HCsAdJPfaqF8cJz231piY5CAMJBqje3GU          0.01 BTC
14R534VhdJKtGsxprPZnC6hZPK8kuMhe1e        0.0095 BTC
                            Total output:   0.0195 BTC

Fee: 0.0005 BTC
```

Figure 4. Sample of a bitcoin transaction as it is registered on the public ledger.[4]

The figure also shows two outputs, one for BTC 0.01 and one for BTC 0.0095, again with their public keys/addresses. The first is the actual payment to my payee's address, and the other is my balance, which is (again) associated with my address. The difference between the sum of the inputs and outputs is the transaction fee, in this case BTC 0.0005 ($15), which goes to the miners (more on which in a minute).

Transactions are broadcast online. Every ten minutes, all Bitcoin

---

[4]   Note: The addresses are (a hash of) 200-bit binary numbers, but rendered here in Base58, which uses all 10 digits plus 24 letters in both lower and upper case (leaving out the o, O, lower case L and upper case i to avoid confusion with 0 and 1).

transactions made during that period – wherever they've taken place – are bundled into blocks of up to 1 megabyte, which represents some 2,500 transactions. Each block contains a summary (called a 'hash') of the previous block. Changing just one digit in a block would change its hash, which in turn would change all subsequent blocks (hence the name 'blockchain'). Transactions are thus recorded on an immutable public ledger, which is open for all to see and inspect.

Before transactions are included in the chain or ledger, they are verified. This verification is carried out by miners, so-called because they are rewarded for their efforts with newly minted Bitcoin. The miners verify that the input tokens are indeed the output of earlier transactions with the same public addresses and that the submitters or 'payers' do actually own the tokens. They do so by checking that the corresponding private keys were used to sign the inputs. To prevent double spending of the same token, the miners also verify that the input tokens have not been used as inputs in other transactions.

Who does the mining? Anyone who wants to be and who has (or can access) sufficient computing power. Does that sound like a recipe for disaster? While miners could, in principle, corrupt the process by adding blocks to the ledger with transactions that assign (big) outputs to addresses they control, there are protections against this. Blocks must be approved by a majority of miners before they are added to the blockchain. To make sure this really *is* a majority – and not a million submissions by the same person – Bitcoin demands 'proof of work', which requires real computing power. A majority is secured not by 51 per cent of the miners' votes but by 51 per cent of the total computing power, which is a lot harder to achieve.[5]

---

[5]   This is perhaps the most difficult part to understand about Bitcoin. The consensus is not achieved by voting. Instead, the miners need to decide which previous block to use as a basis for their verification (since their computations include a hash of this previous block). If there are two competing chains, the one that is picked by miners representing a majority of computing power will likely be the one that first produces the required low hash and thus 'grows' the fastest. Since the miners would spot fraudulent transactions,

For this proof of work, miners solve a puzzle that requires lots of computer time. They take the latest block of 2,500 transactions, add a number of their choosing and then calculate the summary (hash) of the block. This summary is another long number. While calculating this summary takes only a fraction of a second, this hash needs to start with a certain number of 0s (currently 19).[6] The miners have to tweak the number they added to the block until the summary starts with the required number of 0s.

This is a process of trial and error, going through a very large amount of possible numbers; calculating these hashes keeps large computer centres in places like Iceland and Mongolia busy. Their computer power is defined in the number of hashes per second that their specialised hardware can perform; it currently stands at close to 100 'ExaHashes' or 10^{20} hashes per second. To put this into context, a normal PC can perform about 10^{8} H/s, so the total Bitcoin mining power is currently equivalent to 10^{12} PCs, or 100 for every person on the planet. The first miner to successfully come up with a low enough hash gets the reward, which is equal to BTC 6.25 (around $187,500) plus the transaction fees in the block.[7] This process has been described as 'the digital equivalent of a miner striking gold in the ground – while digging in a sandbox'. Believe me, it takes power.

Since there are some 2,500 transactions in a block, the mining reward of BTC 6.25 per block represents some $75 per transaction, in addition to the actual transaction fees, which are estimated to be $3–5 per transaction. Interestingly, this (significant) mining cost/reward is not borne by the payer,

---

a fraudster would need to be backed by 51 per cent of mining computer power. It takes a while to get one's head around it, but it has proved to work in practice.

[6] Formally, the hash needs to be below a certain value, which is driven by the difficulty rate, which is set every two weeks to take into account the computing power of the miners.

[7] This block reward halves every four years, most recently on 11 May 2020 – a week before the transaction in the figure took place, when it halved from BTC 12.5 to 6.25.

but by all Bitcoin holders, who see their stock of Bitcoin diluted the more it is 'mined'.

All this takes time, meaning that Bitcoin is not a convenient way to pay for peak-time tube travel or grocery shopping. Bitcoin transactions become 'final' only after they have been verified by miners, which takes about ten minutes. In addition, payees are advised to wait another sixty minutes before considering the transaction as irreversible.

According to coinmarketcap.com, an authority on all matters crypto, the total value of cryptocurrencies in circulation is around $765 billion. That's not bad considering crypto kicked off only in 2009. And while its adoption as a method of payment has been more limited than the enthusiasts hoped, cryptocurrencies have profoundly reshaped the debate about money and paying. If imitation is the sincerest form of flattery, then the Bitcoin founders should feel flattered (in addition to wealthy). Everyone from BigTech to banks to central banks is now looking to issue their own cryptocurrency.

A dizzying 5,500 cryptocurrencies are in circulation, many of which aren't even currencies in the strict sense – they are coins issued through ICOs. Much as you might buy shares in companies through IPOs, you can now invest in crypto coins that represent some form of ownership in start-ups through ICOs. These crypto coins should therefore really be considered as equity not currency. Others are *utility coins*, which can be used to pay only for specific tasks.

The top four of those 5,500 currencies represent 85 per cent of their total value, and together they demonstrate the different things one can do with a cryptocurrency. So, let's take a look at them, one by one.

Bitcoin

The original cryptocurrency, Bitcoin remains by far the biggest game in town. On 1 January 2021 its value stood at around $540 billion, representing well over two-thirds of the total value of all cryptocurrencies (see Table 4).

Table 4. Largest cryptocurrencies by market capitalisation.

Rank	Currency	Market value ($ billions)	Share of market cap (%)
1	Bitcoin	540	71
2	Ethereum (Ether)	85	11
3	Tether (THT)	21	3
4	Ripple (XRP)	10	1

Source: coinmarketcap.com, 1 January 2021.

Bitcoin allows you to pay someone digitally anytime, anywhere, more or less anonymously and without the intervention of banks or other central providers. Still, there are two important drawbacks that will have to be overcome if the technology is to go mainstream: it is expensive and it is a dream for crooks.

Bitcoin payments are not free – in fact, compared with most other forms of payment, they can cost a lot. Each transaction involves a fee for the sender and mining costs.

Ethereum/Ether

With 11 per cent of the crypto market's total value, Ethereum's Ether is the next largest cryptocurrency after Bitcoin, and the prime example of a utility coin.

Ethereum is a 'distributed computing platform' and a very different animal from Bitcoin. Its currency, Ether, is not used to pay for goods or services. Instead, it is used to buy computer time from participants. In exchange, these participants run code that you give them. The code is submitted by posting it on a public ledger (much like Bitcoin's blockchain), for all to see and inspect.

The big idea behind Ethereum is that it enables smart contracts. These are self-executing contracts through which value is automatically released if pre-agreed conditions are fulfilled: cash on delivery for the crypto world. For example, payments can be scheduled for birthdays or insurance can be paid out to farmers if rain or temperature exceed defined thresholds. The idea is that these contracts are irrevocable: a party cannot withhold payment once the conditions for payment are fulfilled. An important (potential) application is delivery versus payment for securities. If both money and securities were 'tokenised' and transferable through crypto technology, then smart contracts could ensure that the transactions take place only if both tokens are transferred.

Ransomware would seem to be an ideal application for these contracts. The crooks encrypt your files and decrypt them only if you transfer the ransom amount in Bitcoin. How do you trust the hackers to actually decrypt your files once you have transferred the money? It would seem quite feasible to put both the Bitcoin payment and the private key needed to decrypt the files in a smart contract so that they are exchanged simultaneously. As far as we know, it hasn't happened yet – but perhaps it's a business opportunity that the Ethereum coders are quietly working on.

Nor have other applications of smart contracts taken off as yet. Maybe that's because insufficient assets are available in crypto form; the communities that they could solve for are too small or too disparate to reach; or the problems smart contracts purport to solve aren't big enough or don't actually exist. The latter may well be the case for ransomware. The many hospitals hit by ransomware during the Covid-19 outbreak paid up, trusting the crooks. The crooks, perhaps sensitive to the fact that their business model rests on their reputation for responding to ransom payments, reportedly unlocked the systems.

In Ethereum the contracts are submitted as code and automatically executed or enforced. This takes the thinking behind Bitcoin even further. Bitcoin aims to replace money and much of banking: there is no need to put our trust in institutions like (central) banks when we can trust code and cryptography instead. Ethereum would apply this not only to money and banks but to all contracts and intermediaries. Contracts and data are put on shared ledgers, where their integrity can be inspected and verified by a community of users or miners. Code is thus law.

An example of this thinking – and its perils – can be seen in Ethereum's adventures with its investment fund, known as the Decentralized Autonomous Organization (DAO). The idea was to create an investment fund governed by rules encoded as a computer program. Rather than being run by an investment manager, the fund would instead invest based on automated input from token holders. The DAO was crowdfunded through a token sale in May 2016, raising $150 million. A month later, users discovered a vulnerability in the code that enabled them to siphon off a third of that – $50 million.

Under the terms of the contract, withdrawals from the fund were held for 28 days before release, so the money hadn't actually gone yet. In the following weeks an almost religious debate ensued regarding whether the principle of 'code as law' included any vulnerabilities or errors in that code: if it did, then their action was 'lawful'. The result was a schism: a tried and tested way of resolving religious disputes. In this case, it led to a 'hard fork' in the code. The purists branched off into Ethereum Classic, while the pragmatists adapted the code and recovered the funds. The recovered DAO did not live up to its expectations, however, and by the end of 2016 most major crypto exchanges had delisted its tokens from trading. Ethereum Classic still exists, but now ranks #41 on the list of cryptocurrencies, worth only 1 per cent of the value of Ethereum.

While Ethereum's coding language is specifically geared towards smart contracts, few smart contracts have been entered into thus far. But the Ethereum code seems to be quite handy for launching new crypto tokens, as many of the 5,500 cryptocurrencies (mostly ICOs) are built and executed on the Ethereum distributed computing platform.

Tether (THT)

Next up in value we have Tether, worth $20 billion. Tether's THT is the most important of several 'stablecoins', which try to address the issue of price fluctuations. Based in Hong Kong, Tether is the company that issues the currency; THT is the currency. THT maintains a one-for-one link with the US dollar. It does so by issuing THT against payment of an equivalent amount in dollars and offering to redeem THT for dollars, also at par.

According to Tether, the outstanding stock of THT is fully backed by accounts that it maintains with banks (although this claim has been disputed). Tether is certainly active: the daily trading volume in THT is around $20–30 billion, higher than any other cryptocurrency, including Bitcoin.

So, THT is liquid; that's good. Why? Well, Tether's currency is used for trading against other cryptocurrencies – it is the US dollar of the crypto world, if you will. It's been suggested that much of Tether's usage consists of avoiding currency controls on the Chinese yuan. So it's good if you are either into cryptocurrencies as assets or you face difficulties getting your yuan out of mainland China. Not so good is the fact that most of THT's trading happens 'off the chain' through book entry at several large exchanges that maintain accounts for their customers.[8] First, this comes at a cost and involves risk; second, these exchanges use trading platforms that allow 'dark trading', which means you don't get full transparency on pricing.

Ripple/XRP

Fourth on the list is XRP, the currency issued by the California-based tech company Ripple Labs. Ripple's idea is (or was) to radically improve cross-border payments. The initial thinking was that banks would use Ripple's XRP cryptocurrency for all their cross-border transactions, eliminating the need for intermediary correspondent banks, Swift, Nostro accounts and all the rest. XRP would enable transfers to happen in seconds. An American bank needing to transfer money to China would simply buy a suitable

---

[8]   The 'on the chain' transactions happen both on Ethereum, where the majority of THT are issued, and on the Omni channel, for the remaining pool of THT. The Omni channel runs on top of Bitcoin such that Omni transactions are logged on unused fields of (small) Bitcoin transactions.

amount of XRP and send it directly to its Chinese supplier's bank. A neat idea, but there are some practical hurdles.

To enable transfers in this manner, banks would have had to hold sufficient permanent liquidity in XRP, which would have exposed them to the currency's significant price fluctuations. XRP is a new and untested currency controlled by a private organisation. Alternatively, the banks could have left someone else to carry (and charge for) the price volatility, choosing to convert into XRP for each transfer. This way, they could have avoided the long-term price risk, but their overall costs would have mounted because those providing the service to banks would have charged for the price risk they were now carrying. Plus, each time funds were transferred, two costly currency conversions would have to take place. For instance, if a bank in the USA was transferring funds to a bank in Australia, the US bank would have to convert US dollars into XRP and the Australian bank convert XRP into Australian dollars.

Perhaps as a result, Ripple Labs seems to have changed approach. It recently announced that it is engaging with central banks to see how a private version of its XRP ledger could be used to issue Central Bank Digital Currencies (we will cover these CBDCs further on, in Chapter 24). This change in strategy comes as the company faces regulatory action. In December 2020 the much-feared US Securities and Exchange Commission hit Ripple Labs, its chairman and CEO with a seventy-one-page complaint for violating its rules and seeking injunctive relief, disgorgement with pre-judgment interest and civil penalties.[9]

In summary, then, our four major contenders are Bitcoin (big but volatile, with significant running costs and some very shady fans); Ether (presupposes a fluency with coding and the existence of smart contracts

---

[9]   Disgorgement is the legally mandated repayment of ill-gotten gains imposed on wrongdoers by the courts. Funds that were received through illegal or unethical business transactions are disgorged, or paid back, to those affected by the action.

that don't yet have any useful day-to-day applications); THT (stable to the dollar but unbacked by guarantees); and XRP (a currency with big boasts and a small following).

Like cash, many Bitcoin payments take place within the underground economy – although, to be fair, that's not just Bitcoin. Cryptocurrencies have become an indispensable part of an online illicit-transaction ecosystem known as the dark net. Users can access the dark net through TOR, a protocol for anonymous browsing developed by the US Navy on behalf of the US intelligence community.[10] While intended to help legitimate activists living under dubious dictatorships, TOR turned out to be just as handy for illicit activities in legitimate democracies and it's now widely used for anonymously visiting shady marketplaces that sell everything from drugs and weapons to malware, stolen credit card numbers and compromised bank accounts.

Crime is a problem for all cryptocurrencies, but a recent study estimates that half of all Bitcoin payments are used for illicit transactions. Until 2016 as many as 60–80 per cent of transactions were used for this purpose, but don't think that the subsequent decline was down to a come-to-Jesus clean-up – it was because much of the illegal activity shifted to other cryptocurrencies, notably Monero, which was better (and very specifically) designed to obfuscate and hide transaction details.

Cryptocurrencies aren't attractive to buyers and sellers of illicit goods alone: fraudsters love them too. Always quick to swoop on new technologies, fraudsters have made the cryptocurrency world their new backyard. They realised early on that cryptocurrencies are a criminal's dream currency: anonymous, hard to trace and very easy to transfer around the globe. Since making

---

[10]   TOR stands for The Onion Router, so-named because the IP packets are wrapped in several layers of encryption that are removed one by one by the routers it passes through, making traffic virtually untraceable to the computer doing the browsing. Websites accessible through the TOR protocol carry the '.onion' extension instead of .com, .org and so on.

this discovery ingenious fraudsters have been *obtaining* cryptocurrency by, for example, planting malware that uses computing power to mine Bitcoin on other people's computers. The computer owners are usually blissfully unaware, though likely perplexed by higher-than-expected electricity bills. The fraudsters meanwhile reap the rewards. As the joke goes: 'If your Smart fridge starts overheating, it's probably mining Bitcoin.' Elsewhere, there have been many cases in which fraudsters have been able to hack systems to obtain private keys and thereby take possession of someone else's crypto coins.

The biggest frauds, however, have involved crypto exchanges – markets on which you can buy and sell cryptocurrencies. These exchanges often hold both customer funds and cryptocurrencies. Mt. Gox, a crypto exchange operating in Japan from 2010 to 2014, was one such. It was hugely popular and by early 2014 hosted some 70 per cent of all Bitcoin transactions. The first signs of trouble appeared in 2013 when traders started to experience difficulty withdrawing funds from their accounts. Mt. Gox declared bankruptcy in February 2014, claiming that it had been the victim of cyber frauds, apparently dating back to 2011. It revealed that some 850,000 coins were missing, of which 750,000 belonged to customers. The price of a Bitcoin was slightly over $500 at that time, putting the damage at close to half a billion dollars.

Then there's the strange case of Gerald Cotten, founder and CEO of QuadrigaCX, Canada's largest cryptocurrency exchange. Cotten died in India in 2018, leaving a $100,000 trust fund for his two chihuahuas (Nitro and Gully, before you ask), a CAD$9.6 million estate to his wife, but no access to the cold wallets holding US$137 million worth of cryptocurrency for QuadrigaCX's 110,000 customers. Whether he actually died remains an open question: the only apparent certainty is that the money from the accounts is now gone (which, of course, shouldn't have been possible if he indeed took the private keys with him to his grave).

If you aren't yet ready to give up your current account and cards and dive into crypto payments with this somewhat motley crew, don't worry – there are some major would-be players out there, circling the porch.

23. BigTech and banks
enter the fray

If you've always believed that the world's monetary system should sit in the hands of a thirty-something billionaire who likes moving fast and breaking things, give lots of 'likes' (👍) to Facebook's foray into crypto.

In June 2019, Facebook announced plans to issue its own cryptocurrency, the Libra. Garnering front-page headlines in all the business dailies, Libra's mission statement was a bold one: 'A simple global currency and financial infrastructure that would empower billions of people, reinvent money and transform the global economy so that people everywhere can live better lives.'

Wow! All that from our compassionate comrades at Facebook.

Libra (or Diem as it changed its name to in December 2020 – though at the time of writing it continues to be widely referred to as Libra) was intended to be a stablecoin – a crypto instrument that has memorably been described as being 'neither a stable nor a coin', but which (in principle, at least) is directly pegged to the price of a specific asset, in this case several existing currencies. Being tied to a basket of major currencies would allow Libra to avoid being subject to the wild fluctuations of Bitcoin and others. The coin was to be issued by the Libra Association, a company borne out of, but of course entirely separate from, Facebook. Presumably for the avoidance of any related doubt, it was to be based in Switzerland. Transactions would be verified not by miners but by the Libra Association and its partners. These partners would build and run applications that would allow users to buy, hold and sell Libra, and use it in commercial transactions.

Libra announced an impressive list of founding partners – Visa,

Mastercard, PayPal, Uber, Spotify and, of course, Facebook itself. Its users (as well as users of its subsidiary, WhatsApp) could easily send each other money and spend it online. Facebook was to provide the technology, on which fifty engineers had already been working for several months at the time of the announcement.

Facebook's move attracted unprecedented levels of press coverage but also met with a healthy dose of criticism, scepticism and concern – particularly from central banks, which would have been seriously challenged by such a development. Why? Because Facebook's vision raises issues that go straight to the very nature of money and payments. What if people embraced the Libra and decided to use it instead of cash or bank money? What would its impact be on monetary policy, banks and the financial system? How stable would such a coin really be? Could there be a run on Libra if people lost trust and tried to redeem their holdings? Since Libra would be a whole new currency, would it effectively replace existing national currencies as the unit of account – the means by which we measure the value of things, not least our debts and taxes?

Money has three fundamental functions: it acts as a store of value, a medium of exchange and a unit of account. If a particular form of money serves as a unit of account, it means we use it to count everything else: this shirt costs €25.

The unit of account function is the most important one. You can have a store of value without the other two: real estate is generally a good store of value, but it's a terrible medium of exchange and no great unit of value. You can also have a medium of exchange that (tends to be) a good store of value but isn't a unit of account – gold, for instance. But there are hardly any examples of units of account that are not also good media of exchange and stores of value.[1]

---

[1]   One possible exception is the International Monetary Fund's unit of account: its Special Drawing Right (SDR) is a global reserve based on the world's five major currencies, but it is scarcely used outside the organisation.

Much like languages or measures, the unit of account is a convention that is deeply embedded in society. It provides a frame of reference for all economic activity. Changing it throws people off-balance. The euro was introduced virtually in 1999 and notes and coins started circulating in 2002, but as late as 2004 French house prices were still being quoted in francs. Some were even being quoted in ancient francs (worth 1/100th of a new franc), which had been phased out at the end of 1959!

In Britain, the guinea coin was replaced with the pound and the sovereign gold coin in the Great Recoinage of 1816, but for a long period afterwards the name survived as a unit of account because lawyers, doctors and other professionals continued to charge in guineas. (A guinea was worth one pound and one shilling, so apart from anything else, by continuing to charge in guineas they were able to pocket a 5 per cent premium over the pound.) Even today, over 200 years later, horses and some other livestock are still sold in guineas in the UK, with one guinea equating to £1.05. Traditionally, a seller at auction would receive only one pound per guinea, and the remaining five pennies would be taken as commission by the auctioneer. The survival of the guinea was therefore a neat way for auctioneers to factor their commission into a sale.

The unit of account is an extremely powerful tool. It allows a country to increase its competitiveness through devaluation: local costs such as salaries are counted in local currency and a devaluation effectively lowers wages and salaries without the pain of enforcing pay cuts. Messing with the unit of account can also redistribute wealth in an economy, for example through hyper-inflation, which transfers wealth from savers to borrowers: debts 'melt' away, which is good for borrowers, but so do savings, which is of course disastrous for savers. Countries with their own units of account and flexible exchange rates can implement their own monetary policies – raising and lowering interest rates, for instance. And countries tend to be quite attached to the idea of implementing their own monetary policy – look at Britain's aversion to the euro.

A global unit of account, such as Libra was originally envisaged to be, would effectively take us back to the gold standard, when authorities had very little influence on their own currencies.[2] If the Libra served as a global unit of account, countries would find themselves similarly deprived of the ability to set their own monetary policies, such as letting their domestic prices decrease relative to those elsewhere. Most economists regard this as a bad idea because of the universal strictures it would impose on disparate economies. Libertarians (and Doomsday Preppers) tend to think of the gold standard as the best thing since sliced bread, but Libra seems unlikely to suit them either: their preference for gold stems from an inherent distrust of authority – a distrust one could reasonably presume might extend to a BigTech behemoth like Facebook.

The initial euphoria surrounding Libra didn't last long: whether due to public sector pressure or common sense, none of the three blue-chip payment companies (Visa, Mastercard, PayPal) actually signed up as founding members. For a good while the project seemed to be dormant, boasting little more than a snazzy website and a cast of founding members dominated by venture capitalists and blockchainers.

Then – far from moving fast and breaking things – Libra started to rein in its ambitions (it preferred to use the term 'augmenting'). In April 2020 it announced that, instead of tying Libra to a basket of currencies, it would offer digital versions of single currencies, such as Libra dollars and Libra euros. This would certainly be easier for consumers: we wouldn't need to convert prices into and out of a new unit of account every time we bought a pair of socks. Instead, we would just rely on the familiar prices in familiar units like the dollar, euro or pound. Each of these digital currencies would be fully backed one-to-one by cash or cash equivalent. In other words, those

---

[2]   Under the gold standard a central bank could not, for example, devalue its currency (to stimulate the economy in a crisis) as it needed to maintain its value against gold – and therefore against all other currencies.

upstanding fellows at Facebook would take the money we have (protected by deposit insurance) in our banks, place it into their accounts at their bank and give us their digital money in return. Perhaps as a peace offering to wary central banks – or perhaps in a dig at them – Libra also specified that it would be happy to support their digital currencies.

Whatever your views on Facebook and Libra, wouldn't it be simpler if there were one global currency and a single organisation at the centre of the global financial system? It might feel a bit Big Brother, but there'd be no need for Foreign Exchange, Money Transfer firms, Swift, ACHs, RTGSs and many more acronyms besides – and this book would be much shorter. But a social media company at the epicentre, *really*?

Yesterday's transport and mail companies such as Western Union, American Express and Wells Fargo have successfully transformed themselves into today's payment giants, so we should never say never, but a single company with all that power? That is perhaps the bigger issue. And to help us see just how big an issue it is, the European Central Bank published a paper in May 2020 focusing on a disclosure from Libra about what it would do with all our money if we used its currency. Libra had previously announced that its tokens would be backed with investments in high-quality, short-term assets, such as government debt and bank deposits. Libra might have assumed that this proposal would be seen as prudent and favourably received by the central banks. It wasn't.

As described, Libra's portfolio would yield a much lower return than those of banks. This is because the maturity of Libra's assets would be short compared with bank assets (long-term interest rates are generally higher than short-term rates) and government securities yield lower returns than the riskier loans made by banks. Libra would, however, also offer transaction services, which come at a price.

The ECB paper raised the question of whether Libra would be better off as a bank. Of course, it would then have to comply with regulation, but doing so would allow Libra to seek out higher returns on its assets, which could cover the cost of offering the transaction and payment services it first set out to do. It might seem out of character for a European public sector organisation to fret about the private profits of an American company, but it's perfectly reasonable to ask how your payments are going to be funded. However, the ECB's real concern was a different – and arguably far greater – one.

The paper put some numbers on Libra, by comparing it to PayPal and Alipay's Yuebao mutual fund. PayPal users keep an average $70 in their accounts. Extrapolating this to Facebook's 2.4 billion users would give us a total of $170 billion Libra sitting in customers' accounts. While big, this is still small fry compared with bank deposits. But that could change if people started to use the Libra also as a store of value. The average Alipay user has around $230 in their Yuebao fund. If Facebook's 2.4 billion users did the same, it would result in over half a trillion dollars, making it one of the largest funds in the world.

The ECB then looked at an extreme scenario, again taking the Yuebao holdings as its basis. At the fund's peak in 2018, Yuebao holdings averaged at $430 per user. Correcting for purchasing power (GDP per Facebook user is about three times that of Alipay), that gives us a fund of close to $3 trillion. That would be by far the largest fund in the world – approximately the same as the sum of the world's four largest sovereign wealth funds.[3] That would give Libra huge economic clout; its investment decisions could shake financial markets the world over, bringing sovereign borrowers to their knees or affording them reprieves.

If, like the ECB, you think this sort of stuff is better left to banks, you may be reassured to hear that a bank entered stage right, just a few months before Facebook. Oddly though, that bank is led by a man who hadn't previously shown great enthusiasm for cryptocurrencies: Jamie Dimon, president of JPMorgan. Dimon had previously stated that Bitcoin was a 'terrible store

---

[3]   Norway, China, United Arab Emirates and Kuwait.

of value', that it wouldn't survive and that it was a fraud. His final Bitcoin musing concluded: 'I didn't want to be the spokesman against Bitcoin. I don't really give a shit – that's the point, OK?'

Not all cryptocurrencies are Bitcoin and not all digital currencies are crypto. So, OK, perhaps it wasn't that much of a volte-face when JPMorgan jumped into the crypto craze. The company followed a different direction from Facebook, announcing at the offset that its cryptocurrency would be a bank-backed stablecoin – pegged directly to, and backed one-to-one by, the US dollar.

Unlike Libra, JPM Coin appeared to be designed for wholesale payments rather than retail ones. It was intended to serve the institutional market, the idea being that, as a closed currency, JPMorgan clients (such as large corporates and correspondent banks) could use it to settle payments between themselves. Like deposits at the bank, the coin would be backed by JPMorgan. Unlike deposits, however, JPMorgan clients would be able to transfer JPM Coin among themselves without needing to involve the bank. Transactions would simply be registered on JPMorgan's blockchain.

Like Libra, JPMorgan's announcement met with a lot of interest. If anyone could introduce a digital currency for the institutional market, it would have to be JPMorgan. Described as a 'giant money squid', it's the world's most valuable bank and it runs one of the largest correspondent banking networks – if not *the* largest. It's a top-three player in the foreign exchange, bond, derivatives and securities markets, and a top-three global transaction bank, as well as the third-largest securities' custodian.[4] Like Facebook, JPMorgan brings significant marketing power and some impressive technological skills to the table. And like Libra, JPM Coin raises serious issues about how we make payments.

---

[4] A custodian is a financial institution that holds customers' securities for safekeeping in order to minimise the risk of their theft or loss.

Was the bank effectively proposing that its blockchain platform and coin combined could create a closed global ecosystem for wholesale payments, which it would run and dominate? Would JPMorgan want to keep it closed and use it for competitive gain? Could it? On the other hand, if it were open, would its rivals like Citibank and Bank of America want to join or would they instead want to use their own coins and chains?

Let's assume that JPM Coin is a success among its customers, who might value, for example, the ability to use it 24/7 and not be bound by bank opening hours. That might induce them to maintain liquidity in the coin rather than in deposits with other banks. There might even be marketplaces – for, say, foreign exchange or derivatives – that require participants to settle in JPM Coin, further driving adoption and liquidity. (This is a huge might – it's tremendously difficult to build liquidity in these instruments, and more so if they are tied to proprietary assets.)

If JPMorgan appeared to have any measure of success, its competitors would hardly stand idle; they too would launch their own coins, and we would have multiple coins circulating among large corporates and investors (generally, customers of multiple banks). Would these coins trade at different rates, reflecting the creditworthiness of their issuers with, say, $1 million JPM Coin being worth $1,009,546 in crypto coins issued by a less reputable bank? This is effectively what happened during America's so-called free banking era (1837–63). At that time, no US central bank existed; instead, commercial banks issued their own banknotes, which traded at different rates according to the perceived solidity of the issuer. It wasn't great the first time round, so why would a return to 'free banking', this time in digital form, be any better than where we are now?

In short, there are plenty of issues for the bank to work out, and even more for regulators to chew on. There are also the questions of whether the bank's customers would actually adopt and use its currency. Since banks increasingly transfer deposits in real time and 24/7, that's a very real question.

Big on noise but scant on detail, the JPMorgan and Facebook announce-ments leave us, for now at least, with more questions than answers about their planned forays into digital currencies. But they have presented central banks with a challenge they cannot ignore.

24. Crypto for grown-ups: central banks go digital

In his 456-day stint as governor of the Banco Nacional de Cuba, Che Guevara got a lot done. Besides shocking the local bankocracy by signing banknotes as 'Che', he nationalised the central bank, took Cuba out of the World Bank, conscripted armed militias to seize all foreign banks and imposed full currency controls. Apocryphally, Guevara was appointed to the role because Castro had asked if there were any good economists in the room. Having misheard 'good economists' as 'good communists', the physician-cum-Marxist revolutionary shot up his hand and got the job.

It is perhaps just as well that your typical central banker isn't more like Che. Caution, not speed, tends to be their MO. They like to research, investigate, ruminate, ponder, assess, understand, test, trial, postulate, publish and collaborate. Thus it was that 456 days after JPMorgan threw down its digital gauntlet, central banks around the world remained busily engaged in responding to that challenge by exploring the prospect of creating their own central bank digital currencies. To date, most of them have stuck to issuing discussion papers or running 'proofs of concept'. But some central banks – notably, the People's Bank of China (PBoC) – have gone further and started to issue real central bank digital currencies (CBDCs).

Given the power that central banks have over money, CBDCs are a potential game changer. What's the big deal? A CBDC could potentially offer the best of all worlds: all the convenience of Bitcoin – you can send it to anyone anywhere in an instant – but without the price volatility, as CBDCs would be denominated in existing units of account. As the Libra Association belatedly realised, if we are all to adopt cryptocurrencies, they will have to be denominated in national units. So, dollars in the USA, sterling in the UK and so on. A CBDC would be less risky than other cryptocurrencies as its value would be guaranteed by the central bank that issues it. You can think of it as a digital banknote: whoever holds it has the value and it can be passed on without going through the commercial banking system. And where a cash handover requires physical proximity, a CBDC note can be sent over the internet, from mobile to mobile.

Proponents see CBDCs as a solution to many problems, including the disappearance of cash. They see it as a digital alternative to physical money or a way for individuals to directly hold central bank money. For the unbanked, who may be left out in the cold as cash disappears, the theory is that CBDCs could offer access to currency without the need for bank accounts. Instead of sending money through banks or money remitters like Western Union, people could send digital dollars to recipients in other countries. (None of which solves the problem of how those without internet access or suitable devices will deal with the demise of cash, of course. We shall return to this later.)

CBDCs could also solve another persistent headache for central bankers: how to push interest rates well below zero. At the time of writing, several central banks are doing so and more would like to, nudging us all to spend our money rather than save it. But while central banks can get banks to pay negative rates on deposits, meaning they *charge* account holders interest on their balances instead of *paying* it, people have the alternative of keeping their wealth in cash, which effectively pays 0 per cent interest – not more, but also not less. CBDCs would enable central banks to charge interest on CBDC balances, which is something they can't do with cash: a targeted tool for effecting monetary policy.

If it sounds too good to be true, indeed it is, at least as many central banks see it. First, cryptocurrencies are anonymous and therefore a criminal's dream. This is exactly the business central banks are trying to leave by phasing out high-denomination banknotes. Regulators have made it clear that they would not create, or tolerate, what would amount to high-denomination cash on steroids. CBDCs would therefore need to be traceable to real people and businesses, at least by government authorities or someone acting on their behalf, as banks currently do.

Second, CBDCs could weaken commercial banks. Large depositors (who are not covered by deposit insurance) may prefer to convert their bank deposits into CBDCs, especially in times of uncertainty about the banking sector's solidity, as many depositors indeed were at the height of the last financial crisis. Doing so could suck liquidity out of commercial banks, hamper their ability to lend, cause bank runs and exacerbate a crisis.

There are also political considerations. Issuing a CBDC could lead to 'dollarisation' (whereby people start to use the US dollar alongside or instead of their local currency), particularly in countries whose citizens don't trust the national currency. This would be the digital equivalent of what has been happening with physical dollars and euros, many of which circulate in Latin America and Africa (in the case of the dollar) or Eastern Europe (in the case of the euro), as described in Chapter 4.

In Venezuela, where many citizens don't trust the government or the currency, President Maduro's government introduced a cryptocurrency in February 2018, albeit for altogether different reasons. In 2017, the USA had brought in sanctions that excluded Venezuela from the international banking system because of the government's human rights abuses and anti-democratic actions. The petro (₽) or petromoneda, which was supposed to be backed by the country's oil and mineral reserves, was intended to supplement the country's bolívar currency and serve as a useful means of circumventing US sanctions. Two years after its announcement, the system on which it supposedly ran remained down and the only evidence of a petro-anything were the chocolate 'chocopetro' and 'criptochocolate' coins sold by Cacao de Venezuela.

Venezuela aside, the challenge for central banks is that, while reluctant to dive straight in and issue CBDCs, they don't want to be left behind

– and they certainly would not want 'competing' central banks or crypto-currencies to take the lead. The USA would be mortified at the prospect of a 'yuanisation' of Latin American economies, for example. Their ongoing (and widely publicised) experiments with CBDCs can be seen in this light. Central banks are looking for ways to reduce potential risk, for example by de-anonymising tokens and limiting transaction sizes. But they may also want to have their own CBDCs ready to unleash, should a competing currency move aggressively.

These experiments might shed some light on perhaps the biggest unknown: how would people use a CBDC? Would they treat it as a curiosity and use it for limited purposes or would they embrace it as a better form of cash or bank money? That takes us to the crucial question about CBDCs: are they sufficiently better than the options we have now? Would people keep CBDCs in the electronic or mobile equivalent of a physical wallet and use them to pay and get paid? Or would they deposit any CBDCs they receive straight into their bank accounts? There are, after all, good reasons to put ordinary banknotes into bank accounts, and most of them also apply to digital banknotes.

For people to start paying with CBDCs, such currencies would have to be better and/or cheaper than existing methods of payment at helping us to overcome the three challenges we encountered in Chapter 3. They would have to: reduce risk, minimise required liquidity and provide common conventions between both parties.

Let's start with reducing risk. Cash is a bearer instrument, so when you lose it or it gets stolen, it's gone. The same applies to cryptocurrencies: whoever holds the private key, holds the money. As with your cash, you might prefer to let someone else guard your CBDCs, just as banks now guard our cash. And while the bank might go broke, most retail deposits are protected by deposit insurance.

The second challenge that a CBDC would have to overcome is providing liquidity. Normally, we store our money in banks and earn at least some interest from it, while the banks that lend that money out earn a lot more interest in the process. Our deposits furnish their liquidity, which in turn greases the wheels of our payments. Holding on to cash to pay, meanwhile, doesn't earn anyone interest.

One of the neat features of a CBDC is that, unlike cash, central banks can pay, or charge, interest on it. They could, for example, add 1/365 per cent of a per cent to the value each day, effectively paying 1 per cent per year on the balance to whomever holds it. Alternatively, they could shrink the value by that amount, for example as part of a policy to implement negative rates.

By paying interest, central banks could make keeping our money in CBDCs rather than storing it in banks an attractive proposition – we could hold individual accounts with the central bank and keep our currency there. But paying interest would put the burden on central banks to lend out the money, as banks do with our deposits. Turning central banks into banks is a much more radical proposition than it sounds: while central banks have recently been lending out money on a grand scale – by buying corporate bonds, for example – in the long run we would not want central banks in the business of deciding who gets a loan and which companies get to borrow and how much. Nor (with the likely odd exception) would central banks want to.

Another reason to put cash in the bank is to access payment services. You can use the money in your bank account to pay anyone anywhere (with varying degrees of effort, as we've seen, and excepting people without bank accounts). This is where convention comes in. A CBDC would have to establish broad acceptance and enable the information exchange that accompanies a modern payment. When you hand over your credit cards or display QR codes on your smartphone, you are showing the merchants who you are. Presumably a CBDC won't require long public addresses (as is the case for Bitcoin) but will instead work with aliases such as email addresses or mobile phone numbers.

Establishing common conventions requires systems and infrastructure: apps for exchanging the information between transacting parties; wallets for securely storing private keys, initiating transactions and accessing the ledger to check transaction records; systems and procedures to comply with financial crime regulations; customer service centres to handle queries and complaints. You'll recognise many of the activities currently provided by the 'traditional' payment sector. A CBDC may make these cheaper, but it won't be free.

And so we come full circle: a CBDC would really be very similar to cash, for everyone willing and able to use it. It would offer (almost) all the advantages advanced technology can bring – but no answers for those who can't or won't go digital. Most money might still be kept at banks (or providers that look and act like banks), which would presumably facilitate payments by book entry, much as they do now. You could hold CBDCs in your eWallet but, as with cash, there might be instances in which using digital banknotes for payments is preferable to the alternatives, for example because it is cheaper or more convenient.

We can debate the efficiency of the current system, and indeed we have described many of its frictions in the previous chapters. But we can also see that the system is not sitting still. The crucial question is therefore not whether a CBDC will offer better payments than today's bank accounts but whether it will offer better payments than tomorrow's.

And, indeed, while central banks have been toying with CBDCs, new technology has opened up channels for competitors. In Chapter 10 we saw how Alipay and Tenpay have now made paying in stores so easy and cheap for merchants that many are now giving up their card terminals. In Chapter 18 we saw how first PayPal and later Square and Stripe did the same, offering small merchants much more convenient (although not necessarily cheaper) alternatives to the traditional card acquirers. And in Chapter 17, we saw how Hawala, Western Union and newcomers such as TransferWise or Adyen offer more convenient (and somewhat cheaper) alternatives to sending money abroad through banks.

All three instances targeted key weaknesses in banks' offerings. Banks' payment products were developed to support higher-value payments in which liquidity and risk are key considerations. The new competitors came in with much more convenient alternatives for low-value payments. They took business from banks to be sure, but in all three cases they also unlocked new markets: transactions that weren't happening before because there was no convenient way to make them.

It is often pointed out that this dynamic looks just like that famously described by Clayton Christensen in *The Innovator's Dilemma*: competitors with new technology come in at the low end, work their way up and ultimately disrupt and dislodge the incumbents. The analogy isn't perfect, however: while new entrants have 'worked their way up' to larger payments, some important factors have shielded the incumbents, in this case, the banks. First, network effects and customer inertia give banks more time to react; second, risk and liquidity are much more important in larger transactions. This helps banks, partly because their offering is more geared towards these payments and partly because risk and liquidity attract regulatory scrutiny, which banks are well set up to cope with.

It might be interesting to consider how our CBDC would compete with cash at the low end, but there cash is itself being driven out by digital money – by cards, eWallets and operators like Alipay and Tenpay. And the bank-led system isn't standing still either. Perhaps it's only in response to the threat of competition from central banks, FinTechs or BigTechs but it's nonetheless improving and innovating fast. Banks and their infrastructures are increasingly available 24/7, allowing us to make instant account-to-account transfers. APIs enable service providers to tap directly into bank ledgers, making it easier and more enjoyable for us to pay, thereby providing many of the benefits that blockchain technology would bring – and, perhaps, obviating the need for it.

If all these improvements and innovations have been achieved through 'conventional' technology, do you actually need crypto technology to create your CBDC? Could you achieve the same results using conventional databases combined with those APIs described in Chapter 11?[1] Do you need a CBDC at all?

Maybe, maybe not, but the race for the future of payments is on, and no one wants to finish last. Central banks want to be in control, banks want to make profits and tech companies want to grow. What they all know is that technology is making a 'winner-takes-all' scenario a possibility – if not globally, at least in their respective backyards.

---

[1] Conventional in the sense that it does not involve shared ledgers and crypto. The technology used by Alipay and Tenpay is obviously quite advanced.

25. Open access or closed loops: how payment networks compete for customers

If you're a member of an airline loyalty programme you probably spent at least some of 2020 wondering what on earth would become of all those air miles you had accumulated. If you were concerned about the impending nationalisation or collapse of your favoured carrier, you may have investigated how else you could spend them. And if you visited that airline's online miles shop, you might have been disappointed to discover that, say, a small transistor radio could set you back as many 'miles' as a return seat from Paris to Istanbul.

Since American Airlines created the industry's first successful customer-loyalty programme in 1981, almost every carrier has followed suit. Fast forward to 2018, by which time McKinsey estimated that more than 30 trillion frequent-flier miles were sitting unspent in customers' accounts. This was sufficient for almost every airline passenger in the world to redeem miles for a free one-way flight. Air miles and points programmes work because they tie customers in. The companies buy our loyalty and very often inflate their way out of the liability by steadily increasing the number of miles needed for reward flights, or by restricting what we can do with the loyalty points. We, the passengers, have little option but to keep going.

Loyalty programmes are not too far removed from the 'truck system', which was the name given to a set of arrangements under which some form of consumption was tied to workers' employment contracts. Often employees were paid in scrip – 'money' or credit that companies issued in lieu of hard money wages – which could be spent only at the employers' own stores. Sometimes employees *could* exchange scrip for cash, but rarely at face value.

Although the truck system existed for centuries, it did not become an important social and political issue until the nineteenth century. The arrival of labour laws and improved employment standards largely outlawed these practices, with the payment of wages in scrip prohibited, for instance, in Britain under the Truck Act 1831 and in the USA under the Fair Labor Standards Act of 1938.

What scrip and air miles have in common is that they are closed 'currency' systems. Try using your OneWorld miles with SkyTeam or Star Alliance or vice versa and see where you get. The prospect of a crypto future and the increasing involvement of BigTech, be it of the American or the Chinese variety, brings the issue of lock-in and open-versus-closed systems to the forefront. And it's a big issue with payments – after all, it's the system(s) that keeps our economies going.

Where banks have historically run open 'four-corner models' (see Chapter 6), BigTech prefers closed systems. You can talk freely to your friends so long as they are also on Facebook, and Google works great if you sign in with your Google account. Alipay and Tenpay are closed payment systems: it's easy to transact with other users *within* both systems but not *across* them. It's free to pay friends, merchants, even beggars, if they use your system, but you will be charged if you want to transfer your money to a bank or to an account with the other provider. Many Chinese consumers therefore maintain accounts with both Alipay and Tenpay as well as with banks.

This is a reversal of a trend towards keeping payment infrastructures and networks open – a trend that can be traced back to the early 1970s when Swift was still an unrealised plan. Unrealised, that was, until Citibank's competitors recognised that the 800-pound gorilla of banking was planning to build its own electronic correspondent banking network. Citibank's ambition was the catalyst for the other banks to retrieve the Swift blueprint from the drawer and actually build it. When ATMs were introduced it was a similar story, with Citibank once again in a starring role. It was not until the mid-1980s that Citibank's then-CEO John Reed finally opened up the bank's large New York ATM network to the customers of other banks – and then only after he had successfully used exclusivity to expand Citibank's share of deposits in the New York market.

What drives firms to keep their systems closed rather than opening them up? The answer is far from straightforward. In fact, it is remarkably complicated and takes us back to the network effects that we explored in Chapter 9. Firms may choose to open up their networks so that they grow faster; this increases the value for their users as they can now connect with more people (social media), use their cards at more outlets and/or welcome more cardholders in their store (card networks). A good example of this is the way in which Bank of America opened up its BankAmericard in the 1960s, as described in Chapter 8.

Alternatively, firms can keep their networks closed, turning competition into a 'winner-takes-all' game. The classic case was video, where VHS triumphed and Betamax was ignominiously vanquished (for younger readers, videotapes were used to watch movies in the days before DVDs and the internet). Or, in a third variant, large operators may decide they have more to gain by keeping their networks closed in the short term, with a view to opening them up longer term. Citibank kept its New York ATM network closed to outsiders until the other banks' linked networks grew to create an open network that rivalled its own in size and density; only then did it capitulate.

Generally, operators of the largest networks have more to gain from keeping their networks closed than do operators running smaller networks. Alipay, for example, forbids its merchants outside China to sign up with Tenpay, gambling that these merchants will choose Alipay because it has more users.

On the face of it, customers are worse off with closed networks. In the early days of the ATM, the systems of all the different banks were closed.

Gradually, banks started to connect their ATM networks, and today you can insert (almost) any card into any ATM and expect to receive your cash. This is clearly a tremendous benefit to users. But the debate isn't clear cut. Competition between closed networks can foster innovation, as it did with the development of Swift: without Citibank's plans to go it alone, banks might still be sending each other telexes. Similarly, the competition between the two Chinese platforms may ensure they remain competitive on pricing and drive them to innovate faster. This may ultimately benefit consumers and merchants to a greater degree than a common open network.

Furthermore, the 'openness' or 'closedness' of a network isn't always binary. Payment networks can be semi-open – meaning that they don't make it *impossible* to move to another, just difficult. Transfers within the same bank have long occurred more or less immediately, while transfers to other banks have taken more time. Large payment recipients, like utilities, often still maintain accounts at multiple banks so they can see instantly whether customers have paid.

While the open-versus-closed debate has always been relevant, the emergence of BigTech has raised the stakes significantly. This is partly because concentration in tech is much greater than in banking. Launching – and winning – a winner-takes-all game becomes a lot more viable if you control over half the market, which is certainly the case for Alipay and arguably true of Google and Facebook. Banks have nowhere near that market share, even in their domestic markets. (So it may not be entirely coincidental that the largest US banks like JPMorgan are again contemplating closed networks now that industry concentration is so much stronger than it was when the four-corner card and ATM models were launched.)

Open networks are harder to build and maintain than closed ones because they need common standards (and consensus) in order to work. The video war between VHS and Betamax was in effect a standards war. Opening up closed systems – making them compatible with each other – often involves standardising everything from network protocols and information formats, to pricing structures and dispute resolution mechanisms. Despite the complexity, some open payment systems have been hugely successful.

Linking up ATM networks was possible because they mostly used the same standards and protocols to begin with. Correspondent banking similarly rests on a range of common standards for everything from identifiers like the BIC (ISO 9362) and country/currency codes (ISO 3166/4217), to message formats and communication protocols, not to mention the legal frameworks, rules and market practices that support the payment flows.

The triumph of cards has been achieved through rigorous standards, within each card network and across them. At the basic level, these can be as mundane as card size, the way the magnetic stripe and chip work, and how data is formatted. But unlike Alipay and Tenpay, Visa and Mastercard have also facilitated multi-homing for merchants: they don't force merchants to choose one or the other, and since their merchant protocols and message formats are very similar, it's easy for merchants to connect to both. Instead of competing for merchants, they compete for card issuers by, for example, offering higher interchange rates. This is better for the issuers and makes everything more convenient for users, but of course can (and sometimes does) result in higher prices for consumers.

Regulators understandably take great interest in access to networks. Competition authorities have the difficult task of deciding when close cooperation between firms is beneficial to customers (standard setting and network cooperation, for example) and when it isn't (price fixing). In the telecom and energy industries, among others, they have forced incumbents to open up their networks to smaller players much as they have in the UK with Open Banking and in the EU with PSD2 (see Chapter 11).

On this broad battleground it's not easy for regulators to determine where greater competition is needed and where it isn't. In a recent case that some might liken to the pot calling the kettle black, the 'Big Four' Australian banks felt that they were unfairly disadvantaged by restrictions imposed by Apple on the use of the iPhone's 'near field communication' (NFC) controller – the chip that communicates with card terminals at checkout counters. In 2017, they applied to the competition regulator for permission to negotiate collectively with Apple. The banks wanted their digital wallets to be able to use the iPhone NFC, but Apple restricts access to its own digital wallet, Apple Pay, effectively keeping its system closed. Unfortunately for the banks, the Australian Competition and Consumer Commission ruled in favour of Apple, arguing that the technology was in its infancy and that forcing access to the NFC would hamper innovation and reduce competition.

It will be very interesting to see if this argument still holds today. The answer will come from downtown Brussels where, in an otherwise unremarkable building, you will find the ferocious 'DG Comp', the European Commission's competition rottweiler. The Directorate-General for competition has long had an interest in networks, BigTech and payments – and very different views from those of both the Chinese and the Americans when it comes to competition.

The formidable Margrethe Vestager returned to serve a second term as Competition Commissioner in late 2019, with a newly expanded portfolio, now including digital services. No sooner was she back in her seat than she made clear that she had the 'robot vacuum cleaners sucking up data', Google and Facebook, squarely in her sights. In 2020, when the Covid-19 pandemic struck, she urged European countries to buy stakes in their national companies to stave off the threat of Chinese takeovers. She also found time to launch an investigation or two within her first semester – not least into Apple Pay.

Apple's app store has been a phenomenal success, with over 2 million apps available for download. One of the services that Apple offers is payment for 'in-app purchases' through Apple Pay. These might be payments for upgrades from free to premium apps, to fill 'loot boxes' in mobile gaming or to purchase additional content from publishers. Apple can offer this service because it has payment data (typically card information) from its app store customers on file.

You'd think app developers would be overjoyed. And they would be, if it weren't for the fact that Apple charges a fee of 30 per cent of the purchase price, and makes the service more or less mandatory: users can make payments directly to the app developers using their own websites, in which case no fee is payable to Apple, but Apple forbids app developers from mentioning this option in the app. It does very nicely out of doing so; the business rakes in an estimated $20 billion annually, some 7 per cent of the company's total revenue!

Things came to a head in August 2020, when Apple and Google (which uses the same approach for Android apps) removed the popular game Fortnite from their app stores because its makers were encouraging users to pay directly to avoid the 30 per cent fees. Fortnite maker, Epic Games, then sued both Apple and Google, accusing them of breaking antitrust laws.[1] Epic's case comes on top of an ongoing enormous class-action lawsuit on behalf of millions of consumers, which alleges that Apple was using its power to raise the price of its apps by charging its 30 per cent fee. The European Commission is also investigating the practice, following complaints from Spotify regarding Apple's fees.

DG Comp's investigation will take another look at the NFC nut that the Australian banks were unable to crack. But Vestager is casting her net wider and investigating two other issues related to the closed nature of Apple Pay. First, whether the integration of Apple Pay into merchant apps and websites on Apple devices distorts competition and reduces choice and innovation. Second, whether Apple Pay is restricting purchases of rival products. Watch this case because, open or closed, the Commission's findings will affect a far wider payments universe than Apple Pay.

---

[1]   In the wake of Epic's move, Apple announced in November 2020 that smaller developers making up to $1 million would have to pay only 15 per cent rather than 30 per cent from January 2021.

And Vestager has form. In January 2018, the day after she hit the US chip giant Qualcomm with a near €1 billion fine, she was flagged up by billionaire investor George Soros in his annual speech to the World Economic Forum in Davos: 'It is only a matter of time before the global dominance of the US IT monopolies is broken . . . Regulation and taxation will be their undoing and EU Competition Commissioner Vestager will be their nemesis.'

PART VII

POLITICS AND REGULATION

26. Who's running the show?
Rules and regulators

In late 2020, the Chinese government torpedoed what would have been the world's largest-ever IPO. Beijing put a halt to Ant Group's planned share offering just days before Alipay's parent was to list because of 'material matters' relating to a regulatory interview that had been held with the company's founder. Two months later, then US President Donald Trump stormed into the payments arena for altogether different reasons. He issued an executive order banning transactions with eight Chinese apps, including Alipay and Tencent's WeChat Pay, describing the companies as threats to US national security.

Payments matter, and governments care about them for a host of reasons. Sometimes that may be due to the national differences in how we pay, as we have seen. But it is also a reflection of the centrality of payments to so many parts of our lives: within any given country, different branches of government will have different – even opposing – views on payments and their providers. We like to think there are resulting showdowns as akin to the goings on in the American TV comedy *Space Force*, in which the generals of the various armed forces gather to do battle in their testosterone-fuelled command centre.[1] Payment regulation may appear to be an altogether more genteel affair, but the arena is crowded, and tensions can run high. In fact, complete with power struggles and geopolitical frictions, the regulation of payments is arguably every bit as rich in intrigue as any political thriller.

---

[1]   The Netflix series *Space Force* depicts the fictional shenanigans of the people tasked with setting up this sixth branch of the US armed forces to counter threats from space.

The tensions arise partly because payments are fundamental to the way in which the entire financial system operates, but also because different regulators come at payments from many discrete angles, as well as from distinct layers of government. Payments are one of the most highly regulated segments of the global financial system – and, paradoxically, also one of the least. This seeming contradiction can be explained by the essential nature of how we pay. Other than the fairly recent introduction of maximum limits on cash purchases, there is nothing to regulate *how* two parties choose to pay between themselves (other than each other and any limitations imposed on them by the method of payment they use).

When we pay, we are at liberty to select a mechanism that is entirely outside any regulated payment system, provided the other party accepts it; similarly, we can pay in whatever form we collectively agree on. Payment is, after all, only a convention. This dichotomy, together with the future as envisioned by the major players in the current payments war, makes the *what if* facing some of the regulators (national and international) as existential as it is for the banks themselves.

Our economies depend on payments, which is why we have regulators to oversee them. The authorities want to know that things won't blow up à la Herstatt, Northern Rock or Lehman Brothers. They want to know that systems are being run sensibly; that they can withstand peaks and troughs – both financially and technologically. They want to know that systemic risk can be contained if and when disaster strikes; that backups exist, physical and virtual, and that these can withstand attacks – whether kinetic or cybernetic.

Regulators examine how and where data is being housed, whether it can be corrupted and, if so, whether it can be restored. They consider operational, cyber and credit risk, checking that banks are investing in technology and upgrading their systems, and they look at funding to make sure that necessary investments can actually be made. They examine, review, audit and generally kick the tyres on systems, as well as the system operators and participants, and they propagate rules and guidance – sometimes at break-neck speed.

For the most part, central banks are in charge, as the institutions that have long occupied the top of the payments hierarchy. After all, the proverbial buck doesn't just stop with them, it starts there too – they must provide the vital liquidity when things go wrong, as they did so memorably in 2008 and 2020.

We said that central banks manage these considerations 'for the most part' because the above list of regulatory requisites includes how banks conduct their business, an area that is often scrutinised by other dedicated 'conduct' authorities. Bluntly put, 'conduct concerns' are about making sure banks don't screw their customers or serve the wrong ones. Here, conduct regulators tend to look at senior management and corporate behaviours, consumer rights, fairness, money laundering, financial crime and data privacy; and they pry into access modes and pricing, making sure that participation strictures are neither compromising prudential safety nor stifling competition.

But governments tend to have dedicated departments or regulators dealing with these issues and each department generally has overriding authority in its own area of expertise, which it jealously guards. So, they too issue rules that affect payment operators and get to examine and direct their behaviour.

In any given country, this regulatory interest can shake out to a bewildering number of different officials. The USA can have as many as ten regulators for any given bank; in Europe, the numbers can go even higher. Although the EU has spawned its own EU-wide regulators, the national regulators of individual member states haven't surrendered much of their authority.[2]

---

[2]   In the USA, there's the US Treasury, and its offspring the Office of Foreign Assets Control and the Financial Crimes Enforcement Network, as well as the Federal Reserve Banks and Board; then there are the Financial Stability Oversight Council, the Federal Deposit Insurance Corporation, the Office of the Comptroller of the Currency, the

Central banks might seem impregnable and unassailable, with governors who exude sovereign status as though anointed to the job, but they are not in full control of payments, and they face ongoing challenges to their primacy. They are often accused of being too cosy with banks, and not strong enough in terms of ensuring competition and consumer protection. 'Granting the Fed consumer protection authority would create a lapdog for Wall Street, not the watchdog consumers need,' as one US consumer advocate memorably put it. Some have argued that central banks have a conflict of interest when it comes to innovation, especially in respect of new players. If non-bank players are successful, they will presumably take away business or profits from banks: that might make the banks less resilient. Are central banks inclined to shield banks from competition given their prudential mandate? Or, in keeping payments ensconced at banks, are they just trying to hold on to their day jobs?

The cyber defence battleground provides a good illustration of the challenges central banks are facing. Over the past five years, authorities have become acutely aware of the vulnerability of critical infrastructures – electricity, water, healthcare and financial – to cyberattacks. Most countries have given oversight of these critical infrastructures to their ministries of home or interior affairs (or their underlying agencies). The USA, for example, responded to the events of 9/11 by creating the Department of Homeland Security (DHS), whose stated missions cover anti-terrorism, border security,

---

Consumer Financial Protection Bureau, as well as state regulators like the New York State Department of Financial Services. In the EU, banks and other payment providers have to deal with the European Central Bank and the European Banking Authority, as well as the European Commission's Directorate-General for Competition and Directorate-General for Financial Stability, Financial Services and Capital Markets Union. EU member states have their own central banks and their own domestic conduct and competition authorities to contend with (some also have dedicated payment regulators like the UK's Payment Systems Regulator), as well as their data privacy authorities, justice, cyber and, of course, national security authorities.

immigration and customs, and disaster prevention and management. It is also responsible for cyber security. In principle, all of this meant that large banks and financial market and payment infrastructures (which are all considered 'critical') would be subject to scrutiny and oversight by bodies that were fearsome, but not necessarily well versed in finance.

Central banks saw this coming and have largely successfully staked out their territory, extending their supervision of banks and payment systems to include cyber security. The Bank of England, for example, developed its so-called CBEST framework to run intelligence-led cyber-security tests. These include 'red team' exercises, in which qualified IT firms, sometimes staffed by reformed hackers, are tasked with trying to break into financial systems. The ECB later followed suit, launching a similar programme called TIBER-EU. Hoodie-wearing hackers hobnobbing with besuited central bankers may sound unlikely, but the initiative has placed cyber oversight of the financial sector firmly back in the hands of central banks and ministries of finance, and away from the clutches of domestic security departments and interior ministries.

These departments – such as the NSA and the UK's intelligence service, GCHQ[3] – do, however, remain very much involved in cyber *protection* of the financial sector. And their involvement is not necessarily limited to their own domestic institutions. A forensic examination of Bangladesh Bank's computers in the wake of the Lazarus attack (see Chapter 14) found that two other groups were also inside the bank's network. One was apparently a 'nation-state actor' engaged in stealing information in attacks that were described as stealthy but 'not known to be destructive'. In plain English, that's probably spying.

Data privacy authorities are also paying close attention, especially when it comes to cyber incidents that involve payment systems. Swift learned this the hard way in 2013, a few months after American whistle-blower Edward

---

[3]   Through its agency, the National Cyber Security Centre (NCSC).

Snowden had leaked highly classified information from the NSA about covert global surveillance programmes to a consortium of journalists.

On an otherwise quiet September afternoon, the Brazilian weekly television news magazine *Fantástico* broadcast a report about the NSA spying on the state-run oil giant, Petrobras. The news caused immediate uproar in Brazil – but reporters in Belgium picked up on an entirely different angle buried within the story. Alongside Petrobras, the French foreign ministry, Google and Swift, which is headquartered just outside Brussels, were also named as NSA targets. The Belgian media was primed for newsworthy Snowden revelations at the time, as it had emerged only a week earlier that GCHQ had been targeting the Belgian national phone company, Belgacom, under an associated eavesdropping programme called 'Operation Socialist'.

Belgium is a quiet sort of place – more Hercule Poirot than James Bond – and not used to being at the centre of transcontinental espionage upsets, so the news that another of its corporates was tied up in the Snowden affair immediately garnered national headlines. Excitement brewing in the Belgian media doesn't generally spill over to an international audience, but it does tend to reach Belgium's smaller neighbouring countries.

The Dutch duly took heed and it wasn't long before the head of the Dutch Data Protection Authority appeared on the scene, announcing on national television that his agency would launch an investigation. The Dutch body could claim jurisdiction on the issue because one of Swift's European data centres was located in the Netherlands. A long investigation concluded in the following May with a terse, and far less newsworthy, announcement that the agency had not found any security violations at Swift.

So, who *is* in charge of our payment systems? Arguably, everyone and no one. *Everyone*, because banks face the massed ranks of regulators with an interest, or purported interest, in payments: federal and state financial regulators in the USA, national- and EU-level regulators in Europe, conduct and competition authorities, data protection and privacy folk, justice, civil liberty, cyber security, domestic and national security, and more. And *no one*, because as payers and payees, we can do exactly what we want, where we want, how we want, with whatever we want when we pay each other – unless our chosen payment providers (like Stripe or Square) choose to limit what we can do, or perhaps if we want to pay large amounts in cash.

In the middle somewhere sit the non-bank providers like FinTechs, which, alongside the banks' many outsourcers and service providers, are able to operate through lighter-touch regulatory sandboxes and/or face only light-touch regulation. Finally, in regulatory never-never land we have (or *had*, until recently) Alipay and Tenpay in China, both of which, at least in their early days, escaped any significant form of regulation or oversight and yet (or *thus*) have grown to become as big or even bigger than banks when it comes to payments.

Therein lies the rub. If virtual overseas non-banks become bigger than national banks in payments, there are any number of national authorities whose roles and responsibilities could be compromised, not least central banks. But beyond our regulators' employment prospects, does it matter who owns the pipes? For the most part, perhaps not. Business is business, after all. But it matters very much if they stop working or, indeed, if the home countries of these providers come into conflict with yours. Your country's data could be scrutinised or somehow used against it; its access to cloud services impaired; its routers and software left unpatched or not upgraded; its encryption broken. In extremis, an entire country's ability to make payments could simply be taken away. It's odd that, despite all the current concerns over who is equipping our 5G mobile networks, few voices other than those of the regulators are raising similar fears about our payment technologies.

Nations do not even have to be at loggerheads for problems to arise. Compatibility can also be an issue. Perhaps the home nation of one of your country's key payment plumbers (a card network, say, or an eWallet provider) has different privacy laws from your own, different views on the limits of free speech, lower resilience standards or less cyber-security expertise.

By allowing foreign companies in to provide payment services, control over those payments is not the only thing nations stand to lose. A country may be handing over hugely valuable data pools, providing rivals with the fuel to power their own artificial intelligence ambitions, thereby jeopardising jobs as well as revenue. It may be inhibiting the ability of its own law-enforcement agencies to access potentially vital information or giving access to foreign agencies unfettered by judicial procedure. It may be offering foreigners carte blanche to hike payment prices at will.

With geopolitical tensions on the rise, the fight for multinational tax revenue intensifying and payments becoming increasingly borderless and technology-dependent, the struggle for control is already under way. Restrictions on where payment data can be stored have been raised everywhere from Brazil to Indonesia, to Europe and beyond; already there are small-print prescriptions on who can design systems, where code has to be written and by whom. So far, such measures tend to be hidden from public view in detailed documentation or debated behind closed doors. But watch this space: it could rapidly bubble up and become every bit as volatile as the 5G debate.

27. Europe gets a phone number: how EU regulators reshaped payments

Henry Kissinger is famously said to have asked, 'Who do I call if I want to speak to Europe?' This apparently apocryphal question is regularly trotted out by those pushing for greater centralisation of authority in Brussels, but those close to the man himself say that if Kissinger had a concern about Europe, it was the exact opposite: he was fed up with having to deal with a president of the European Council he regarded as incompetent and ineffectual, even though he represented the whole EU.

If Kissinger wanted to 'speak to Europe' about payments regulation he'd be spoilt for choice on who to call. In addition to the central banks of nation states within Europe, there's the European Banking Authority, the European Commission and the European Central Bank, not to mention the different national financial conduct authorities. Banks in the UK might not feel beholden to the ECB (although the ECB says otherwise, if they deal in euros), but they need not feel short-changed: they have their own purpose-built authority, the Payment Systems Regulator.

Looking at things from the perspective of the European consumer, this overabundance of overseers hasn't done a bad job. Their cards work right across Europe and mostly for free; they have real-time payment services; their bank transfers, standing orders and direct debits can be executed across the continent freely and pretty much instantly; and their foreign exchange fees have been capped and made transparent. Plus, they have a range of bricks-and-mortar banks, neobanks, eBanks and eWallets to choose from.

From the European investor's point of view, things don't look quite so rosy. As we saw in Chapter 13, the price earnings of European banks are among the lowest in the world and their revenue growth is dwarfed by their peers in China and the USA. No matter, you might say, European investors can put their money into non-bank payment providers instead. They could, though with a few notable exceptions they would be investing in Chinese or American providers.

How is it that European consumers can pay abroad as efficiently as if they were at home, and yet their providers cannot match the growth and economies of scale of their American and Asian competitors? In a sense, the answer is provided in the question: payment pricing has been pushed down in Europe but the banks have remained national. European banks are therefore squeezed on both sides: they can't charge (much) for payments due to the caps on fees and they can't lower costs because they lack scale.

For this situation, banks and consumers have regulators to thank. Back in 2001, the European banks woke up to find they had a brand-spanking-new regulator. The EU had adopted the 'virtual' euro two years earlier and the new euro banknotes were poised for release at the end of the year. But European payment systems remained stubbornly national and sending money to another euro-area country was no easier or cheaper than sending it to the other side of the world. European banks charged significant fees for ATM withdrawals and card purchases in other euro countries, a practice they had every intention of continuing after the physical currency was introduced. It was bad enough that they were going to lose the foreign exchange margins in these transactions; they were damned if they were going to give up the fees as well.

Unfortunately for the banks, those fees were a particular source of annoyance to the many expats staffing the EU bureaucracy in Brussels. A good number of these eurocrats retained their national bank accounts and were using their foreign-issued cards to shop and withdraw cash in Belgium. Many of their cards didn't work in Belgium at all, and those whose cards *did* work were charged for using them.

Just two weeks before the introduction of euro banknotes and coins in December 2001, impatient with the banks' lack of progress, the European Commission implemented EU Regulation 2560/2001 to apply to cross-border payments in euros. The name is unlikely to mean anything to you, but if you are European or live in Europe this regulation will have made a big difference to your pocket. By abolishing any difference in price between domestic and cross-border euro payments, including transfers, ATMs and card purchases, it ensured that banks had to charge the same for cross-border euro transfers as they did for domestic ones. Since many banks didn't charge for domestic transfers, they had little choice but to make cross-border euro transactions free as well. The European Commission also made it clear that more draconian measures would follow if banks did not get their act together quickly and create a true single-payments area.

The banks were caught off guard. They were used to new EU rules in the form of directives, which had first to be transposed into national law before taking effect. Directives gave companies both breathing space and room for manoeuvre. In contrast, EU Regulations take immediate effect and cannot be moulded to national requirements or interests. The banks were also used to dealing with (and influencing) domestic governments, regulators and overseers, not EU ones. To the extent that the banks had organised themselves, they had done so at a country level, sitting together on the boards of national clearing houses and other infrastructures. Their advocacy or lobbying was led by national banking associations. While there was (and is) a European Banking Federation, it is an 'association of associations' and its members are the national banking associations of the EU member states rather than the banks themselves. Confusingly, it represents only the large commercial banks; savings banks and cooperative banks each have their own similarly federal EU representations.

Banks also lacked European infrastructures. A few years earlier, in 1998, the fifty-two largest European banks had created EBA Clearing, a transfer system to clear large-value euro transactions, much like the

US CHIPS does for dollars.[1] But there was no clearing house for cross-border euro retail transfers, and products like direct debit worked only at the national level.

Amid the confusion, some forty representatives from the payments sector – including about twenty banks, the three federations and infrastructures like EBA Clearing – got together in a Brussels hotel in March 2002. Over two days, the participants hammered out an outline of what was to become the deep plumbing of the Eurozone's Single Euro Payments Area (SEPA) project. The banks appointed their own European Payments Council (EPC) and mandated it to create, among other things, a pan-European scheme for credit transfers and direct debits. The bank-owned EBA Clearing would use its existing Step2 system to clear the payments.

The European Commission took note but clearly wasn't overly impressed; it continued to assert itself by issuing further regulations and directives. In 2007, the Payment Services Directive[2] formalised the concept of a payment services provider and limited the time allowed to process transfers within the Eurozone to two days.[3] Its second iteration – PSD2, which we learnt about in Chapter 11 – followed in 2016, mandating banks to grant access to third parties, including the new FinTech players that we met in Chapter 18. Now these FinTechs could make payments and check balances on behalf of customers, in direct competition with the banks.

It wasn't just the Commission keeping the banks and their lobbyists busy. The European Central Bank was also devoting considerable energy to payments at the same time. The ECB had signposted its ambitions in the infrastructure area in 1999 when it established TARGET, the large-value central bank payment system. It did so by drawing together euro members'

---

[1]   The Clearing House Interbank Payments System (CHIPS) is the largest private-sector, US dollar-based, money transfer system in the USA.

[2]   PSD, or EU Directive 2007/64/EC.

[3]   A payment services provider is an entity that carries out regulated payment services.

– in some cases, fairly different – RTGS systems (see Chapter 16) into a single network.

Developed as part of the new European monetary policy, TARGET would also, the ECB claimed, make large-value payments throughout Europe faster and more secure. TARGET wasn't in place long before the ECB set about revamping it, citing a decentralised technical structure and lack of IT consistency. Even before the system's second iteration, TARGET2, was up and running, the ECB announced its intention to build yet another one: a securities settlement system called TARGET2 Securities.

The ECB has not been slow to point to (and take credit for) TARGET's success as an integrated European system, and has made clear that it and other regulators are not willing to simply stand by and wait for further integration in payments. As board member Gertrude Tumpel-Gugerell succinctly put it during a speech in Madrid in the summer of 2006, 'Action by authorities is warranted in the event of market failures.'

In short, while Europe's consumers are spoilt for choice, its banks are spoilt for regulators, meaning it's a less than ideal place for a business to get big in payments. There are the fee caps and other regulatory restrictions to worry about, consumer expectations regarding low fees, a host of regulators to keep happy and the idiosyncrasies of twenty-seven-odd member states to accommodate.

Of course, a few non-bank European payment giants have emerged. We've already looked at TransferWise, which has flourished by turning the foreign exchange hurdle into a business opportunity; Adyen, which has grown mostly by serving e-commerce giants abroad; and Klarna, which made it big by integrating credit in the payment process. But they are the exception, not the rule. Most payment giants hail from outside the EU.

This situation is due partly to the stubbornly national payment habits of individual EU member states, as well as the many legal, linguistic and locational challenges. It may also reflect a simple failure of imagination by the private sector. But, in large part, it comes down to the penchant of

Europe's legislators and regulators for promoting competition and choice over building up regional or national providers, and for keeping down the cost of payments. Advocates of their approach see it as in the best interests of European consumers; critics counter that their long-term interests may be better served by a stronger home-grown payment sector.

28. How payments became weaponised

The rash of regulators presiding over a surfeit of systems is not limited to Europe. The same picture is replicated around the world. Is anyone *actually* in charge, you may well ask? For once there is a succinct answer. Yes. The USA is, whether the rest of us like it or not.

We're spoilt for choice for examples, so let's go for a dramatic one that pitted the USA against its biggest ally, the EU, and resulted in the anointment of the first 'geopolitical Commission'. In May 2018, President Trump announced that the USA was withdrawing from the nuclear agreement that his predecessor, President Obama, had signed with Iran. Painstakingly negotiated in 2015 – by the USA, France, Germany, the UK, China, Russia, the EU and Iran – the Joint Comprehensive Plan of Action (JCPOA) promised Iran sanctions relief in return for limiting its nuclear development. The deal was hailed as a great diplomatic achievement, heralding the prospect of eventually normalising relations with Iran.

One of the sanctions that Iran sought relief from was the exclusion of its banks from the global payment system. The US and EU had achieved such exclusion by forbidding their financial sectors from processing almost any transactions to and from Iran, effectively barring the country from accessing the international financial system. Iran wanted assurance it would be let back in – a *sine qua non* of its signing. At the time, Obama was in the White House, the Democrats were on a seeming pre-electoral roll and the Republicans (many of whom were vocally opposed to the deal) were in some disarray. What could possibly go wrong?

As 2018 dawned, it rapidly became apparent that quite a bit could go wrong. The Trump administration began exiting the JCPOA, while the other signatories remained hell-bent on sticking to it. The European signatories remained united in their insistence on keeping the JCPOA in place. This put them on a direct collision course with the USA, which was equally intent on re-imposing all the financial sanctions that had been lifted. And it put the EU financial sector right in the middle.

The problem wasn't immediately obvious because European firms are subject to EU law. However, many of the transactions that are executed through European entities are denominated in US dollars, which means they go through the US clearing system and its banks. Defying US edicts would thus subject even European financial firms to US sanctions and ultimately exclude them from access to the US payment system, leaving them unable to serve their customers.

Diplomatic wheels whirred in overtime over the following months as the European and other powers first tried to ascertain how far Trump would go, then to plead reason and finally to moderate the impact. With Trump in power and John Bolton heading up the National Security Council, the plaintiffs knew they'd have their work cut out, but they kept their hopes up until the eleventh hour. The EU even put in place a blocking regulation to shield European organisations from US sanctions, presumably hoping that even if this didn't give its financial sector legal protection against US enforcement, it might at least give Trump and Bolton an elegant way out.[1]

Nice try, but no cigar. In November 2018, Trump's Treasury Secretary Steven Mnuchin announced the re-imposition of all the financial sanctions that Obama had waived, making it clear to the EU that the USA would not hesitate to take action against anyone conducting prohibited transactions.

---

[1] The blocking regulation sought to protect EU businesses and individuals, charities or voluntary bodies carrying out lawful activities outside the territory of the USA from the impact of the listed extraterritorial US sanctions relating to trade with Iran.

While hoping for the best, the EU had prepared for the worst. Just as the EU financial sector was pulling back from Iran, the Commission unveiled plans to build a special-purpose vehicle to handle non-US dollar transactions with Iran to avoid breaking US sanctions. Designed by diplomats, the Instrument in Support of Trade Exchanges (INSTEX) would, in theory, allow European companies to continue to do business with Iran while the EU could claim to be upholding the spirit, if not the letter, of the JCPOA.

Much to their chagrin, however, the architects of INSTEX soon discovered that the banks had no appetite to do business with Iran, even if none of it had to go through the US banking system. The best that INSTEX could therefore offer was to serve as a ledger that would work so long as: (a) the value of EU imports of Iranian goods perfectly matched the value of EU exports to Iran; (b) none of these goods violated specific US prohibitions on imports and exports; and (c) EU banks were happy to credit and debit the associated amounts flowing between EU companies. The diplomats were to be disappointed on all three fronts.

A good year after its inception, INSTEX remained unused. Dismissed by one observer as a 'dysfunctional insurance vehicle for small carpet traders', it was not until March 2020 that France, Germany and the UK confirmed the first INSTEX transaction: the export of medical goods to help combat the Covid-19 outbreak in Iran. But it was too little, too late. By that point, Iran had already announced that it too was withdrawing from the JCPOA and restarting nuclear development. Although it wasn't for want of trying, the EU had proved itself powerless in the face of US sanctions.

How is it that a single country can prevent transactions between two other countries anywhere in the world? We come back to the inescapable reality that payments are, in some important ways, a single global system. The USA's enthusiasm for flexing its financial muscle may be an extreme example of the risks inherent in this interconnectivity, but it brings us back to the serious point we touched on in Chapter 27: it *matters* who owns, controls and pays for the plumbing behind our payments.

Even so, why do banks in other countries have to comply with US sanctions when they are handling payments that don't go anywhere near the US? The answer comes down to the US dollar and its unique role in the global payments system. The dollar is so omnipotent that it can be mobilised as the ultimate embargo: preventing adversaries – individuals, companies, countries – from using the US dollar effectively excludes them from the international payments system. US sanctions can leave targets unable to conduct *any* economic activity with an international dimension.

In part, this is because most international trade is conducted in US dollars. Swift measures the share of the currencies used in the payment instructions that it processes and periodically publishes updates on their relative shares. It consistently finds that the dollar is used for almost half of all international payments. In trade finance payments, the dollar is used for an overwhelming 90 per cent of all transactions. In a way, the dollar fulfils the role of a global standard, much like the English language. It provides a common frame of reference, a lingua franca, to global business.

The dollar also dominates foreign exchange markets. It acts as a global hub for almost all travel between other currencies. There is no liquid market for directly trading, say, Indian rupees against Russian roubles. This also explains why most trading is done against the greenback. A holder of, say, British pounds looking to buy the Mexican peso will find it a very costly exercise because there aren't enough buyers and sellers in the currency pair. For each pound they might get 25 pesos, but for each 25 pesos they may find they get only 76 pence back: the difference between these buy and sell prices is the so-called 'spread'. They'll do much better if they first trade their pounds for US dollars, and then sell these US dollars for Mexican pesos; both these markets are much more 'liquid', with lower spreads. This further reinforces the position of the dollar in foreign exchange trading.

But there's more to the dominance of the US dollar than that. The dollar is the currency in which other countries keep their foreign reserves.

Countries that run a trade surplus, like Germany, Japan and China, keep most of their savings abroad in US dollars, much of it in US government debt. When governments and large corporates borrow abroad, they also tend to denominate their bonds in dollars. Why? Investors like to invest in dollar-denominated debt because the market for dollar payments is the most liquid, making it easier to buy and sell them. It's also because dollar-based government bonds will keep their value even if the issuing governments decide to devalue their currencies. The dollar is also – often counterintuitively – seen as a safe haven. When Lehman collapsed and the US housing and financial sectors were in total disarray, where did investors park their money? In US dollars.

Why do investors see US dollars as safe? In part, simply because they know that everyone else does. More importantly, perhaps, the US economy is big, strong and resilient; it still has strong institutions at home and it has hard power abroad: the USA spends as much on defence as all other countries combined. Liquidity is also key. The USA has by far the biggest and most established domestic securities market, so there are plenty of liquid assets in which to keep your surplus dollars if you don't want to leave them with banks.[2]

With the status of global reserve currency comes 'exorbitant privilege': the USA is the only country that can borrow almost limitless amounts in its own currency, which effectively shields it from devaluations and speculators. It can also print money to repay its creditors, something no other country can do at the pace and in the volumes it does.

This phenomenon is neither recent nor accidental. Two world wars and some adroit moves in their aftermath helped the US dollar to usurp the pound sterling in its role as the world's reserve currency. Nor was the USA

---

[2]   The US securities market is as big as those of all other countries put together. US securities account for close to half of the market value of all securities: $85 trillion out of $180 trillion.

slow to appreciate that reserve currency status comes laden with power. When the USA left the gold standard and devalued its currency in 1971, then US Treasury secretary John Connally famously declared at a G10 conference: 'The dollar is our currency, but it is your problem.' Connally was a straight-talking Texan who was in the car with Kennedy in Dallas and survived two bullets; as he would doubtless have noted, the problem's only grown bigger since then.

Part of the US dollar's exorbitant privilege is that any major bank, no matter from which country, needs to process dollar payments in major volumes. To do that, a bank needs access to dollar liquidity and clearing, which is available only in the New York interbank market. If a bank wants international business, it either needs a US subsidiary or branch that participates directly in the large-value dollar payment systems or a correspondent that has such access. This may explain why Citibank and JPMorgan are the world's largest correspondent banks; they enjoy the home advantage.

Whichever way you look at it, the dollar gives the USA huge leverage over the payments system, able to effectively block transactions at every level. This system has proved more effective than its inventors can ever have imagined, and, above all, it is because of the dollar's role in payments. Take a theoretical example. A German supplier sells entirely legitimate building equipment to Iran. No US or EU sanctions prevent them from selling the goods or dealing with the buyer they have in mind. So how do they get paid?

Iran still has several hundred million euro in the Europäisch-Iranische Handelsbank (EIH), a German bank that serves the (large) Iranian community in Hamburg, so the Iranian buyer could pay through EIH. Except they can't, because no German banks will now deal with EIH. The best the bank can do is to tell the supplier that the funds are there: all they have to do is collect them. The German supplier could drive to Hamburg or Frankfurt and pick up the cash from EIH or the Bundesbank, put it in a few briefcases and motor back on the Autobahn. They would then need to provide the Bundesbank (affectionately known as Buba) with evidence that the withdrawal complied with its rules on money laundering, sanctions and terrorist finance – rules that Buba put in place in August 2018, doubtless under US pressure.

Having passed this test, the German supplier would then have a briefcase or two of cash to deal with, which even in cash-loving Germany is a problem. If they want to use those euros to pay their own suppliers and employees, they would need to deposit them in their own account, but their bank will (or certainly should) ask where they come from. When the bank is told of their origin, it will refuse to bank the euros because they have come from an Iranian bank and that would mean breaking US sanctions.

The USA has thus turned its currency and, most significantly, its sway over the payments system into a powerful foreign policy tool, sometimes referred to as the 'weaponisation of finance'. Although this fits into a centuries-old tradition of weaponising trade and its tools, American history is more recent. Its much feared Office of Foreign Assets Control (OFAC) was born out of the Foreign Funds Control (FFC) unit, which was itself established in 1940 following Germany's invasion of Norway in order to prevent the Nazis from accessing the overseas holdings of the countries they occupied. Once the USA entered the war, the FFC went on to freeze enemy assets. Then, in December 1950, when China entered the Korean War and President Truman declared a national emergency, OFAC came into being. Its first act was to block all Chinese and North Korean assets subject to US jurisdiction.

It wasn't until much later, however, that the USA began to appreciate the true power of targeted financial restrictions. In 2005, the US Treasury designated Macao's Banco Delta Asia as an entity of 'primary money laundering concern' because of its extensive dealings with North Korea. This designation was unsupported by evidence and was unaccompanied by the final US Treasury rule needed to implement it. Despite this, but perhaps encouraged by 'outreach' from US Treasury and OFAC officials, Chinese and other foreign banks stopped dealing with Banco Delta Asia for fear of being next. When the USA saw how the spill-over effects were helping to prevent North Korean banks from accessing the financial system altogether, it knew it was on to something big. As described in the *International Herald Tribune* two years later: '[T]he bank's fate serves as a warning that a threat from Washington alone can wreak financial havoc.'

Perhaps encouraged by this success, OFAC further developed its capabilities, and it now has seemingly limitless powers to trace payments and finance flows and designate people or entities as a threat to US security and foreign policy. Collectively, these are termed Specially Designated Nationals (SDNs); once listed, their assets are blocked and all 'US persons' (a broad category that goes well beyond having a US passport) are generally prohibited from dealing with you. The USA also developed and fine-tuned its legal frameworks to bring 'bad' actors to justice, impose fines and insist on remediation programmes. But it transpires that this was just the start; so-called secondary sanctions have now come into the picture and are taking things to a whole new level.

Primary (or 'bog-standard', if you prefer) sanctions prohibit transactions with targets that have a direct connection to the issuing country, in this case the USA. They might, for instance, prevent Iranian oil transactions from being cleared in US dollars and/or prevent US entities from dealing with Iranian ones. Secondary sanctions make the effects of primary sanctions go further; entities – no matter where they are in the world – can be targeted with secondary sanctions purely because they have engaged with those designated under primary sanctions. As in our German example, these secondary sanctions can effectively bar any bank, anywhere, from processing payments with any other bank, anywhere, in any currency.

All this is well and good when there is general agreement on the 'bad guys'. The US efforts have helped identify and stem terrorism, track down its sponsors and more – and no countries or banks should want to be in that business. But of course there isn't always multilateral agreement on these things. And herein lies the tension; the world needs a policeman, but everyone wants it to be *their* policeman.

Adding to the geopolitical tension resulting from the status quo, is the fact that the rules around these secondary sanctions are often deliberately ambiguous, requiring costly (and often indeterminate) legal advice. This ambiguity, combined with the US Treasury's influence and the spectre of expensive and heavy-handed enforcement, coalesces into a perfect fear factor, resulting in 'overcompliance'. No case has yet been brought before the US Supreme Court and the rules and sanctions have never really been challenged. Many of the ultimate threats that have been bandied about in draft legislation and the like – such as designating the ECB, the Bank of England or the People's Bank of China as SDNs – appear somewhat unrealistic and could do with being tested, but no company has dared to yet.

One company that may yet push the envelope on all this is China's largest telecom company. The USA has long harboured deep suspicions about Chinese telecom giant Huawei, in particular the equipment it supplies to the new 5G networks that Western telecom providers are currently rolling out. The fear is that Huawei – and, by extension, the Chinese authorities – could snoop on sensitive Western data as it passes through its equipment. It would also position Huawei out in front of US providers, giving China an industrial as well as an economic edge.

The USA had made clear its feelings about Huawei for some time, but it still came as a shock when, in December 2018, Huawei's chief financial officer Meng Wanzhou – who also happens to be the daughter of Huawei founder Ren Zhengfei – was arrested in Canada on charges of bank fraud at the request of the USA. Canada was acting on an extradition request from the USA but, under the terms of the US–Canada extradition treaty, the alleged crimes behind any such requests must be illegal in both countries. Canada therefore has first to convict her of a crime before extraditing her.

The US extradition request concerned Huawei's dealings with Iran, which violated US sanctions against that country. Canada had no such sanctions in place at the time of the alleged crime. Currently under house arrest in Canada, Meng is fighting the charges, arguing that the alleged violations do not pass the double-criminality test.

How did the USA know what Huawei had or had not done with Iran? Ironically, given American concerns about Huawei's snooping, the USA had obtained information from one of the company's banks.

HSBC (Hongkong and Shanghai Banking Corporation) is a British bank, but much of its business is in Hong Kong. Like all large international banks, it must process dollar payments and maintain access to the global financial system. The USA is therefore well placed to demand data on its customers' transactions, wherever they live, which puts HSBC in the invidious position of having to bite the hand that feeds it: providing evidence against the country that gave it its name and supplies a good chunk of its profits.

Will frequent unilateral use of this mighty weapon blunt it as some, including many of Obama's former advisers on sanctions, claim? This could happen in two ways: first, the accelerated demise of the dollar as the world's only reserve currency; and second, the development of alternative means to pay for sanctioned transactions. The first seems a stretch right now. As we saw earlier, the power of the dollar rests on several pillars, none of which is likely to crumble any time soon. In addition, there are the network effects (described in Chapter 9) to contend with: much of the value of the dollar rests on the fact that everyone uses it as a global unit of account and lingua franca. Contesting this position would not be trivial.

So, what about the second option? It's certainly more possible, but alternatives would take time to develop and it's pretty much guaranteed that the USA would prepare itself against them in the interim. When the USA left the JCPOA, Iran made it clear that it would be happy to accept crypto payments as an alternative. No sooner had it done so, however, than OFAC was on the case. Now, whenever OFAC adds individuals or companies to its SDN list, it also helpfully publishes any related Bitcoin addresses it can find, warning Bitcoin exchanges and others not to deal with any funds traceable to its targets.

One could, conceivably, see the emergence of a parallel system of banks that have correspondent relationships only with each other. They could then clear payments directly between themselves without having to go through the correspondent banking system.

Any banks participating in such a parallel system, however, would still be susceptible to US secondary sanctions and not many of them (if any) would be willing to take on that risk. This is likely to remain the case for as long as the dollar holds its power. To understand why, imagine for a second that there *is* such a parallel network of banks. This group of 'pariah' banks would slosh sanctioned dollars or other currencies between themselves, using them to pay for Iranian oil and Venezuelan minerals. These funds might therefore find their way to oil importers in, say, China, who would be able to send them back to Iran, closing the loop. So far so good, but it would be only a matter of time before the USA got wind of this, given its well-developed financial intelligence capabilities, which include hundreds of analysts at OFAC and FinCEN. All the companies involved – including those Chinese oil importers – would then be at risk of secondary sanctions. You'd soon be needing a pariah corporate sector as well. And of course, if those pariah banks and corporates conducted business of any sort with their 'clean' fellow nationals, they'd soon join them on the USA's blocklist. It's no slam-dunk, which is probably why it hasn't happened.

Could it ever? If the USA goes far enough, then maybe – but who wants a world *without* a policeman? The alternative presents the inevitable challenge of working out who's in charge of (and paying for) any new system. Would China be happy to depend on a Russian system or India on a Chinese one? And where would Europe stand?

Europe has clearly stated its ambition to make the euro an equal to the dollar as a reserve and international trade currency. And, ever since the 2018 US exit from the JCPOA, it has been very clear that sovereignty over its own foreign policy, its banks, payments – and even card networks – is a clear motive for this. Just as we've seen the emergence of a new European card network, perhaps we might see a second instance or second incarnation of a vehicle like INSTEX. But even in setting out its ambitions for a stronger euro and greater 'strategic autonomy', Europe is treading carefully to avoid upsetting its NATO partner. Disappointing those hoping for a sanctions free-for-all, it has made clear it aims first and foremost for coordination and alignment on sanctions.

Until one of these options gets off the ground successfully, it seems safe to conclude that the USA will continue to call the shots in the global payments system. In the meantime, geopolitical gurus could do worse than watch the payments system as closely as people in payments have been watching geopolitics: changes in payments' power could change everything.

29. Follow the money: payment trails and the fight against financial crime

'We've been doing this backwards. We've been following the drugs to get to the bad guys. What if we chased the money?' With that change in approach, US federal agent Robert Mazur and his team exposed Pablo Escobar's drug network, an act that led to the indictment of eighty-five drug lords and corrupt bankers and the collapse of the Bank of Credit and Commerce International. One of the largest money-laundering banks in the world, with branches in seventy-eight countries, BCCI's downfall not only showcased how informative payment trails can be, but also evidenced their politically charged international nature.

Following the money has become a very big thing since Deep Throat urged Bob Woodward to do it during the Watergate probe.[1] The USA, which has historically led the way in tracking financial transactions, has developed significant capabilities for doing so. Alongside the NSA, which does the listening, it has two bureaus within the US Treasury: OFAC and FinCEN, both described in Chapter 28. These two departments employ just 500 staff but their impact is felt the world over, engendering the sort of fear that tax inspectors can only dream of.

Following the money inevitably involves tracking payments: that's how money 'moves' in the first place. More often than not it's the payments that lead authorities to uncover illicit finance, and many of the high-profile fines

---

[1]   Or at least that's what he said in the 1976 film, *All the President's Men*.

handed out by the USA to foreign banks have been for international payments sent through the US dollar clearing system.

The USA doesn't have an exclusive on following the money – authorities around the world are busy trying to watch as it winds its way through the financial plumbing. But, for the most part, they are playing catch up and some of them have a long way to go. Following the explosion of Europe's biggest money-laundering scandal in 2018, the European Banking Authority increased its financial crime staff by 500 per cent – from two to ten!

Those eight new hires have Danske Bank to thank for their day jobs. In September 2018, the Danish bank published an internal investigation into money laundering at an overseas outpost. The investigation centred on Danske's Estonian branch, a small outfit that Danske had inherited when it acquired Finnish Sampo Bank in 2007. Finding that the branch effectively functioned as a 'laundromat', the investigation concluded that it had processed over $200 billion in suspect transactions over the previous nine years. Some $3 billion in payments was for a fund owned by Azerbaijan's ruling elite, for instance, some of which went through shell companies in Cyprus, the UK and New Zealand; other payments allegedly went to European politicians and lobbyists.

Following the announcement, Danske's CEO stepped down. By late 2018, the chairs of the board and audit committees had also fallen on their swords and the bank's share price had halved as it found itself under investigation by the US Justice Department, as well as by authorities in Denmark, Estonia, France, the UK, the EU and more.

The Danske scandal was a textbook example of how *not* to handle a potential money-laundering case. Repeated warnings of malpractice, both internal and external, were ignored until the bank's hand was finally forced by a whistle-blower, which then led to a series of protracted investigations, a nosediving share price, eventual penitence, resignations, fines and a very long stint in the naughty corner.

As early as 2007, the Russian Central Bank had warned Danske that

Sampo's clients 'permanently engage in financial transactions of doubtful origin'. That warning seemingly fell on deaf ears. Even more surprisingly, alarm bells failed to ring four years later when the Estonian branch generated a staggering 11 per cent of Danske's total pre-tax profits, despite accounting for only 0.5 per cent of its assets.

Things started to get lively in 2014, when a whistle-blower at the Estonian branch filed a report stating that the branch was knowingly dealing with criminals. The bank investigated and the resulting recommendation was to stop serving foreign nationals, many of whom were living in Russia or former Soviet republics (hence the suspicions of the Russian Central Bank). Not so fast. Management and board found it 'unwise to speed up an exit strategy' because this might 'significantly impact any sales price'. Thus it was that Danske did not close the bulk of the branch's non-resident activities until 2015, and then only after Estonian financial regulators had pushed it to do so.

By 2016, the Danish regulator was involved, reporting the bank to the police for not having identified and reduced 'significant money laundering risks in its Estonian branch'. In what must have been a fit of penitence and an eye to what was likely to come down the line, the bank engaged Promontory, a top-notch American consultancy, staffed by former US regulators. It duly reported 'major deficiencies in controls and governance' at the Estonian branch. Soon after, criminal investigations were launched in Estonia and Denmark, and the other authorities piled in.

At around the same time that reports emerged estimating that Danske's total fines would come in at some $2 billion, an entirely avoidable PR disaster occurred. In early January 2020, Danske released a review on the rich returns of the last ten years, titled 'Goodbye to the golden decade: Will the next be just as good?' Judging by the public response to the report's title, it's safe to say it probably won't be.

Financial crime is big business, accounting for an estimated $5.8 trillion in 2018, or close to 7 per cent of global GDP, of which some $4.4 trillion is available for money laundering. Close to half of this is fraud of various types, some $450–650 billion is drug trafficking and another $1.6 trillion is proceeds of counterfeiting and piracy – including $216 billion in pirated movies, music and software, and $34 billion in counterfeit toys. At $350 million, currency counterfeiting seems almost small beer. And these figures don't include the estimated $2 trillion worth of bribes and corruption or the $4.3 trillion in tax evasion that goes on.

You might assume that much of the proceeds of financial crime is transferred through payment methods that are hard to track – crypto, cash or Hawala. Actually, these payments represent only a fraction of the problem. For large-value transactions, on the scale of billions, you need banks. Most illicit money flows through the financial system at some stage.

This situation puts banks in the front line of the fight against financial crime – and when they fall short, the penalties, not to mention the reputational damage, can be huge. Authorities have collected some $36 billion in fines over the past ten years. Of that, the vast majority – almost 80 per cent – has been handed out (and raked in) by the US: $21 billion for sanction violations and another $5.4 billion for money laundering. Almost all European fines, by contrast, have been for money laundering – but the lines between money laundering and sanction crimes are sometimes blurred, and invariably sanction-related violations ultimately involve some form of money laundering or misdeed.

The size of the US figure is testament not just to the strength of the dollar in payments and to America's keen exercise of the power that the dollar affords it (which we explored in Chapter 28), but also to its deft ability to follow the money and its determination to enforce sanctions and hold banks accountable.

The USA has an army of authorities to assist in this endeavour: the fines are handed out by multiple institutions, sometimes to the same bank. In August 2012, Standard Chartered, which is headquartered in the UK but conducts its main activities in Asia, the Middle East and Africa, found itself under investigation by the New York State Department of Financial Services (NYDFS) regarding violation of sanctions against Iran. It transpired that the bank was operating its dollar-clearing activities under a licence from the NYDFS, which the department was threatening to revoke at extremely short notice. Within a week, the bank settled for $340 million.

Later that year, Standard Chartered paid another $132 million to OFAC, $100 million to the Federal Reserve and $227 million to the New York District Attorney's office – all for the same dealings. In 2014, French bank BNP Paribas agreed to a settlement of $8.9 billion for violating sanctions against Sudan, Iran and Cuba. Of this, the NYDFS received $2.24 billion, $963 million went to OFAC and $448 million to New York's District Attorney.

US fines are often accompanied by 'consent orders' and 'deferred prosecution agreements' (DPAs), whereby the banks commit to extensive remedial programmes, overseen by outside monitors appointed by the authorities. This was the case for Standard Chartered. In 2014, its monitor found that the bank had violated the terms of its DPA, after which the bank paid another $300 million to NYDFS.

Many US fines have been issued to banks found to be engaged in the practice of 'payment stripping' (those involved are referred to as members of the 'strip club'). Knowing that dollar payments would be screened for sanction compliance when they went through the New York dollar-clearing system – and in an attempt to thwart efforts to 'follow the money' – these banks hid the true nature of dollar payments to and from sanctioned countries and customers. They could do so by 'stripping out' the name of the sending customer and filling the field with 'one of our customers'; instead of names, they relied on reference information, such as invoice numbers, to allow receiving customers to reconcile the payments.

No country should want its financial industry to facilitate crime, and most are now taking it more seriously – but a crime in one country isn't necessarily illegal in another. Which brings us to one of the perverse effects of the 'export' of crime (or at least criminal proceeds): money is most scrupulously inspected when it crosses borders. Perhaps this is why, when it comes to illicit finance, authorities on both sides of the Atlantic show a marked tendency to fine banks other than their own.[2] In the case of the USA, the targets have mostly been European banks (HSBC, Standard Chartered, Deutsche Bank, BNP Paribas, to name a few).

The Europeans have expressed some surprise at the apparent faultlessness of US banks and chronic culpability of EU ones, but they have the USA to thank quite a bit of the time for pointing out who has taken what from whom. European countries have also been pretty dexterous themselves when it comes to penalising other countries' banks. In 2019, for instance, the French authorities fined Swiss bank UBS \$5.2 billion, while the Belgian central bank fined the UK's HSBC \$336 million. In both cases, the banks were fined for facilitating tax evasion by the host country's citizens. Notable exceptions to such cross-border fining are the Nordic countries and the Dutch authorities, which, in 2018, handed out a fine of close to \$1 billion to the Dutch ING bank for facilitating money laundering.

While the sums are hefty, the fines aren't the most severe punishment meted out on European banks by US authorities – for that, we have to head to Latvia.

In February 2018, ABLV Bank – then Latvia's third-largest lender – was brought down by a simple press release issued by the US Treasury stating that it had evidence of extensive money laundering by the bank. This effectively denied ABLV access to dollar funding and triggered a run on the bank. Within a week, it was forced into liquidation and shut down.

---

[2] The USA has handed out billions in fines to its own large banks for conduct-related misbehaviour, notably the mis-selling of securities backed by mortgages: \$56 billion to Bank of America (which includes Merrill Lynch and Countrywide, acquired by BofA), \$27 billion to JPMorgan (which includes Bear Stearns and Washington Mutual (WaMu)) and \$12 billion to Citibank for manipulating the Libor interest rate benchmark.

How this obscure Latvian bank came to the US Treasury's attention isn't clear but it may have been linked to the bank's involvement in what would later be described as 'the heist of the century'. Twenty-eight-year-old businessman Ilan Shor had begun laying the foundations for this in 2012. He took control of three Moldovan banks, serving as chairman of the largest, using the position to extend a series of loans worth $2.9 billion to companies linked to . . . himself and his allies. The required liquidity was provided by deposits by, among others, Moldova's state Health Insurance Fund.

In late November 2014, a week before the parliamentary elections, some $750 million was transferred abroad, the majority to previously unused accounts owned by UK companies with registered addresses in Russia and Ukraine and held at banks in Latvia – including ABLV. The day after the money left, a van belonging to Klassica Force (a company that Shor also owned), was transporting twelve sacks of bank files when it was stolen and torched.

The transfers knocked a big hole in the balance sheets of the Moldovan banks, forcing the central bank to step in. All in all, the fraud is estimated to have cost the central bank around $1 billion, some 12 per cent of the country's GDP. The fraud created a huge scandal and led to no fewer than seventy-seven judiciary proceedings, resulting in the imprisonment of several central bank officials, the former prime minister and more. ABLV's role in this may have been relatively minor but according to the US Treasury's findings, it had 'institutionalised money laundering as a pillar of the bank's business practices' and was involved in large-scale illicit activity connected to North Korea, Azerbaijan, Russia and Ukraine.

Scandalous it may have been, but what happened in Moldova is not the only illicit money case in which bankers have ended up with prison sentences. In 2014 it came to light that the Spanish government-owned Bankia had issued so-called 'black cards' ('tarjetas black') to its senior executives, high-ranking politicians, government officials and labour union leaders. Arguably the most exclusive cards in history, they carried the ultimate perk of neither needing to be paid off nor ever coming into the purview of the tax authorities, and were used to pay for everything from jewellery and lingerie to furniture and holidays. Payments instruments are normally used to pay bribes, but here the payment instrument *was* the bribe. When the scandal broke, it emerged that the bank had issued these cards to some eighty-five people, who between them had spent over €15 million. The bank had administered the cards manually and hidden the spending in a general 'computer errors' account – all of which might have been helped by the fact that members of the control committee were among the cardholders. Among those sentenced was Rodrigo Rato, president of the bank, a former government minister and former managing director of the IMF.

Cleaning up dirty money requires concerted action – even with right-minded staff and proper controls, no single bank or even country can do it alone. For the last thirty years countries have been coordinating their fight against illicit finance, most notably through the Paris-based Financial Action Task Force (FATF). Founded in 1989 by the G7, the FATF focuses on fighting money laundering and terrorism finance. FATF's Recommendations and Special Recommendations are (or should be) closely followed by banks and authorities across the world.

Part policymaker, part watchdog, the FATF also maintains lists of high-risk jurisdictions. The 'call for action' list requires immediate remedial action by those listed (currently Iran and North Korea), and recommends that other countries 'apply counter-measures' when (or if) dealing with them. The 'grey list' currently features sixteen countries, each of which has 'deficiencies' they have committed to resolving.

Banks have responded to all this by ramping up their own capabilities to monitor accounts, transactions and customers. For global transaction banks – or any other bank caught in flagrante – it is now standard practice to recruit former US Treasury, OFAC or FCA officials, on top of the several thousand financial crime compliance staff they employ, the software they rent and the services they buy in.

While the former regulatory staff are wheeled out in public to say the right thing, the rest of the staff are (presumably) busy performing know your customer (KYC) checks. These include tracing the beneficial owners of legal entities, something they do by going through multiple layers of holding companies and checking them against lists of sanctioned individuals and politically exposed persons (PEP – such as family members of government officials), as well as looking for adverse media coverage on their customers. They also screen payments to make sure they comply with sanctions issued by multiple countries.

Much of this process is automated through filtering software, but such systems tend to generate large amounts of hits: most turn out to be false positives, but each one must be checked by an analyst. Most effort, though, is expended in filing suspicious-transaction reports and looking for money-laundering patterns. Some may be easy to spot, such as the small butcher who deposits $350,000 per week or receives frequent back-to-back transfers from tax havens; the much used laundering technique of over- or under-invoicing otherwise legitimate trade flows, however, is much more difficult to detect. The task is made harder by the fact that money launderers change and adapt their methods in a constant game of cat and mouse.

So, what *did* US Customs agent Robert Mazur eventually find when he decided to follow the money instead of the drugs? The Danske case may be Europe's biggest fraud but it pales in comparison to what Mazur unearthed some thirty years earlier. In 1986, he infiltrated BCCI's private client division in Florida, finding out that it was actively soliciting business from drug traffickers. Famously, he organised a fake wedding in Miami, inviting drug dealers and BCCI officials from around the world, all of whom were promptly arrested.

You couldn't make BCCI's charge card up: 'money laundering, bribery, support of terrorism, arms trafficking, the sale of nuclear technologies, the commission and facilitation of tax evasion, smuggling, illegal immigration, and the illicit purchases of banks and real estate; . . . a panoply of financial crimes limited only by the imagination of its officers and customers'. BCCI's clientele included a stellar cast of baddies – the Medellin cartel, Saddam Hussein, Manuel Noriega and Abu Nidal, to name but a few. Among the US security agencies BCCI was known as the Bank of Crooks and Criminals International. They would have been in the know; the CIA itself held accounts at BCCI to finance covert operations, while the National Security Council used the bank to channel money and arms during the Iran–Contra affair.

Amid a flurry of criminal investigations spread over three continents, expensive litigation and some $13 billion in missing funds, BCCI's downfall exposed a number of public figures, not the least of whom was Clark Clifford.[3] Advisor to four US presidents and Secretary of Defense under Lyndon Johnson, Clifford had become chairman of First American Bankshares after leaving public office. The largest bank in Washington DC, First American turned out to be illegally owned – through proxies – by BCCI. Awkwardly, if not (apparently) damningly, Clifford's law firm was retained as the bank's general counsel and handled most of BCCI's US legal work. During the investigation Clifford summed up his predicament to a reporter: 'I have a choice of either seeming venal or stupid.' He opted for the latter, but his ill health ultimately excused him from trial, leaving his fellow citizens to make up their own minds which of the two he was.

---

[3]   Deloitte, in its role as BCCI liquidator, sued the Bank of England for £1 billion but lost and had to reimburse its legal fees of £73 million.

30. No way to pay: excluded from the payment system

How is that banks keep serving the wrong customers, processing illicit payments and paying staggering amounts in fines? Are they staffed by the immoral or the incompetent, or do banks simply face mission impossible? There will always be some bad eggs, but for the most part, it's the latter: few banks want to be in bad business. Most, if not all, have significantly stepped up their efforts to crack down on illegal activity. But criminals will always find new ways to hide their money. And right now they are helped by globalisation and new technology, which make it easier to manage bank accounts remotely, and to hide behind legal entities in friendly jurisdictions.

Meanwhile, efforts to increase regulatory scrutiny of banks and to enforce substantial punishment have had an unintended but significant consequence: the exclusion of certain groups from the banking system.

Authorities in both the USA and Europe recognise the problem and have been trying to fix it. The US Treasury permits banks to accept foreign identity documents at their discretion, allowing them, for example, to recognise the 'matricula' issued to Mexican immigrants by Mexican consulates in the USA.[1] But potential bank customers must also *want* to be bank customers: a lack of trust among immigrants from countries with less robust banks and currencies means that many remain wary.

The EU has been pushing for increased access to payments through its Payment Accounts Directive, which stipulates that consumers should be guaranteed access to a range of basic payment services. Among other things,

---

[1]   The US Treasury's application of Section 326 of the Patriot Act.

the directive mandates banks to offer basic payment accounts to all EU residents, asylum seekers and others who may not have residency permits. Banks can refuse customers only if they fail to provide information required under anti-money-laundering and anti-terrorism financing rules or if opening an account for them would pose a threat to national security and public order.

Clearly visible here is the tension between financial inclusion and strictly enforced regulations that are aimed at *excluding* criminals. When the EU directive was discussed in the Dutch parliament, several representatives pointed out that it had become impossible for certain groups, such as sex workers, to get bank accounts. Could the parliament be assured that banks would now provide them with accounts or was there a danger that banks would instead claim that people in these groups could be considered a national security or public order issue?

The wider issue came to a head in 2018 when large numbers of Syrian refugees arrived in the Netherlands, mostly with little or no documentation. Syria was under strict sanctions and the banks were reluctant to offer Syrian refugees accounts in case any of them had links to ISIS. The Dutch government nevertheless made it clear to the banks that they needed to provide the refugees with accounts and should suspend strict KYC procedures if these were slowing things down too much.

A similar tension exists at the political level. Banks are required to apply additional screening measures to politically exposed persons and monitor them closely. But risk profiles can change overnight and today's liberators all too often seem to become tomorrow's oppressors. Similarly, banking diplomats can prove a risky endeavour.

In 2010, the Angolan embassy in Washington DC suddenly found itself without banking access when all its accounts with US banks were shut down. Angola was rated among the fifteen most corrupt countries in the world and, given the inherent ties between an embassy and its home regime, banks found banking the embassy almost impossible to square. But the Angolan mission to the USA wasn't alone; over thirty-five other embassies faced a similar threat. The press got hold of a letter in which JPMorgan informed diplomatic missions it would close the division that served them. For the bank, the business was not worth the risk.

Without access to payments, the embassies immediately appealed to the US Department of State and then US Secretary of State, Hillary Clinton. Oh, to have been on the line during the flurry of calls that followed! US financial regulators duly clarified that they expected banks to provide embassies with continued access to the payment system and stated that, 'financial institutions have the flexibility to provide services to foreign missions while also remaining in compliance'.

Excluding customers because of the compliance risk and burden they present (as opposed to any evident misdeeds) is referred to as 'de-risking'. Like the ill-fated embassies in Washington, banks in several countries have found themselves de-risked by their correspondent banks. In part this is because banks' compliance responsibilities have been extended to 'know[ing] your customer's customer'. In practice this means that correspondents now need to ensure not only that the banks they service are kosher, but that the customers these banks serve are *also* kosher.

Always quick to look at the risk–reward ratio, correspondent banks will now often write off entire geographies because doing business with them is not worth the risk. The problem this presents is that some countries' access to the global payment system has been compromised.

Research by the Bank for International Settlements, for example, concluded that the number of correspondent relationships fell by 20 per cent between 2011 and 2018. The Financial Stability Board (FSB) similarly keeps track of the development of correspondent relationships and publishes an annual report on the topic. It too has found that 'access to correspondent banking relationships remains a critical issue in some regions and jurisdictions'.

While there are many factors involved, the research found that banks withdrew more from countries with high rates of corruption than from countries with lower corruption rates. At the very least, this indicates some de-risking. As the researchers point out, the retreat of correspondent banks might hinder efforts to improve access to banking for all, raise the cost of cross-border payments or drive them underground – at a time when technology promises to do quite the reverse.

While several measures have already been taken – such as issuing regulatory clarifications, building domestic capabilities in the affected countries and introducing measures to reduce compliance costs – the FSB has made clear that it reserves the right to take further action should the situation deteriorate further. Quite what actions those will be is unclear: there are limits to what FSB members (largely central banks) can do to deflect edicts imposed by their fellow national authorities – law enforcement, national security agencies and the rest.

All the while, banks are caught between a rock of strictly enforced financial crime regulation on one hand and the hard place of political pressure not to exclude customers on the other. Regulation on one side of the world can jar with political sympathies on the other. It's a tricky balance, especially with avaricious shareholders to keep sweet. The problem is clearly a serious one, but sometimes the art of turning customers away simply requires a certain panache, as a senior banker once explained. During his time working as a branch manager in The Hague, the girlfriend of the city's most notorious mobster walked into his bank to open an account. The banker clearly knew his customer and wanting neither her business nor the wrath of the mob for refusing it, he improvised: 'We can't open any new accounts because the computer is full.' It did the trick.

Epilogue: What's next?

'So what's the endgame in payments?'

It's a straightforward enough question, you might think, and the BigTech executive who asked it during a virtual conference of payment professionals in 2020 was no doubt looking for a straightforward answer. Unfortunately there isn't one. Given how fast things are changing and what's at stake, wanting to know what will happen in the future is understandable. But in payments even the short term is difficult to predict.

Many of the key developments over the past ten years seemingly 'came out of nowhere'. Who could have predicted that thanks to two super apps, China would be processing the majority of the world's electronic payments? Who would have guessed that mobile phones would transform the developing world's access to payment services or introduce a third of the global population into financial services? That central banks would seriously consider a world without cash, and experiment with cryptocurrencies? Or that payment providers such as Visa, Mastercard, PayPal, Square and Adyen – some of which did not even exist ten years ago – would now be worth more than most banks?

Only a decade ago BigTech was at best MediumTech. Amazon was worth less than $100 billion and Facebook was valued at about $25 billion, both of them far less than the world's biggest banks. Today Facebook is worth close to $800 billion, while Amazon has surpassed $1.5 trillion. In other words, Facebook is worth a little less and Amazon just a bit more than the sum of the six largest banks in the entire world.

Much of the technology now driving changes in payments is little more than a decade old. The iPhone was introduced only in 2007, while the first

Android smartphone didn't make its debut until 2008. Cryptocurrencies came on the scene with the arrival of Bitcoin in 2009, a year in which cloud computing was but a small cloud on the horizon (Amazon launched its 'Elastic Compute Cloud' in 2006), and only programmers knew what APIs were.

Cybercrime similarly went from fringe to mainstream in an even shorter timeframe. In 2013 criminals were dealing in small change when they stole data on credit cards; the next year they began using a single piece of malware through which, in a string of attacks across multiple countries, they minted over $1 billion; and by 2016 they were ready to try stealing the same amount in a single hit, with an attack on Bangladesh Bank.

At around the same time that the cyber criminals were getting their teeth into e-payments, the USA was beginning to crack down on money laundering and sanctions evasion like never before, raising fines from the mundane to the seemingly stratospheric. In 2012 alone, two British banks, HSBC and Standard Chartered, agreed to pay almost $2.6 billion in fines as part of record settlements with US authorities over such allegations.

The full implications of many of these developments have yet to play out and yet the pace of technological innovation means more change is certain to come – much of it doubtless unforeseen.

Some change we will resist. The disappearance of cash is a case in point. Cash use is falling on average across the world but even in the most advanced of economies, consumers aren't ready to say goodbye to it just yet.

Other changes will be unavoidable. Countries such as the UK that have stubbornly resisted national identity schemes will see the rapid adoption of digital IDs – either that, or they'll be left far behind. The geopolitics of payments will get uglier. As payments get swept up in the ongoing fourth industrial revolution – 5G, the Internet of Things, big data, AI and crypto – they'll become part of the technology arms race between the world's superpowers. Payments data and technology will be weaponised in much the same way as finance has been; as we write this, the USA is threatening to remove the WeChat app and its payment facility Tenpay from the Apple and Android app stores. But it won't just be the Americans and the limits won't just be on private enterprise.

Central banks around the world are already worried about China's CBDC. Already available to millions of consumers in Shenzhen, some fear it might be used to 'Yuan-ise' other countries. And it won't just be the dollar versus the yuan and the euro: it will be Apple and Facebook versus Alibaba and Tencent; Motorola and Qualcomm versus Huawei; and the EU versus all of them, as it tries to get a foot in the door. Take all this to its extreme, and you won't be able to pay or get paid in China with an American phone or vice versa. In such a scenario, we'd be changing phones at airports instead of currencies.

Despite the already testy geopolitics, BigTech firms are currently riding high, at least in part because of their ambitions in payments. The likes of Amazon and Google have the skills and scale to fundamentally reshape the landscape in a way that banks can't. But the assumption that the BigTech forays and FinTech payment valuations rest on is that there *is* an endgame: that they *can* provide solutions at scale, across multiple countries/regions and at profitable margins.

Three actions taken by regulators on three different continents give us an indication of just how tough realising that assumption will be. In July 2020, the European Commission and European Central Bank heralded the arrival of the European Payments Initiative. A pan-European payment system and interbank network, EPI is intended both to rival Mastercard and Visa and to eventually replace national European payment schemes. Just four months later, the Indian payments regulator imposed a cap of 30 per cent on the total share of UPI transactions that any third-party provider (think Google or Amazon) could process and launched an antitrust investigation into Google and Google Pay. And within days of that, the Chinese authorities blocked the planned public listing of Alipay's parent Ant Group – stopping what would have been the largest public offering to date. A month later they then went further and launched an antitrust investigation into Ant's parent,

Alibaba. We can quibble over whether the Indians and Europeans were rooting for domestic champions or whether the Chinese were upset by Jack Ma's rhetoric and Ant's forays into consumer lending – but the three regulators' actions demonstrate that however keen they are on having efficient tech-driven payment systems, they plan to keep them in check.

The winner-takes-all dynamic that the tech revolution is bringing to payments is upping the ante for everyone, particularly with the declining use of cash. True, the payments landscape is stubbornly local, which restricts the potential of global platforms – but network effects and scale economies can still play out in domestic or regional markets. That's a problem for the regulators as we've seen, but it's also a problem for banks.

You may have noticed that while this book claims to be about payments, much of it is about banks – there is no escaping them! You may also have inferred that we hold a somewhat unfashionable viewpoint on the banking sector's role in payments. This book is not intended to be a defence of banks. But we do believe banks have an important, irreplaceable role in payments. Not necessarily the banks we know and love to hate, but banks nonetheless.

Moving money involves risk and requires liquidity: for all the alchemy technology brings to the table, these two elements can't be magicked away. Liquidity and risk will continue to shape payments, especially higher-value ones. Big money movements (including those arising from the accumulation of smaller payments) require sizeable liquidity and entail significant risk. Given the sheer scale of the sums involved, it is difficult to envisage countries or central banks tolerating anyone handling the business without the benefit of a bank balance sheet and a good dollop of regulation behind them.

Banks will thus likely keep the accounts and deposits that fuel payments, but their role in providing the actual payment services – and the revenues these generate – is clearly under threat. Non-bank providers are doing what banks did (or could or should have done) better. The very real prospect of payments being separated out from current accounts could relegate banks to the status of glorified utilities: they would end up running the basic infrastructures and checking compliance with money-laundering regulations, while non-banks take the customer interface and many of the commercial opportunities that come with it.

That scenario would deprive the banks of much of the money to be made from payments and thus their ability to invest in the infrastructures that make payments possible. And in that context it is not impossible that domestic regulators could begin championing domestic banking giants, something that was until recently unthinkable from a competition stand-point. Central banks meanwhile may well follow China's lead in rolling out their own CBDCs.

How we pay ten years from now will be forged in the collision between these opposing forces, where innovation meets prudential regulation and where technology crashes into legacy infrastructure; where the data opportunity bumps into privacy rights and where private profits plough into consumer interests, national interests and geopolitics.

Tools and technologies that we are already using in other parts of our lives could be brought into payments – and altogether new ones may emerge. Perhaps we shall see new paradoxes added to the ones mentioned in the introduction to this book: payments becoming ever more imperceptible – perhaps totally invisible – yet ever more relevant. We may only ever notice payments when things go wrong.

Behind the scenes, government and private enterprise will be jostling for our data and fees, as well as for certain people, activities or countries to be included or excluded from payments. As the act of paying becomes less explicit and more abstracted, the philosophical divides and geopolitical battles will become increasingly evident and more heated. Different parts of the payments' technology stack will become disputed territory; today it's chips and communications devices, phones, networks and currencies. Tomorrow, who knows?

Experiencing the next evolution in payments is guaranteed to be an exciting ride. It's a journey for which we can best equip ourselves (and for which we hope this book has equipped you) by understanding what's at stake and by preparing to 'expect the unexpected'. The only certainty, as the adage goes, is death and taxes – and with those, payments. But, far from having an endgame, payments are a story without end – except, perhaps, in heaven where, supposedly, you can count your blessings but not spend them.

Acknowledgements

First and foremost we must thank our families who put up with the long hours, endless travel and (apparently) 'boring' conversations, not to mention all that went into the gestation and birth of this book. A particular thanks to Chris Owen who made considerable time (if not great speed) in (in his words) 'improving' the text.

With an accumulated six decades in and around the world of money, there are more people we owe a debt of gratitude to than it would be decent to list – we know who you are, and we thank you. Thanks must also go to those who read versions of the book and provided valuable comments: Alec Nacamuli, Gerard Hartsink, Douwe Lycklema, Chiel Liezenberg, Jack Stephenson, Olivier Denecker, Ron Berndsen, Paul Taylor, Joanna Bamford, Dominic Hobson and Mitchell Feuer.

This book wouldn't have happened without the vision of Elliott & Thompson. In particular Lorne Forsyth, who must have seen something in the (now unrecognisable) manuscript he first received, and Olivia Bays who ran with it and patiently brought it into its current form. Thank you both, and all the team at E&T.

Finally, since what you write about is inevitably informed by what you read, we must acknowledge what we've been reading. The interested reader will find a list of texts on subjects that we touch on in the book (and a few other adjacent topics) that we have read, enjoyed and been informed by. See www.thepayoffthebook.com for this and more.

Sources

Chapter 1

For more on Penywaun and access to cash in south Wales, see University of Bristol report: 'Identifying Vulnerable Communities in a Case Study of South Wales', January 2020, https://cpb-eu-w2.wpmucdn.com/blogs.bristol.ac.uk/dist/3/599/files/2020/01/2020-01-Geographies-of-Access-to-Cash.pdf

For the story on van Halls, see: https://toritto.wordpress.com/2018/10/10/banker-to-the-resistance-walraven-van-hall/ and the 2018 film, *The Resistance Banker* [*Bankier van het Verzet*] (www.imdb.com/title/tt4610378/).

Twain, M. (1893). *The Million Pound Bank Note*. Berlin: Langenscheidt ELT.

For more on the Irish banking strike, see: Krüger, M. (2017). 'Money and Credit: Lessons of the Irish bank strike of 1970'. ROME Discussion Paper Series ISSN 1865-7052, No. 2017-13, June.

Kyotaki, N. and Moore, J. H. (2002). 'Evil is the root of all money', *American Economic Review*, 92(2), 62–6.

Chapter 2

For the story on the London bus ticket, see: www.ft.com/content/e8a177d4-dfae-11e9-9743-db5a370481bc

'It's time to talk about money', speech delivered by Sir Jon Cunliffe, Deputy Governor Financial Stability, Member of the Monetary Policy Committee, Member of the Financial Policy Committee and Member of the Prudential Regulation Committee, at the London School of Economics, 28 February 2020; see: www.bankofengland.co.uk/speech/2020/jon-cunliffe-speech-followed-by-panellist-at-chinas-trade-and-financial-globalisation-conference

Chapter 3

The valuation of Stripe is based on a November 2020 financing round through which the company was seeking investors at a valuation of $70–100 billion. Since the round had not yet concluded at the time of writing we took the lower end of the range.

Chapter 4

Figures from Report by the Comptroller and Auditor General, National Audit Office (2020). 'The production and distribution of cash', HM Treasury, Bank of England, The Royal Mint, the Financial Conduct Authority and the Payment Systems Regulator, September 2020.

For more on the Swiss CHF1,000 banknote, see https://www.swissinfo.ch/eng/nota-bene_thousand-franc-note-is-a-hidden-treasure/36439396

On the cash shipments to Iraq, see: 'New York Fed's $40 billion Iraqi money trail', *CNBC*, 25 October 2011 (www.cnbc.com/id/45031100).

On the foreign use of euro notes, see: N. Bartzsch, G. Rösl and F. Seitz (2011). 'Foreign demand for euro banknotes issued in Germany: Estimation using (in)direct approaches', Deutsche Bundesbank, Discussion Paper Series 1, Nos 20 & 21; 'Why is the €500 banknote about to disappear?' Interview with Dr Johannes Beermann, Member of the Executive Board of the Deutsche Bundesbank, published in *Frankfurter Allgemeine Sonntagszeitung*.

Figures on global financial crime, lower estimate, taken from US Treasury (2018): https://home.treasury.gov/system/files/136/2018NMLRA_12-18.pdf; upper estimate taken from RAND Corporation's annual survey: www.rand.org/news/press/2019/08/20.html

For cocaine on bank notes, see: www.theguardian.com/world/2009/aug/17/cocaine-dollar-bills-currency-us

For large denomination bank notes and their use in the underground economy, see: K.S. Rogoff (2016). *The Curse of Cash*. Princeton, NJ: Princeton University Press.

Figures on gold taken from the World Gold Council (www.gold.org)

Chapter 5

For the 'war on cash', see: 'Why elites are winning the war on cash', *UK Uncensored*, October 2019 (https://ukuncensored.com/why-elites-are-winning-the-war-on-cash/); https://dailyreckoning.com/elites-winning-war-cash/

Willem Buiter's quote is taken from: W. Buiter and E. Rahbari (2015). 'High time to get low: Getting rid of the lower bound on nominal interest rates', *Citi Research Economics*, *Global Economics View*, 9 April.

Figures in cash from Albania taken from: World Bank Group and Bank of Albania (2018). 'The retail payment costs and savings in Albania' (www.bankof albania.org/rc/doc/WB_RetailPmt_Albania_WEB_Final_12074.pdf); INSTAT-Institute of Statistics provided in Independent Balkan News Agency (2015). Salaries in Albania, drastic gap between the minimum and maximum pay (https://balkaneu.com/salaries-albania-drastic-gap-minimum-maximum-pay/)

Data on cash usage in various countries from McKinsey: 'Attacking the cost of cash' (2018). www.mckinsey.com/industries/financial-services/our-insights/attacking-the-cost-of-cash

For more on access to cash in Bristol, see: 'Mapping the availability of cash – a case study of Bristol's financial infrastructure', University of Bristol, http://www.bris.ac.uk/geography/research/pfrc/themes/finexc/availability-of-cash/

Figures on cost of cash taken from: 'Access to Cash Review', final report (2019). www.accesstocash.org.uk/media/1087/final-report-final-web.pdf

For the quotes on printing money, see: www.nytimes.com/2020/03/23/upshot/coronavirus-fed-extraordinary-response.html; https://twitter.com/AsILayHodling/status/1241008225924845568; www.reuters.com/article/us-health-coronavirus-ecb-qe/ecb-primes-money-printing-gun-to-combat-coronavirus-idUSKBN21D0J4

For the story on Sweden's cash decline and resistance, see www.spink.com/media/view?id=338; Kontant Upproret, 'The cash uprising – the voice of cash in society' (www.kontantupproret.se)

Björn Eriksson was quoted in D. Crouch (2018). 'Being cash-free puts us at risk of attack: Swedes turn against risk of cashlessness', *Guardian*, 3 April (www.theguardian.com/world/2018/apr/03/being-cash-free-puts-us-at-risk-of-attack-swedes-turn-against-cashlessness)

For the UK Chancellor's 2020 announcement on access to cash, see: www.gov.uk/government/publications/budget-2020-documents/budget-2020

For Puerto Rico during Hurricane Maria and the Fed's response, see: www.nytimes.com/2017/09/29/us/puerto-rico-shortages-cash.html; www.americanbanker.com/news/feds-emergency-cash-plan-swings-into-action-in-puerto-rico

Chapter 7

For the story on BankAmericard and Joe Williams, see: Joe Nocera (1994). 'The day the credit card was born', *Washington Post*, 4 November (https://www.washingtonpost.com/archive/lifestyle/magazine/1994/11/04/the-day-the-credit-card-was-born/d42da27b-0437-4a67-b753-bf9b440ad6dc/)

For the story on the Parrys and the invention of the magnetic stripe, see: www.ibm.com/ibm/history/ibm100/us/en/icons/magnetic/

Figures on global spending on pre-paid cards are taken from: www.mercatoradvisorygroup.com/Reports/U_S__-Canada_-and-U_K_-Prepaid-Markets--Similarities-and-Differences/

Chapter 8

For the Durbin Amendment, see: https://fas.org/sgp/crs/misc/R41913.pdf

For SEPA and its impact, see: https://ec.europa.eu/info/business-economy-euro/banking-and-finance/consumer-finance-and-payments/payment-services/single-euro-payments-area-sepa_en

Chapter 9
For the story on Citibank and the $900 million error, see: https://dockets.justia
.com/docket/new-york/nysdce/1:2020cv06539/542310; for Deutsche Bank's
$35 billion error, see: https://money.cnn.com/2018/04/19/investing/deutsche-
bank-35-billion-mistake/index.html; and for Oliver North's mix-up, see:
www.nytimes.com/1987/05/13/world/north-s-10-million-mistake-sultan-s-
gift-lost-in-a-mixup.html

For the story on the mix-up of Barclays' sort codes, see: www.theguardian.com
/money/2019/dec/07/i-lost-my-193000-inheritance-with-one-wrong-digit-on-
my-sort-code

For the UK introduction of confirmation of payee, see: www.which.co.uk/
news/2020/03/confirmation-of-payee-which-banks-are-ready-to-offer-vital-
name-checking-service/

For an overview of network effects and their impact, see: O. Shy (2001).
The Economics of Network Industries. Cambridge: Cambridge University Press.

Chapter 10
Estimate for card transactions based on the twenty-five CPMI (Committee
on Payments and Market Infrastructures, part of the Bank for International
Settlements (BIS)) countries, which have a population of around 4.5 billion
(2019).

The figures on global transactions per person are based on the 25 CPMI
countries, which have some 4.5 billion inhabitants. The Committee on Payments
and Market Infrastructures (CPMI) is the part of the Bank for International
Settlements (BIS) that establishes and promotes global regulatory/oversight
standards for payment, clearing, settlement and other market infrastructures, and
monitors and analyses developments in these areas. The 25 CPMI members are
Argentina, Australia, Belgium, Brazil, Canada, China, France, Germany, Hong
Kong, India, Indonesia, Italy, Japan, Korea, Mexico, the Netherlands, Russia,
Saudi Arabia, Singapore, South Africa, Spain, Sweden, Switzerland, Turkey,
United Kingdom, United States. (The BIS provides separate data for China
and Hong Kong, but they are counted as a single country.)

Data on Alipay and Tenpay are for 2019 and taken from the PBoC. An English-language version of the report can be downloaded from: www.pbc. gov.cn/en/3688241/3688663/3688681/3861364/3993121/index.html. The report mentions 720 billion online payment transactions by non-bank agencies (mostly Alipay and Tenpay) but that includes transfers from banks to the wallets so there may be double counting. The report also mentions 378 billion transactions for the Nets Union platform, through which the two super apps have to route all 'QR code' payments. The true number of super-app transactions therefore lies in between 378 and 720 billion. We have taken the conservative approach and used the lower figure.

Data in Figure 3 are for 25 CPMI countries and taken from BIS, except the Chinese data, which are taken from the PBoC. The data for the Eurozone represent the total for the six Eurozone countries in the CPMI 25.

Transaction fees for the Chinese super apps are taken from: www.chinadaily. com.cn/bizchina/2016-09/13/content_26778445.htm

For the story on QR codes replacing tin cups, see: www.brookings.edu/ research/is-chinas-new-payment-system-the-future/

For QR codes on uniforms, see: www.businessinsider.co.za/chinese-troops-qr-codes-on-body-armor-massive-parade-2019-10

For the story on Alipay's Yuebao fund, see: www.forbes.com/sites/ywang/2020 /01/17/ant-financial-is-shifting-away-from-chinas-76-trillion-online-payments -market/

Chapter 11

For an overview of instant payment systems in fifty countries, see: www.fisglobal.com/flavors-of-fast

The number of UPI transactions is taken from the National Payments Corporation of India (NPCI): www.npci.org.in/product-statistics/ upi-product-statistics

Chapter 12

Figures on global payment revenues taken from McKinsey and BCG: 'The 2020 McKinsey Global Payments Report' https://www.mckinsey.com/~/media/mckinsey/industries/financial%20services/our%20insights/accelerating%20winds%20of%20change%20in%20global%20payments/2020-mckinsey-global-payments-report-vf.pdf; 'Global Payments 2020: fast forward into the future' https://web-assets.bcg.com/7c/e0/596af1214f32820093f1f88c05f0/bcg-global-payments-2020-fast-forward-into-the-future-oct-2020-1.pdf

How much consumers account for payment revenues depends on who you ask. Both BCG (2019) and McKinsey (2019) put consumer revenues from payments at around $1 trillion, but McKinsey has much higher estimates for payment revenues from corporates: some $900 billion, more than double BCG's $400 billion. Much of that difference is driven by a single number: the interest margin on corporate accounts in China, which McKinsey estimates at $275 million. This chapter uses mostly the McKinsey figures because they provide the more detailed breakdown.

For the psychology of interest rate compounding, see the S&P Global FinLit Survey: https://gflec.org/wp-content/uploads/2015/11/3313-Finlit_Report_FINAL-5.11.16.pdf?x22667

Data on Cardtronics taken from: www.link.co.uk/about/intro/; http://www.cardtronics-uk.com/about/Our-ATM-Network.aspu

Chapter 13

Payment industry figures are taken from McKinsey. 'The 2020 McKinsey Global Payments Report': https://www.mckinsey.com/~/media/mckinsey/industries/financial%20services/our%20insights/accelerating%20winds%20of%20change%20in%20global%20payments/2020-mckinsey-global-payments-report-vf.pdf

US overdraft charges are taken from the US Centre for Responsible Lending.

Payment revenue growth is taken from Oliver Wyman: www.oliverwyman.com/content/dam/oliver-wyman/v2/publications/2020/January/Oliver-Wyman-State-of-the-Financial-Services-Industry-2020.pdf

For China's cap on interest rates paid on deposits, see: www.ft.com/content/997c735c-4482-11e8-803a-295c97e6fd0b

Figures on Alipay and Tencent deposits at PBoC are taken from: www.pbc.gov.cn/diaochatongjisi/116219/116319/3750274/3750284/index.html

Figures on UK credit card debt are taken from: www.theguardian.com/money/2006/sep/27/debt.creditanddebt

Chapter 14
For the story on Ubiquity networks, see: N. Vardi (2016). 'How a tech billionaire's company misplaced $46.7 million and did not know it', *Forbes*, 8 February.

For the story on dating-app fraud, see: https://www.interpol.int/en/News-and-Events/News/2021/Investment-fraud-via-dating-apps

Chapter 15
For more on early clearing, see: www.frbatlanta.org/-/media/documents/research/publications/economic-review/2008/vol93no4_quinn_roberds.pdf

For the Herstatt failure, see: https://academic.oup.com/ehr/article/129/540/1129/2769724

Chapter 16
On the Bank of England's response to the unveiling of CHAPS, see the Gilbart Lecture delivered by Governor, Sir Edward George, 'Steady Eddie', organised by the Chartered Institute of Bankers, 22 October 1996: www.bankofengland.co.uk/-/media/boe/files/quarterly-bulletin/1996/risk-reduction-in-the-payment-and-settlement-systems.pdf

Ernst & Young estimate that the capital of the top 200 banks is $5.5 trillion, up from $2 trillion in 2007. See Global Banking Outlook, 2018: www.ey.com/ Publication/vwLUAssets/ey-global-banking-outlook-2018/$File/ey-global-banking-outlook-2018.pdf

For stories on the CHAPS outage, see: www.bbc.co.uk/news/business-29687904; www.independent.co.uk/news/business/news/homemovers-stranded -after-bank-of-england-mortgage-payment-system-crashes-9806619.html

Share of real estate purchases in total CHAPS volumes is taken from: www.ft.com/content/995c892e-5869-11e4-942f-00144feab7de; www.bank ofengland.co.uk/-/media/boe/files/report/2015/independent-review-of-rtgs-outage-on-20-october-2014.pdf

Quote taken from A. Greenspan (2007). *The Age of Turbulence: Adventures in a new world*. London: Penguin.

Bank rankings from: https://www.spglobal.com/marketintelligence/en/news-insights/trending/robdlgca1gbjyjrx3sdcjg2

For the story on why KfW became known as Germany's dumbest bank, see: www.nytimes.com/2008/09/18/business/worldbusiness/18iht-kfw.4. 16285369.html

For the *Alphaville* comments on the CHAPS outage, see: https://ftalphaville. ft.com/2016/01/29/2151327/rtgs-and-the-story-of-batches-instead-of-blocks/

The value of JPMorgan wholesale payments is taken from: www.jpmorganchase. com/corporate/investor-relations/document/line-of-business-ceo-letters-to-shareholders-2018.pdf

Chapter 17

For the reputation of cross-border payments, see: M.L. Bech and J. Hancock (2020). 'Innovations in payments', *BIS Quarterly Review*, March, 21–36. The authors describe cross-border payments as 'slower, more expensive and more opaque'. The IMF, according to a speech given by its deputy director, Dong He,

sees them as 'costly and cumbersome . . . opaque and slow' (www.imf.org/
en/News/Articles/2017/11/01/sp103017-fintech-and-cross-border-payments).

For Hawala volume estimates, see: http://www.treas.gov/offices/enforcement/
key-issues/hawala/; www.un.org/esa/desa/papers/2002/esa02dp26.pdf
(calculation based on TransferWise's published statistic of £5 billion per month
in transfers).

Figures on value of Swift payments based on McKinsey estimate of cross-
border volume: 'A Vision for the Future of Cross-border Payments'. See:
https://www.mckinsey.com/~/media/McKinsey/Industries/Financial%20
Services/Our%20Insights/A%20vision%20for%20the%20future%20of%20
cross%20border%20payments%20final/A-vision-for-the-future-of-cross-border
-payments-web-final.ashx

Figures on volume of Swift payments based on FSB Correspondent Banking
Data Report (2017) combined with BIS figures on number of Swift MT103
payment messages, and their mix of domestic and cross-border. Average value
follows from dividing value by volume. See: https://www.fsb.org/wp-content/
uploads/P040717-4.pdf; http://stats.bis.org/statx/srs/table/PS6

For more on public sector efforts to enhance cross-border payments, see the
work of the FSB.

For the full G20 report, see: www.bis.org/cpmi/publ/d193.pdf

Chapter 18
Figures on FinTech investment taken from: https://news.crunchbase.com/
news/q4-2018-closes-out-a-record-year-for-the-global-vc-market/

Figures in growth of payment revenues taken from 'The 2020 McKinsey
Global Payments Report': https://www.mckinsey.com/~/media/McKinsey/
Industries/Financial%20Services/Our%20Insights/Accelerating%20winds%20
of%20change%20in%20global%20payments/2020-McKinsey-Global-Payments
-Report-vF.pdf?shouldIndex=false; and Oliver Wyman, 'The State of the
Financial Services Industry 2020': www.oliverwyman.com/content/dam/oliver

-wyman/v2/publications/2020/January/Oliver-Wyman-State-of-the-Financial-Services-Industry-2020.pdf

Market shares Citi and JPMorgan Chase from: https://www.spglobal.com/marketintelligence/en/news-insights/trending/ujwgp8yqefmy0vzsndwjaa2 and Statista.com

Figures on N26 taken from: https://n26.com/en-eu/blog/n26-raises-more-than-100-million-dollars-in-extension-of-its-series-d-funding

Figures on banking numbers taken from: https://ogury.com

Chapter 19
For the story on Stripe's founders, see: www.wired.co.uk/article/stripe-payments-apple-amazon-facebook

For more on non-acceptance of some businesses by FinTech acquirers, see: https://stripe.com/blog/why-some-businesses-arent-allowed; https://squareup.com/gb/en/legal/general/ua

For more on Klarna, see: www.klarna.com/knowledge/articles/how-klarna-won-over-80-million-shoppers-hearts/

For JPMorgan on payments, see: www.jpmorgan.com/country/GB/en/merchant-services/consumers-prefer-breachless-payments-to-frictionless

Chapter 20
For the plot of the movie *The Joneses*, see: https://www.imdb.com/title/tt1285309/

For the litigation between Amazon and Barnes & Noble over 1-click shopping, see: https://knowledge.wharton.upenn.edu/article/amazons-1-click-goes-off-patent/

For the story of thirteen-year old Cameron and his in-app purchases, see: www.dailymail.co.uk/news/article-2298771/Policeman-Doug-Crossan-reports-13-year-old-son-Cameron-FRAUD-running-3-700-iPad.html

For Professor Prelec's research, see: https://web.mit.edu/simester/Public/Papers/Alwaysleavehome.pdf

For research on exposure to credit card logos, see: R.A. Feinberg (1986). 'Credit cards as spending facilitating stimuli: A conditioning interpretation', *Journal of Consumer Research*, 13(1), 348–56.

For figures on BigTech and trust, see: M. Bijlsma, C. Carin van der Cruijsen and N. Nicole Jonker (2020). 'Consumer propensity to adopt PSD2 services: Trust for sale?', DNB Working Paper (www.dnb.nl/en/binaries/Working%20paper%20No%2E%20671_tcm47-387219.pdf)

For figures on Open Banking in the UK, see: www.openbanking.org.uk

Chapter 21
For more on Lana Swartz, see: http://llaannaa.com

For the plot of the movie *The Circle*, see: www.imdb.com/title/tt4287320/

For ING Bank's attempts to use customer data for marketing, see: https://fd.nl/frontpage/ondernemen/10864/ing-geeft-adverteerder-inzicht-in-klantgedrag and www.finextra.com/newsarticle/34092/dutch-banks-told-to-stop-using-payments-data-for-personalised-marketing

For more on the UK Competition Market Authority and Open Banking, see: https://assets.publishing.service.gov.uk/government/uploads/system/uploads/attachment_data/file/885537/Notice_of_proposed_changes_to_the_open_banking_roadmap_-_web_publication_-_cma_gov_uk_---_May_2020_-.pdf

For the story on hedge funds using data from screen scrapers, see: www.politico.com/news/2020/02/07/banks-fintech-startups-clash-over-the-new-oil-your-data-112188

For a scientific article arguing that Big Tech may want to own banking subsidiaries, see: M. Brunnermeier, H. James and J.-P. Landau (2019). 'The digitalization of money', Working paper 26300, National Bureau of Economic Research.

For *The Economist* article, go to: www.economist.com/leaders/2020/10/22/ how-to-deal-with-free-speech-on-social-media

Chapter 22
For the plot of the movie *The Big Short*, see: www.imdb.com/title/tt1596363/

Quote on mining as striking gold in a sandbox from: https://greatestideaever. wordpress.com/category/tales-from-the-crypto/

Figures on market capitalisation of cryptocurrencies are for 15 June 2020, taken from CoinMarketCap.com

For illicit activity on Bitcoin, see: S. Foley, J.R. Karlsen and T.J. Putniņš (2019). 'Sex, drugs and Bitcoin: How much illegal activity is financed through cryptocurrencies?', *Review of Financial Studies*, 32(5), 1798–835.

For the link between Tether and Bitcoin. see: J. Griffin and A. Shams (2020). 'Is Bitcoin really untethered?', *Journal of Finance*, 15 June.

Chapter 23
Quote on Libra taken from: www.iosco.org/library/pubdocs/pdf/ IOSCOPD650.pdf

For the Bank of England discussion paper on CBDC, see: 'Central Bank Digital Currency: Opportunities, challenges and design', Discussion Paper, 12 March 2020 (www.bankofengland.co.uk/paper/2020/central-bank-digital-currency-opportunities-challenges-and-design-discussion-paper)

For the ECB discussion paper on Libra, see: M. Adachi, M. Cominetta, C. Kaufmann and A. van der Kraaij (2020). 'A regulatory and financial stability perspective on global tablecoins', *Macroprudential Bulletin, European Central Bank*, vol. 10.

Figures on large sovereign wealth funds taken from: www.swfinstitute.org/fund-rankings

Jamie Dimon quotes on Bitcoin taken from: www.pymnts.com/blockchain/bitcoin/2018/jpmorgan-chase-jamie-dimon-dapper-labs-funding/

Chapter 24
For more on Che Guevara's stint as Cuba's central bank governor, see: https://sociable.co/web/fidel-castro-appointed-che-guevara-bank/

Chapter 25
Figures on global frequent flyer miles taken from: www.mckinsey.com/industries/travel-logistics-and-transport-infrastructure/our-insights/miles-ahead-how-to-improve-airline-customer-loyalty-programs#

For Citibank and its New York ATM network, see: https://www.cgap.org/sites/default/files/Interoperability_in_Electronic_Payments.pdf

For the EU investigations into Apple Pay and Qualcomm, see: https://ec.europa.eu/commission/presscorner/detail/en/ip_20_1075; https://ec.europa.eu/commission/presscorner/detail/en/IP_18_421

George Soros delivered this remark at the World Economic Forum, Davos, Switzerland, 25 January 2018; see: www.georgesoros.com/2018/01/25/remarks-delivered-at-the-world-economic-forum/

Chapter 26
For US Executive Order banning eight apps, including Alipay and WeChat, see: https://www.federalregister.gov/documents/2021/01/08/2021-00305/addressing-the-threat-posed-by-applications-and-other-software-developed-or-controlled-by-chinese

Carmen Balber, Washington Director for Consumer Watchdog, made the suggestion that the Federal Reserve Board consumer watchdog would be a lapdog (https://www.prnewswire.com/news-releases/dodd-proposal-to-give-the-federal-reserve-consumer-protection-authority-would-create-an-industry-lapdog-not-a-public-watchdog-85971237.html)

For forensic analysis of the attack on Bangladesh Bank, see: www.reuters.com/article/us-usa-fed-bangladesh-investigation/exclusive-bangladesh-bank-remains-compromised-months-after-heist-forensics-report-idUSKCN0Y40SM

Chapter 27
For comment on INSTEX, see: W. Münchau (2019). 'America's "exorbitant privilege" is Europe's sin of omission'. *Financial Times*, 26 May.

Quotation on ECB's TARGET2 taken from: 'Drivers for change in payment and securities settlement systems', speech delivered by Gertrude Tumpel-Gugerell, Member of the Executive Board of the ECB, speaking at the Banco de España, Madrid, June 2006 (https://www.ecb.europa.eu/press/key/date/2006/html/sp060609.en.html)

Chapter 28
For more on the EU's 'geopolitical Commission' see 'The European economic and financial system: fostering openness, strength and resilience', European Commission, 19 January 2021: https://ec.europa.eu/finance/docs/policy/210119-economic-financial-system-communication_en.pdf

The figures from Swift on the US dollar share in international payments exclude payments within the Eurozone. Taken from: www.swift.com/file/67981/download?token=9jCDTPae

For more on the huge privilege afforded the dollar, see E. Eichengreen (2011). *Exorbitant privilege: The rise and fall of the dollar*. Oxford: Oxford University Press.

For the story on Bundesbank rules on money laundering, see: www.ft.com/content/24feb850-98a1-11e8-9702-5946bae86e6d

For early use of the term 'weaponisation of finance', see: Ian Bremmer of Eurasia Group (@ianbremmer on Twitter, 5 January 2015)

Stories on Macau's Banco Delta Asia and early North Korean sanctions taken from: www.treasury.gov/press-center/press-releases/Pages/hp315.aspxu; www.piie.com/blogs/north-korea-witness-transformation/juan-c-zarates-treasurys-war; www.nytimes.com/2007/01/18/world/asia/18iht-north.4255039.html

Story on Iran's use of cryptocurrency to evade sanctions taken from: https://cointelegraph.com/news/iranian-general-calls-for-use-of-crypto-to-evade-sanctions; https://home.treasury.gov/news/press-releases/sm556

Chapter 29

Figures on OFAC/FinCen taken from: www.reuters.com/article/us-usa-sanctions-ofac-insight/u-s-agency-overseeing-sanctions-faces-brain-drain-added-work-idUSKCN0QC0CN20150807; www.fincen.gov/frequently-asked-questions

Stories on Danske Bank taken from: www.theguardian.com/world/2017/sep/04/uk-at-centre-of-secret-3bn-azerbaijani-money-laundering-and-lobbying-scheme; www.theguardian.com/business/2018/sep/21/is-money-laundering-scandal-at-danske-bank-the-largest-in-history; www.reuters.com/article/us-danske-bank-moneylaundering-timeline/timeline-how-danske-banks-estonian-money-laundering-scandal-unfolded-idUSKCN1NO209

Figures on financial crime taken from: https://thefinancialcrimenews.com/global-threat-assessment-2018-by-john-cusack/

Figures and stories on fines handed out to banks for financial crime taken from: www.fenergo.com/resources/reports/another-fine-mess-global-research-report-financial-institution-fines.html; www.businessinsider.com/r-bank-settlements-create-windfall-for-us-and-wrangling-over-how-it-is-spent-2014-24?IR=T; www.justice.gov/opa/pr/bnp-paribas-agrees-plead-guilty-and-pay-89-billion-illegally-processing-financial; www.theguardian.com/business/2014/aug/20/standard-chartered-fined-300m-money-laundering-compliance; www.dw.com/en/financial-crisis-bank-fines-hit-record-10-years-after-market-collapse/a-40044540

For the story on the Moldovan bank heist and its links to a Latvian bank, see: www.forbes.com/sites/francescoppola/2018/02/28/why-the-u-s-treasury-killed -a-latvian-bank/

For the story on ABLV and the US Treasury, see: https://www.fincen.gov/ news/news-releases/fincen-names-ablv-bank-latvia-institution-primary-money- laundering-concern-and

For the story on BCCI fraud, see: https://fas.org/irp/congress/1992_rpt/bcci/ 01exec.htm; http://news.bbc.co.uk/2/hi/business/5056056.stm

Chapter 30
For US policy on banks accepting foreign IDs, see: http://financialservices. house.gov/media/pdf/062603sb.pdf

For Dutch parliament discussion on financial exclusion, see: www.parlement airemonitor.nl/9353000/1/j9vvij5epmj1ey0/vk5dmnhjv5ui

For financial exclusion of embassies, see: www.transparency.org/cpi2018; https://foreignpolicy.com/2010/11/19/37-embassies-in-washington-face- banking-crisis/; www.reuters.com/article/us-financial-embassies/banks-can- keep-embassy-accounts-u-s-regulators-idUSTRE72O3ID20110325; www.federalreserve.gov/supervisionreg/srletters/sr1106a1.pdf

For BIS and FSB on decline in correspondent banking relationships, see: T. Rice, G. von Peter and C. Boar (2020). 'On the global retreat of correspondent banks', *BIS Quarterly Review*, March, 37–52; www.fsb.org/ 2018/11/fsb-correspondent-banking-data-report-update-2/

Epilogue
For the cap imposed on UPI transactions processed by third-party providers in India, see: https://www.npci.org.in/PDF/npci/press-releases/2020/UPI- balances-consumer-experience-with-growth-for-TPAPs.pdf

Index